English Catholic Historians and the English Reformation, 1585–1954

For my parents

English Catholic Historians and the English Reformation, 1585–1954

John Vidmar OP

sussex
ACADEMIC
PRESS
Brighton • Chicago • Toronto

4 6 8 10 9 7 5 3

First published 2005, reprinted 2008 and 2019 in Great Britain by
SUSSEX ACADEMIC PRESS
PO Box 139
Eastbourne BN24 9BP

Distributed in North America by
SUSSEX ACADEMIC PRESS
Independent Publishers Group
814 N. Franklin Street
Chicago, IL 60610

British Library Cataloguing in Publication Data
A CIP catalogue record for this book is available from the British Library.

Library of Congress Cataloging-in-Publication Data
Vidmar, John.
English Catholic historians and the English
Reformation, 1585–1954 / John Vidmar.
p. cm.
Includes bibliographical references and index.
ISBN 978-1-84519-007-1 (hbk. alk. paper)
ISBN 978-1-78976-028-6 (pbk. alk. paper)
1. Reformation—England—Historiography.
2. England—Church history—16th century—
Historiography. 3. Historiography—England.
4. Catholic historians. I. Title.
BR377.V54 2004
274.2′06′072042—dc22

2004007295

Typeset and designed by Sussex Academic Press, Brighton & Eastbourne.
Printed and bound by CPI Group (UK) Ltd, Croydon, CR0 4YY

CONTENTS

ACKNOWLEDGEMENTS

This project has a long history, and my gratitude to the various people who helped goes back almost twenty years. First of all, thanks are due to my brothers in the Dominican Province of St. Joseph in the United States for allowing me three and one-half years of time and the financial means to carry out the research and writing for this book. I am also very grateful to my brothers in the English Province of Dominicans for their hospitality, especially those who lived in the Edinburgh and London houses; and to Fr. Allan White, OP, who was the superior of the Edinburgh house and whose wise advice was always helpful. I would also like to thank my brothers at the Angelicum in Rome for their hospitality and moral support.

The archivists and librarians of the following institutions are deserving of my profound gratitude: The archives of the Archdioceses of Birmingham, Southwark, and Westminster, the English College in Rome, Boston College, the Jesuit Archives at Farm Street, Ushaw College, Downside Abbey, the Duke of Norfolk; the Bodleian Library at Oxford, the National Library of Scotland, the Cambridge University Library, the Vatican Library, the Angelicum Library in Rome, the Phillips Memorial Library at Providence College.

I wish to thank David Cressy and Lori Anne Ferrell for directing a National Endowment of the Arts Summer Institute on Early Modern England, and to my fellow-participants. Gratitude is also due to Anthony Grahame of Sussex Academic Press for encouraging me in this project and for so expeditiously seeing it through to publication. Two Altars from Augustus Welby Pugin's *Contrasts* (1863 publication), pages 92–3 herein, courtesy of The Victoria & Albert Picture Library, London.

Abbreviations and Notes

Abbreviations

BAA   Birmingham Archdiocesan Archives

BC   Boston College Archives

DA   Downside Abbey Archives

ECA   English College Archives, Rome

FSA   Farm Street Archives of the Society of Jesus, London

SAA   Southward Archdiocesan Archives

WAA   Westminster Archdiocesan Archives

Notes

1 In the pages which follow the terms the "Church", the "Catholic Church", and the "English Catholic Church", all refer to the Roman Catholic Church and should not be confused with the Church of England.

2 The term "temporal authority" or "temporal power" (lower case) of the popes refers to their temporal "pretensions" or their claims to temporal power made throughout the centuries. The term "Temporal Power" came to refer specifically to the pope's dominion over the Papal States. I have maintained the lower and upper cases in order to distinguish the two.

Introduction

HISTORY AND RELIGION

Christian religion, by which I mean the combination of theological belief and religious practice, has a unique relationship to history. Lord Acton maintained that religion was the "key of history", and twentieth-century Catholic historians have supported Acton's claim. Christopher Dawson wrote, "The great civilizations of the world do not produce the great religions as a kind of cultural by-product; in a very real sense the great religions are the foundations on which the great civilizations rest."[1] An understanding of religion, not an acceptance of it, is essential to the understanding of history. More specifically, an understanding of the Catholic religion is essential to an understanding of the history of the West. Historians may not believe that God works in and through history, nor might they hold particular tenets of that religion, but they must accept its presence and its impact on society. Historians who neglect this do so at their own peril. Edward Gibbon, in his *Decline and Fall of the Roman Empire*, attempted to describe a phenomenon – Christianity – which he simply could not comprehend. Dawson pointed out that Gibbon had "no understanding of religious value . . . the fundamental concepts of religious faith and divine revelation – in short the idea of what Christianity was all about".[2]

When it comes to the English Reformation, this understanding of religion is especially important in understanding what happened in England, and why. Historians who have tried to focus primarily on political, materialistic, or societal causes, have largely missed the point. Certainly, there were political, materialistic, and societal *effects* on the people of England, but what caused the Reformation, what drove it, and gave it its main direction, was religion.

Catholic historians of the English Reformation, writing over the last four hundred years, have come to that realization gradually, by a process of elimination. Initially and immediately, even as the Reformation was happening, Catholic historians pointed to politics as the principal cause of the Reformation, seeing in the reign of Queen Elizabeth its epicentre. But slowly, as the political effects of the Reformation began to wear off, they started to see its other underlying causes. Almost as layers are peeled from an onion, so did Catholic writers eventually get to the core of England's religious revolution, which they identified as theological, and specifically as the spiritual authority of the papacy.

These Catholic historians took their Reformation seriously, because it had jeopardized the very existence of the Catholic community, called into question the Catholic claim to continuity with the Early Church, and even made the civic loyalty of Catholics suspect. Hilaire Belloc, writing in 1936 with his customary excess, stated that the English Reformation was "the most important thing in history since the foundation of the Catholic Church 1,500 years before".[3] Whether or not Belloc was correct in his appraisal is not the issue, and would be impossible to prove in any case; what is at issue is that an English Catholic historian thought so much of the English Reformation that he had the audacity to make such a sweeping claim.

I have chosen Catholic historians writing between the years 1585 and 1954 because they fall within a unique spectrum beginning with the very first history of the Reformation by a Catholic, Nicholas Sanders' *Rise and Growth of the Anglican Schism*, published in 1585, and ending with the last truly Ultramontanist history written by Philip Hughes (*The Reformation in England*) in 1954. Thereafter, the Reformation debate entered a new phase with the ground-breaking work of A. G. Dickens and G. R. Elton (non-Catholics) and the Catholic scholars Dom David Knowles, J. J. Scarisbrick, and Eamon Duffy. The period 1585–1954 also represents a span of time which saw the Catholic Church spiral downward into near non-existence – in 1780 the Catholic population of England was 1 per cent – to a dramatic and somewhat triumphalistic recovery in the first half of the twentieth century. By studying this group of historians, and studying them as a complete entity, we will see patterns and directions of thought which would otherwise look like unrelated moments of Catholic thinking.

This kind of study has, very simply, not been done before. It is possible that the formidable Geoffrey Elton scared students away by disparaging historiography as becoming "unfortunately" popular, though he spared it his severest rebuke, namely that it was being practiced in the United States.[4] It has been done in related areas – most notably John Burrow's *A Liberal Descent: Victorian Historians and the English Past* (1981), John Kenyon's *The History Men* (1983), and Rosemary O'Day's *The Debate on the English Reformation* (1986) – but the Catholic contribution has been consistently and, I believe, unwisely neglected. This comes as no surprise to English Catholics, since it follows the pattern set by G. P. Gooch in his monumental *History and Historians in the Nineteenth Century* (1913), which mentioned only Lord Acton at any length, and dismissed Aidan Gasquet as one who "related the dissolution of the English Monasteries".[5] More recently, Jasper Ridley's biography of Queen Elizabeth I supplied a lengthy summary of the historical literature on the subject and studiously avoided the mention of a single Catholic author.[6] Rosemary O'Day managed both to ignore the contributions of several Catholic authors and to misunderstand the ones she did mention, especially Lingard. She did not mention a single Catholic historian from the time of John Lingard (d. 1851) to J. J. Scarisbrick, whose important biography of Henry VIII was written in 1968. Granted, this was to ignore a lot of small-fry who wrote questionable or mediocre history, but it was also to ignore the likes of Lord Acton, Aidan Gasquet, John Hugerford Pollen, Hilaire Belloc, Philip Hughes and, last and certainly not least, David Knowles.

This book is an attempt to correct a glaring neglect. The injustice of the omission of Catholic authors from the Reformation debate becomes evident when one studies the Catholic histories themselves, and here we discover what issues concerned the writers of these histories: What did Catholic writers say about the English Reformation over the last four hundred years and why did they say it? What characters and events of the Reformation did they find important? Did their opinions change over time? Were there any opinions on which they agreed consistently and across political lines? Were there any patterns or trends of opinion which emerged? What contemporary issues affected their reflection on the past?

The English Reformation began when Henry VIII abandoned hope that he would sire a son by his wife, Catherine of Aragon. Arguments employing scripture and canon law were used in an attempt to have the marriage annulled, all in vain. The pope, under some (but not complete) constraint by King Charles V of Spain, Catherine's nephew, refused to grant the annulment. Henry, making use of his newly-appointed Archbishop of Canterbury, Thomas Cranmer, had the case tried in England, where he was granted his wish and was now free to marry Anne Boleyn in 1533. There followed a succession of laws which hamstrung the Church in England, beginning in 1532 with the Act of Submission of the Clergy (whereby all clergy who had papal appointments had to resign their benefices and be re-appointed by Henry), and becoming more draconian with the Act of Supremacy in 1534 (effectively making Henry the head of the Church in England), and the Acts of Dissolution of the Monasteries in 1536 and 1539. Thomas Cromwell became a major figure after the resignation of Sir Thomas More as Chancellor in 1532, master-minding the dissolution, which had the two-fold effect of providing the king with necessary cash and eliminating the most vocal opposition to his supremacy and marriage. The Pilgrimage of Grace in the winter of 1536–37, an amazing rebellion of northerners with economic and religious grievances, only gave Cromwell and the King the pretext for closing down *all* of the religious houses.

Henry's death in 1547 marked a new era in the Reformation. His next two very different successors – Edward VI and Mary Tudor – occupied the throne for roughly five years apiece. The pace of Protestantizing increased dramatically under Cranmer and the boy-king, Edward, but was reversed by Mary, who made the very unpopular mistakes of executing people (282 of them) for heresy, and marrying a Spanish king.

Elizabeth took the throne in 1558 and arrived at a religious compromise called the "Anglican Settlement", whereby she hoped to satisfy both Catholic and Reformed parties within the Church. An Oath accompanied the restored Act of Supremacy, and was required of anyone holding ecclesiastical, political, or military office, and it could be demanded of anyone seeking to be a lawyer, teacher, or medical doctor. This Oath had many different manifestations during the next centuries and was a huge obstacle on the path to Catholic Emancipation. The ancestor of Elizabeth's Oath was the Oath of Supremacy, drawn up under Henry VIII to enforce compliance with the Act of Supremacy. An essential part of declaring himself the Supreme Head of the Church in England, was declaring that the pope was not. The various oaths which succeeded Henry's initial Oath, (which became known with time as the Oath of Allegiance), sought different formulae, but all agreed that the central issue to be included was a denial of the authority of the pope in England, the *sine qua non* of Catholic relief.[7]

As cries for Catholic Emancipation grew louder in the late 1700s, the Oath became the sticking point. There had been a lengthy Oath attached to the 1778 Relief Act, which was virtually the same Oath as had been affixed to an Irish relief bill in 1774, which omitted the objectionable clauses of the Test Act of 1673, including its denial of Transubstantiation, and toned down the objections to the pope's spiritual jurisdiction in England. The pertinent phrases read: "I do declare, that I do not believe, that the Pope of Rome, or any other foreign prince, prelate, state or potentate, hath, or ought to have, any temporal, or civil jurisdiction, power, superiority, or pre-eminence, directly or indirectly, with this realm".[8] This was quite a concession on the part of the government when one realizes that the last Oath of Allegiance (1689) was worded: "I do declare, that no foreign Prince, Person, Prelate, State or Potentate, hath, or ought to have, any jurisdiction, Power, Superiority, Preheminence or Authority, *Ecclesiastical or Spiritual*, within this realm."[9]

Partly to appease public unrest, the government sought to toughen the oath in the next round of negotiations. A new Oath, proposed for the Relief Bill of 1791, re-introduced some of the old codewords (e.g. spiritual power of jurisdiction) which had been dropped in the 1778 oath, and introduced others (e.g. Infallibility) which had not been seen before. The proposed Oath read, in part:

> That no foreign prelate . . . hath . . . any spiritual power of jurisdiction . . . within this realm that can directly or indirectly affect or interfere with . . . the liberties, persons, or properties of the subject thereof.

> That I do from my heart abhor, detest and abjure as impious and heretical, that damnable Doctrine and Position that Princes excommunicated by the Pope or by Authority of the See of Rome, may be deposed or murdered by their subjects.

> That I acknowledge no infallibility in the Pope.[10]

Needless to say, the Catholic bishops found these provisions objectionable and saw that they were either dropped or so amended that they lost their meaning. A good example of the bishops' skill at qualification is the statement on infallibility, which the bishops changed in this way: "I acknowledge no Infallibility, right, power or authority in the Pope, save in matters of Ecclesiastical doctrine and discipline only."[11]

The debate on the Oath of Allegiance continued almost to the time of Catholic Emancipation in 1829, and involved all sorts of ingenious proposals. John Lingard, writing in 1821, suggested including the explanatory clause, "limiting the spiritual authority abjured, to such authority as may affect the civil rights of the king and his subjects". This clause, he added, needed only to be approved by Parliament, and need not be spoken aloud when the Oath was taken, since it would be assumed to be the approved meaning of the Oath.[12] When Catholic Emancipation finally came in 1829, no such Oath was required.

At one time, during the reign of Henry VIII, many Catholics had reluctantly signed the Oath, but their opposition hardened under Elizabeth and became increasingly belligerent, threatening the peace which Elizabeth had worked so hard to achieve. Missionaries, trained abroad by Jesuits, began to arrive in England in the 1560s in order to sustain the now underground Catholic Church. A rebellion in Ireland in 1579, followed by the news in 1580 of the arrival the first two Jesuits on English soil, caused the queen to become alarmed. Penal laws directed against Catholics began to be enforced, and 180 Catholics were executed during her reign. Mary Queen of Scots was executed by Elizabeth's order in 1587, and the

Spanish Armada attempted an invasion of England the following year. By 1603, the year Elizabeth died, legislation was in place which forbade Catholics to vote, hold office, inherit property, send their children to school, etc. That legislation would remain in place until 1778, when the first of three relief acts was passed, culminating in the Third Relief Bill (otherwise known as Catholic Emancipation) of 1829.

The Reformation was a catastrophe for the traditional Church by anyone's reckoning, and English Catholics tried immediately to lay blame for their plight. Whose fault was it? Could it have been averted? Could its extent have been lessened? The attention of Catholic historians focused initially on the reign of Elizabeth, because that is where their civil disabilities began. Two different opinions emerged from the ashes. The first was driven by Exiles, those Catholics (especially priests) who had been forced to flee to the continent and would favour an aggressive policy in restoring the Faith. They were aided in this by the Society of Jesus, newly-founded in 1540, an almost militaristic group owing its allegiance to the pope. They placed the blame squarely on Elizabeth and her ministers. The second group was made up of those who remained behind in England – especially the small group of diocesan priests imprisoned in Wisbech Prison who sought to negotiate with the government about their release. They were known as Appellants. They blamed the Jesuits for exciting Elizabeth to take action against Catholics and were groveling in their protestations of loyalty to the crown.

That scenario – Exiles/Jesuits versus Appellants/Diocesan clergy – would remain the historical battleground among Catholics until Catholic Emancipation in 1829, when disabilities against Catholics were almost entirely removed. Prior to 1829, histories of the Reformation written by both of these groups were written with an eye towards freedom. They were concerned almost solely with matters of state – with insistence on loyalty to the crown, assurance that the Catholic religion was not of itself a threat to the government, and that the disabilities inflicted on Catholics were unjust. Catholics lived in the shadow of the Reformation, and not only saw it as the source of their current plight, but searched it for clues to a solution.

Histories of the Reformation in 1830 could hardly be divided between those written by non-Catholics and those written by Catholics. There had been only two full-scale Catholic histories of the English Reformation written before Lingard in the 1820s – Nicholas Sanders's *De Origine ac Progressu Schismatici Anglicani* (1585) and Charles Dodd's *Church History of England* (1737–42). The former was not translated into English until 1877 and the latter was very difficult to obtain, so that their impact on English public opinion was negligible.[13] Besides, as we shall see, they also disagreed completely over the causes and effects of the English Reformation.

The histories written by non-Catholics dominated the field. They emphasized the political victory of England over Spain and Rome or the moral and theological improvement of the nation's religion. These histories divided roughly into those which thought that the Reformation was primarily a political event, and possibly an unsavory one, which brought England into the modern age (Henry Hallam, Thomas Babington Macaulay), and those who thought its overthrow of medieval religion a moral triumph (Robert Southey, Sharon Turner).[14] Among this latter group High Church historians had the worst of it because they needed to defend the Reformation against the Roman Catholics in order to preserve their ecclesiological identity, but also against the Low Church and Enlightenment historians in order to preserve their theological integrity.

Historical writing, at the time Lingard put pen to paper, was still heavily influenced by the Enlightenment tradition, which often saw history as an adjunct to other more important disciplines. Of those who wrote history, David Hume had been a philosopher, as had lesser lights such as the Catholic priest Joseph Berington. Henry Hallam and Charles Butler were lawyers. Sharon Turner was a lawyer turned philologist and Robert Southey was a poet. Yet all of them wrote some sort of history of the English Reformation at about the same time as Lingard, who was trained to be a philosopher. The day of the professional historian was still generations away.

Hume's six-volume *History of England* (1754–61) held the field and would remain the standard work for nearly a hundred years, and is still in print today – supposedly more for its style than its content. It was a typical product of the Enlightenment, formed as it was by a cynicism about theology generally and about the Roman Catholic Church in particular – especially the institution of monasticism – as well as by Hume's personal animus against the priesthood. In Hume we find an almost conscious avoidance of the Middle Ages, a prejudice which had its English roots at least as early as 1693, when the historian Gilbert Burnet boasted that he knew almost nothing about the period.[15] This attitude grew to an art-form in the Enlightenment period. G. P. Gooch observed that Enlightenment historians practically ignored the Middle Ages. "Hume", he wrote, "dismissed the Anglo-Saxon centuries, the time of the making of England, as a battle of kites and crows. Voltaire declared that the early Middle Ages deserved as little study as the doing of wolves and bears".[16] Histories written in this manner were often derivative and relied unashamedly on previous historians, who were quoted as unassailable authorities. English Catholics countered by using the same methods.

Joseph Berington, like Lingard a secular Catholic priest, stated in his *State and Behavior of English Catholics* (1780) that his sources were Burnet, Hume, Clarendon, and Dodd, and he never once questioned what he drew from them.[17]

But with Lingard and emancipation, a change came over the writing of this history. In fact, the further in time Catholic historians got from Elizabeth, the more they saw the heart of the Reformation in earlier reigns. Attention first began to be given to the reign of Edward VI and the liturgical changes which his reign inaugurated. Catholics suddenly found themselves staring at a problem they had not previously had the luxury of addressing: the Church of England or the Anglican Church. Anglicans were in the throes of a crisis themselves – brought on by emancipation, which legally allowed Catholics and even non-Christians to hold office in Parliament, and therefore to vote on matters pertaining to the established Church of England. This anomaly led quickly to the Oxford Movement, which began with John Keble's Assize Sermon in 1833, entitled "On the National Apostasy", and which, in an almost domino-like series of events, involved the Roman Catholic Church. What had appeared to be an intramural squabble between Anglicans was rudely interrupted by a Catholic priest named Nicholas Wiseman, who wrote in 1838 that the debate would henceforth need to include Catholics, and that the issue would be the Reformation:

> Ours was a conservative reform; we pruned away the decayed part; we placed the vessel in the furnace, and, the dross being melted off, we drew it out bright and pure. Yours was radical to the extreme; you tore up entire plants by the roots, because you said there was a blight on some one branch; you threw the whole vessel into the fire, and made merry at its blaze.[18]

Lingard's history was key because it bridged both major periods of Catholic historical writing. His first edition (completed in 1830) was written with emancipation in mind, but his next editions became more outspoken and confident. He was the first Catholic to turn his attention to the Reformations which preceded Elizabeth's.

This process continued through the nineteenth century, and included a defense of the monasteries by Aidan Gasquet toward the end of the century, and an assessment of the Anglican liturgy by Gasquet and Edwin Bishop, but took a new turn with the appearance of Hilaire Belloc and his thesis that the heart of the Reformation was theological and involved Henry VIII's problem with papal authority. Philip Hughes made Belloc's thesis respectable by supplying the research and the footnotes.

Until the historical work of Belloc and Hughes, these Catholic histories were written oftentimes by amateurs. If there is a sense in which theology comes from "below", it is certainly manifest in this period of Catholic thought. Few of the Catholics who wrote about the Reformation within the period 1585–1954, especially during the first 300 years of that period, were trained either as historians or even theologians. Instead, they were philosophers, polemicists, lawyers, and ecclesiastical administrators. Most of them were what might be best described as "hack" writers, whose principal interest was in defending the Faith or their Church, and not in exposing historical truth. Even Lord Acton, regarded by most as the most brilliant historian of the lot, never wrote a book. Belloc received his historical training at Oxford, but almost immediately became, and ever after remained, a journalist. But, almost despite themselves, they moved ineluctably toward a historical truth, which was that religion stood at the core of the English Reformation, and that core was the pope's claim to spiritual authority and jurisdiction.

A certain breadth is necessary to make that point, which could not be made by examining only the works of an individual author. It is only in comparing one author to another, and in showing thematic progressions in the writing of Catholic history during this period, that this thesis is able to be sustained. Someone might note that this book is neither fish nor fowl, that it is not a history of the Reformation, nor is it a history of Catholicism from 1585 to 1954; rather, it is an examination of the Catholic histories of the Reformation and the writers and the issues behind them. Christopher Dawson once commented, "We cannot fully understand an age unless we understand how that age regarded the past, for every age makes its own past."[19] If he is correct, then this study will help to fill a gap, albeit in a small way, in our knowledge both of the English Reformation and of the Catholic Church in England during this period.

Chapter I

EXILES AND APPELLANTS

E ven as the English Reformation was happening, two groups of Catholics contested for the right to assign blame for their plight. Their assessment of the Reformation would be very different, and it would affect future Catholic writing of the Reformation until the twentieth century.

The Exiles and the Jesuits

The Exiles were priests who had fled England in the reign of Elizabeth when it became illegal and dangerous for them to remain. They might also be students who had been educated on the continent, with the idea of some day returning to England as priests.[1] And finally, some of these Exiles might belong to a new religious order, known as the Society of Jesus. The fact that they styled themselves "Exiles" meant that their stay abroad was to be hopefully temporary. They planned to return to England when the ecclesiastical situation had returned to its pre-Reformation status. Some of these Exiles did, in fact, return to England, even in the midst of severe penal legislation. Catholic priests, if caught in England, would be exiled for a first offense, and executed for a second.

Regardless, Exile priests, secular as well as Jesuit, returned to England and became the stuff of heroic stories – entering in disguise, sometimes very bold ones, and traveling from one safe house to another, administering the sacraments at great peril to their lives, ruthlessly hunted down by a nervous government using the services of spies, informers, and, alas, members of the secular clergy. Some of them, for various reasons, did not attempt to return to England and face death, and were the ones responsible for what I shall label "Exile History".

Their alienation from the English crown was not evident in the early years of Elizabeth's reign. These men, who would later become Exiles, had hoped that Elizabeth would continue the reforms introduced by Mary and make good on her promise to conform to the Catholic Church. They became increasingly confrontational when it became apparent that she had no such intention. As they fled to the continent in the 1560s in increasing numbers, they imbibed the new spirit of the Council of Trent (1545–63), which had sought to enforce discipline and clarify the doctrine of the Church.[2] Even diverse local liturgical rites were suppressed, making the Roman Rite normative throughout the world.[3] Thus we find a typical Exile priest, Edward Rishton, ordained in 1577, saying his first Mass in the Roman Rite, "in obedience to the decrees of St. Pius V", thus signifi-cantly abandoning the Sarum Rite "to which [his] forefathers had been accustomed in England".[4]

The Society of Jesus, founded by Ignatius Loyola in 1534 and approved by Pope Paul III in 1540 just five years before the Council of Trent began, proved to be the principal agent by which the reforms of the council were promoted throughout the world. The Society's ties to Rome were neces-sarily strong, and the constitution of the Jesuits, submitted in 1550, specified that the services of the Society should be at the disposal of the pope, going so far as to add a fourth vow of special obedience to the pope.

In all of this could be seen a new confidence in the ultimate victory of the Roman Church and an accompanying aggressiveness in attacking its enemies. These Exiles had the pope's ear, and they urged on him the momentous decision in 1570 to excommunicate Elizabeth – thinking that such action would force the queen to comply or, in the case of her refusal, provide the legal basis for her removal. It was more than an excommuni-cation; it was a declaration of war.

The first legal step in any overthrow of a prince was excommunication. It was a weapon which had become blunted from overuse in the past – the Council of Trent mandated that it be used much less often – but still carried with it enough bite to cause discomfort and even alarm. When Savonarola was excommunicated in 1497, he attempted to negate the penalty by claiming that the pope who issued it was invalidly elected himself, and therefore no pope. This ploy did not work, and the city council of Florence had him executed. Even Martin Luther, in boldly burning the writ of his excommunication, knew he had a patron, Frederick the Wise of Saxony, to protect him. Elizabeth was more exposed and, though she might scorn an excommunication, she knew that the rulers of other countries (especially France and Spain) might not. They could very well honour it and allow it to serve as a pretext for interfer-ence in England's affairs.

The excommunication issued by the Dominican Pope Pius V in 1570,

Regnans in Excelsis, was quite pointed as far as the English were concerned. Elizabeth was declared a heretic, and an encourager of heretics. The pope revoked every "right, dignity, and privilege" which belonged to her, and freed her subjects from any oaths made to her, obligations of allegiance, fealty, and obedience. He concluded, "We command all . . . never to venture to obey her monitions, mandates, and laws."[5] The Exiles had hoped that this document would be a call to arms. Only one major Exile figure, Nicolas Sanders, became directly involved in a rebellion against the crown, but several others were certainly involved indirectly – usually by encouraging foreign countries to threaten war against England. The extent of their involvement in these seditious schemes has long been a subject of dispute, and the number of priests involved in these plots was exaggerated by Elizabeth's ministers. However, those who were involved had intentions which could hardly be called innocent.

Even Reginald Pole was involved in one such scheme as early as 1538, when he tried to gather support for the excommunication of Henry VIII by forming an alliance between the pope and the kings of France and Spain. The excommunication was drawn up but never issued, because the two kings balked at waging war against England. But Pole's action set a dangerous precedent, so that when it became apparent that Elizabeth would not be converted, the Exiles engaged in similar entanglements, especially with Spain. Thus Sanders landed with Spanish troops in Ireland in what was known at the Desmond Rebellion of 1579. He died in 1581, pursued by English troops. The belligerence of the Exiles took a further blow when the brilliant Jesuit Edmund Campion was arrested and executed in 1581. In the same year, Pope Gregory XIII issued a "Mitigation" of the excommunication – stating that English Catholics were not bound to it until such time as "circumstances changed". It was an admission that the excommunication had been a tactical failure as far as Elizabeth was concerned, and that it had placed Catholic lives in mortal danger. For the excommunication gave Elizabeth the pretext to kill Catholics for treason instead of heresy. But the Mitigation did not soothe the English government, which regarded it (quite rightly) as wordplay. The Exiles were in full retreat and did not recover any of their lost ground until the 1800s.

The principal Exile figures were the Jesuits Edmund Campion and Robert Persons (or Parsons),[6] Cardinal William Allen, and Nicolas Sanders. Campion and Persons have similar stories: both were educated at Oxford, both became Catholics when they left Oxford, both joined the Society of Jesus within two years of each other and returned to England together in 1580. Campion was captured and executed in 1581, while

Persons returned to the Continent, where he eventually became the Rector of the English College in Rome from 1597 to 1610.[7]

William Allen was a Fellow of Oriel College in Oxford, during the reign of Mary Tudor, and left England for Louvain in 1561, only to return to England the following year and be exiled permanently in 1565. He helped to establish the English Colleges at Douai, Rome, and Valladolid. Because of this, he came to be regarded as the *de facto* head of the English Catholic community. Having been promoted to Cardinal, he became embroiled in the Spanish Armada, as it was thought he had written a manifesto of sorts, called *Admonition to the Nobility and People of England*, to accompany the invaders in 1588.[8] Because of the explosive nature of this manifesto – calling Elizabeth a bastard and no queen – his authorship was called into question by the secular clergy, eager to distance Allen and themselves from such an incriminating document.

Nicolas Sanders graduated from New College in Oxford in 1551 and fled to the Continent when Elizabeth ascended to the throne in 1558. He was ordained priest in 1560, and the next year accompanied Cardinal Hosius to the Council of Trent. In 1572 he became a consultor to Pope Gregory XIII on English affairs, and wrote the most complete "Exile" history of the Reformation, *De Origine ac Progressu Schismatici Anglicani*. He did not finish the project, but left notes for its completion in 1579, when he set out on his ill-fated mission to Ireland. His manuscript was edited by Edward Rishton, another Exile priest, who added new material and published the work in Cologne in 1585. It was not translated into English until 1877 by David Lewis, and published as *The Rise and Growth of the Anglican Schism*. Both the date of the translation and the choice of the word "Schism" by Sanders and Lewis would prove to be significant indicators of how the Catholic Church viewed both itself and the Church of England in the late 1800s.

Exile history, as written by Sanders, Allen (in his *Admonition*), and Persons (in his *Responsio Edictum* of 1593) was all about Queen Elizabeth. Henry VIII was important to them only insofar as he fathered her by Anne Boleyn, someone who was not legitimately his wife. Henry's Reformation was dismissed by the Exiles as temporary, and something which he came to regret. Edward VI and his protectors were vigourous in promoting the cause of Protestantism, but did not endure long enough to make their changes lasting. Elizabeth, on the other hand, by consistent policy and sheer longevity (both of which would have been known by Persons, Allen, and Rishton, if not by Sanders), was able to form the schism into something permanent and of her own design. Hence, she would receive the brunt of the Catholic Exile attack, which encompassed her policies, her person, and her mother.

The first business of Exile history was to establish the illegitimacy of Elizabeth's birth and, by extension, that of her reign. Henry had married Anne Boleyn contrary to the laws of the Church, making the marriage invalid and all the children of that marriage bastards. This was not enough for some Exiles, who proposed that Anne Boleyn was not only the invalid wife of Henry VIII, but his daughter as well. Thus, Elizabeth's birth violated both the laws of the Church and natural law.

Nothing was bad enough for Anne Boleyn. Her immorality was another subject on which the Exiles dwelt – making mention of her sinning first at age fifteen with her father's butler, then with his chaplain, then with the gentlemen Norris, Weston, and Brereton, her musician Mark Smeaton, and her own brother. Sanders wrote, "She appeared at the French court, where she was called the English mare, because of her shameless behaviour; and then the mule, when she became acquainted with the King of France."[9] Even Anne's physical appearance became a target. Sanders continued,

> Anne Boleyn was rather tall of stature, with black hair, and an oval face of sallow complexion, as if troubled with jaundice. She had a projecting tooth under the upper lip, and on her right hand six fingers. There was a large wen under her chin, and therefore to hide its ugliness she wore a high dress covering her throat.[10]

The real target here was not Anne Boleyn, but Elizabeth, the inference being "Like mother, like daughter". William Allen wrote that the court of Elizabeth was run in the midst of an "unspeakable and incredible variety of lust".[11] Elizabeth herself, according to the Exiles, was immoral – entertaining any number of suitors. Furthermore, she was a heretic who denied the pope's authority; she was a perjurer who violated her coronation oath which provided for the defense of the Catholic faith; she was a bastard and never claimed the crown as her birthright, but intruded by force; she was, therefore, a usurper who did not merit loyalty.

But had Elizabeth submitted to the pope, the Exiles would have forgiven her other sins. It was her heresy in assuming the supremacy of the Church of England which was the heart of the matter, and for the Exiles the issue was very clear: obey the pope and we will be your lawful and loyal subjects; disobey him and we will seek to overthrow you.

The sources from which the Exiles drew their historical account of the Reformation consisted of diplomatic reports, information passed on by newly-arrived Exiles, and news from letters. Any information obtained in this manner was bound to be sprinkled with rumour, fabrication, and exaggeration, all of which was complicated by the fact that the Exiles tended to credit every story which was derogatory to their enemies. For they were not merely compiling a record of the events surrounding England's break from Rome; they were trying to argue that the break was entirely wrong. They were convinced that the English Reformation had sprung from evil motives and was proceeding on a course which was disastrous. In this cause they occasionally used doubtful material, which earned for Sanders the nickname "Dr. Slanders", and drew from the historian Jeremy Collier the rebuke that "he was almost as bad an historian as he was a subject".[12] His charge that Anne Boleyn was the daughter of Henry VIII was labeled by the Catholic John Lingard as "ridiculous", a criticism which is given support by Sanders's penchant for repeating every negative charge against Anne Boleyn used by the government at her trial – a source which, in other circumstances, Sanders would have found to be highly unreliable.

Exile bias also manifested itself by omission. Sanders, for example, never wrote a word about the heresy burnings carried out by Mary Tudor. Exile historians also overlooked, or positively denied, the role played by some of their number in fomenting foreign mischief.

But, more than any other flaw, Exile historians could not resist employing a black-and-white approach to the issues, which similarly marred Protestant histories written at the same time.[13] Protestants, or any person who promoted the Protestant cause either directly or indirectly, were found almost always to be in the wrong. Conversely, Catholics were found to be in the right. The consequences for Protestants could be quite dramatic:

> Among the memorable events of these times, in which innocent Catholics were everywhere made to suffer, is that which took place in the city of Oxford. One Rowland Jenks was arraigned as a Catholic, found guilty, and being but one of the common people, was condemned to lose both his ears. But the judge had hardly delivered the sentence when a deadly disease suddenly attacked the whole court; no other parts of the city, and no persons not in the court, were touched. The disease laid hold in a moment of all the judges, the high sheriff, and the twelve men of the jury . . . The jurymen died immediately, the judges, the lawyers, and the high sheriff died, some of them within a few hours, others within a few days, but all of them died. Not less than five hundred persons who caught the same disease at the same time and place [Oxford], died soon after.[14]

This approach led to a reductionism by which all complex motives and effects were consigned to the single sphere of religion. Thus, Catholics were persecuted solely on the grounds of their being Catholic. The Pilgrimage of Grace became, for Sanders, a revolt on behalf of religion. He noted:

When, therefore, they [Catholics] saw that under the cloak of banishing superstition nothing else was meant but stealing the sacred vessels, the silver
crucifixes, the chalices that held the blood of Christ, together with all other
things by which the churches were adorned, they took up arms.[15]

Modern scholarship has joined the fray over this matter of the
Pilgrimage. A. G. Dickens said of the Pilgrimage that it "is agreed to have
been a social and economic affair, little related to any aspect of the
Reformation".[16] That it was not as universally "agreed" as Dickens
thought, is testified by J. J. Scarisbrick, who wrote that the Pilgrimage
"was 'religious' in the widest sense of the word, that is, it was a protest
on behalf of the old religion (above all in defense of the monasteries),
though the reasons for clinging to the old ways may well have ranged from
the highest and most unworldly to the most profane".[17] The point here is
that Sanders was incapable of such qualification. When he expressed a
point which was arguable, he deliberately ignored any nuance which
might have clouded his purpose.

The matter of the trials of priests is a similar case in point. Persons and
Campion attempted to formulate a more subtle reduction – but a reduction nonetheless – that the prisoners who were being put to death for
treason were, in reality, being put to death for their religious beliefs.
Consequently, their historical accounts of this process concentrate on the
tortures, interrogations, and executions of the "martyrs", as they called
them, who had been arrested for no other reason than that they had dared
to practice their religion. There was a clear and necessary distinction
between the dictates of conscience and those of loyalty to the state. Only
because Henry VIII, Edward VI, and Elizabeth claimed supremacy over
the Church in England, had the distinction become blurred. Try as they
might, the Exiles could not convince the government to recognize the
distinction. The government countered by claiming that the pope had
muddied the waters by presuming to pronounce an excommunication and
deposition, thus freeing the crown's subjects from their loyalty, and
converting a specifically religious issue into one of civil allegiance. It is
likely that the government even welcomed the pope's bull of excommunication, and sought to exploit the resulting confusion. Now the
government was free to eradicate the opposition by a process which might
otherwise have proved tedious and embarrassing.

Exile history was too close to the event itself to be more than lengthy
editorializing, but its main tenet – that the pope's authority was what the
Reformation was all about – was a conclusion which would be reached
again, after sophisticated research and the high ground of perspective was
reached, almost 400 years later.

The Appellant Approach

"Appellants" or "Appellant Clergy" were those diocesan (i.e. secular) priests who were imprisoned at Wisbech Prison and got their name from their numerous appeals to Rome for the removal of certain clerical representatives. Not having any bishops of their own after 1559, the secular clergy increasingly looked to William Allen as their spokesman in Rome. Upon Allen's death in 1594, George Blackwell was appointed by the pope as an "archpriest", to take Allen's place and exercise authority over the secular clergy in England. Blackwell pursued policies which these secular clergy perceived as being pro-Jesuit and overly strict. Redress was sought in Rome, where an appeal for his removal was sent, signed by thirty-one priests, headed by William Bishop. It was unsuccessful, but two more appeals followed in 1601 and 1602. Blackwell was eventually reprimanded, but not removed immediately. Bishop and twelve other priests also drew up a Protestation of Allegiance" to the queen in 1603 and repudiated the notion that England could be converted by political means. In 1603 Blackwell took the extraordinary step of taking the Oath of Allegiance to Elizabeth's successor, King James I, which discredited him and got him replaced by George Birkett. Though the controversy over leadership died with the arrival of Birkett, the scars remained and would be re-opened periodically, not only in the writings of Charles Dodd and Joseph Berington in the seventeenth and eighteenth centuries, respectively, but even well into the nineteenth century with the writings of Charles Butler, John Lingard, and Mark Tierney.

The Appellants looked on themselves as the guileless victims of a tug-of-war between the Society of Jesus, recently-arrived on the scene, and the government of Queen Elizabeth. But it was the Society of Jesus, and not the government, which was the cause of their problems – from the general state of religious persecution throughout England, to their own specific imprisonment in Wisbech Castle. Their histories of the Reformation reflected this animosity. Before the Jesuits had come in 1580, life for Catholics had been relatively peaceful, they maintained. William Watson, the principal spokesman for the Appellants, wrote:

> It cannot be denied that, but that for the first tenne yeares of her Majesties raigne, the state of Catholikes in England was tolerable, and after a sort in some good quietnesse. Such as for their consciences were imprisoned in the beginning of her coming to the Crowne, were very kindly and mercifully used . . . [18]

The Appellants saw what followed as a series of ill-advised provocations, beginning with the Rising of the North in 1569, followed quickly by the bull of excommunication in 1570, and the pope's attempt to foment the rebellion by sending his own agent, Ridolphi, from Florence, soliciting the help of Spain, and assigning the Duke of Norfolk to lead the uprising.[19] Jesuit influence in this interference was obvious to the Appellants, who charged the pope with being "mis-informed, and indirectly drawn to these courses".[20] It would not do to tread too heavily on a former pope, since the current pope was the one to whom they were making their "appeal".

Thus, the Appellant histories place most almost all of the responsibility for the lowly state of Catholics on the Jesuits, even before they were personally present in England. Watson wrote: "[The Jesuits] have bin the chiefe instruments of al the mischiefes that have bene intended against her Majestie, since the beginning of her reigne, and of the miseries, which we, or any Catholikes, have upon these occasions sustained."[21]

Despite these provocations, they thought, Elizabeth reacted with surprising moderation. The Law of 1571, though strict, was sprung from a just cause and was never effected with such cruelty as it might have been. Watson continued:

> [Once the excommunication had become known], there followed a great restraint of the said prisoners: but none of them were put to death upon that occasion: the sword being then onely drawne against such Catholikes, as had risen up actually into open rebellion. Wherein we cannot see what her Majestie did, that any Prince in Christendome in such a case, would not have done.[22]

Catholics, according to the Appellants, persisted in their ingratitude. In 1572, Sanders wrote *De Visibili Monarchia*, defending the Rising of the North, and in 1580, the ultimate provocation saw the arrival of the first two Jesuits in England, Campion and Persons. This, combined with the news of the Desmond Rebellion in 1579, settled what had previously been a doubtful issue. Elizabeth and her ministers now had little choice but to come down brutally against the Catholics of England. Watson wrote, "[The government] had great cause as politicke persons to suspect the worst".[23]

Watson claimed that he was not opposed to the Society of Jesus as such, but it is clear that he thought good Jesuits the exception rather than the rule. He wrote, "The order of that society being approved by the Pope is to be honoured of all good Catholikes, and the men themselves are to be reverenced; such we mean as live according to their calling and first institution: which few of them do".[24] The Jesuit association with Spain was problematic. Ignatius Loyola was a Spanish soldier, and the Society was dominated by Spanish Jesuits who could hardly avoid a loyalty to the

Spanish crown. Any Spanish scheme of invading Ireland or England necessarily implicated the Jesuits.

Nor was this all. According to the Appellants, Jesuits sought only "to advance and increase their owne societie"; they were known to have stolen money destined for secular priests;[25] they exaggerated their tortures, and both lied and dissembled under interrogation; finally, they opposed the appointment of abbots and bishops-in-ordinary, wanting instead "to fixe Vicars [so that the Jesuits] shall have the Land, Mannors, Lordships, Parsonages, Monasteries, and whatsoever, into their own hands".[26]

The object of this venom was Robert Persons, who embodied for the Appellants everything devious, grasping, and pernicious about the Society of Jesus. He was, according to Watson, "by his birth a bastard, begotten upon the bodie of a very base woman by the Parson of the parish where he was borne: and his right name is not Parsons, but Cowbuck".[27]

Evaluating the Appellant and Exile Histories

At first glance, the Appellants do not seem to offer anything more than a crude assault on the Society of Jesus. Watson says of the Jesuits, "The ignorant sort of their foolish Enamorades have nothing but their back, or *Posteriora*, that is the fruits of their labors to judge them by . . . ."[28] Yet, polemic aside, the Appellants exhibited a consistent view of the Reformation which bears a closer look. They saw it, first of all, as a purely Elizabethan phenomenon. Nowhere do they mention the Henrician or Edwardian Reformation. For the Appellants, the Reformation was an undecided affair certainly before 1570, and even before 1580. It was only during Elizabeth's reign did the Reformation begin to take a definite shape.

Next, the forces which caused this definite shape to take place were predominantly Catholic. The Appellants regarded Elizabeth and her government as neutral factors on which the negative influence of the Jesuits, Exiles, and popes was exercised. Thus, Elizabeth did not initiate the Reformation practices of her reign, but rather was compelled to act as she did by forces quite outside her control. Watson asked, "Who then gave the cause that you [Catholics] were troubled? When her Majestie used you kindly; how treacherously was she dealt with by you? Did not *Pius Quint.* practise her Majesties subversion; the [good lady] never dreaming of any such mischief?"[29]

Thirdly, the Catholic forces had more to do with politics than with religion. The English Reformation was, for the Appellants, primarily a quarrel about jurisdiction. Very little allusion is made by them to reformed religions and their influence on or within Elizabeth's government.

This is in sharp contrast to the Exile view, which saw the Reformation more in religious terms. Persons could describe the excommunication as "an act of jurisdiction between two superiors, the one Ecclesiastical, the other temporal", and in so doing attempt to trivialize its effect.[30] But Persons, probably because he had the advantage of European experience, saw the Reformation in England in the context of the general European movement toward revolt. Persons saw the Reformation as the complicated mixture of politics and religion that it was. He frequently wrote on the heretical nature of the Reformation, the truth of Catholicism, and the reasons why Catholics could not attend the new English service. These were not solely questions of jurisdiction, but matters of theology, and were hardly mentioned by the Appellants.

The loyalties of the two groups are instructive. The Exiles and Jesuits were loyal primarily to the pope, and saw Elizabeth as expendable, because she was not loyal to the pope. Any English regent who succeeded her and conceded the pope's spiritual authority in England would have their undying loyalty. The Appellants were loyal primarily to the queen, but not to the point of throwing over the pope. They did not, it must be emphasized, ever conform to the new liturgy or abjure the pope, which would have been very easy to do. But their starting point was loyalty to the crown, and they would attempt to work their loyalty to the pope around that initial commitment.

The Appellants were between a rock and a hard place. They were actually in England and in jail. The Exiles, on the other hand, had the luxury, if it could be called that, of being on the continent and out of harm's way. It was far easier for them to make impossible demands on the English people, to speak grandly about theological issues, and to pontificate (if you pardon the expression) on the authority of the pope. It was not so easy for the Appellants to make any claims about their allegiance to the pope. The fact that they remained Roman Catholic priests was allegiance enough. Their desperate situation called for a different approach. When some Exiles began returning to England as missionary priests, and began getting arrested, interrogated, and tortured, they also began to look for some qualification of the terms of the excommunication, and for some way to get around the pointed questions about their dual loyalty – to their English queen or to a foreign prince.

The Appellants have been accused of playing politics, of downplaying the important of the Reformation simply in order to gain toleration.[31]

Evidence is not wanting to support this thesis, notably the groveling protestations of loyalty made by the Appellants to the government. Watson wrote:

> We ought to have carried our selves in an other manner of course towards her, our true and lawfull Queene, and towards our countrie, then hath bene taken and pursued by many Catholikes, but especially by the Jesuites. And therefore . . . we have thought it our parts, (being her Highnesses naturalle born subjects,) to acknowledge the truth of the carriage of matters against us, and the apparent causes of it. . . .[32]

The Appellants became pawns of a government which, without offering much incentive, convinced them to inform on the whereabouts of missionary priests and to write a defense of the Crown so conciliatory as to be almost indistinguishable from the writing of William Cecil, Elizabeth's chief minister.

Yet, to concentrate on this "capitulation" is to oversimplify the Appellant position, which was a consistent program, though never systematically expressed, for the improvement of relations between the Catholic religion and the English state. The pope, they believed, was to refrain from intruding into areas (e.g. the deposition of princes) over which he had no jurisdiction.[33] Bishops-in-ordinary were to be appointed in order to provide an ecclesiastical court of appeal within England as well as an ecclesiastical body more in tune with the needs of the English people. The Jesuits were to be removed both from England and the seminaries throughout the continent.

One Appellant mistake was to imagine that the ecclesiastical world which they remembered was possible of immediate reconstruction, and that Elizabeth wanted to reconstruct it. To think that bishops-in-ordinary, presumably approved by the pope, would be coming back to England anytime soon was a very unrealistic dream. How would Elizabeth have accepted this without conceding her spiritual jurisdiction to the pope? In a way, the Appellants wanted what the Exiles wanted, but without having to go through all the necessary steps to get it done.

Another Appellant mistake was to associate the pope's jurisdictional quarrel with Elizabeth (i.e. did he have the right to excommunicate and depose her, and to command her obedience in spiritual matters to him) too closely with the Reformation itself. It was an issue, granted, and a very significant one, but one which could not be taken in isolation. Related to this, the Appellants saw the Reformation narrowly as co-terminus with England. The Exiles and Jesuits had an advantage here, because they saw the causes and effects of the reform movement in continental terms, and therefore as larger issues. But this could also be seen as a disadvantage, since the Exiles and Jesuits wanted to apply a continental solution to what may have been a specifically English problem. Person's solution was a sweeping eradication of heresy and the restoration of the Catholic religion, while the Appellants, perhaps more realistically in this case, sought only the toleration of their faith.

The final Appellant mistake was to think that the Catholic Church was totally in control of the situation. Get rid of the Jesuits, and Elizabeth will somehow come back to the Roman Catholic Church. Do this, and life as we knew it under Mary, will return. They seemed unable to admit that times had changed and that they were in jail for good, no matter what Rome decided.

In any case, the programs of both parties – Exiles and Jesuits on the one hand and Appellants and Secular Clergy on the other – persisted as late as the mid-nineteenth century, and greatly influenced divergent Catholic historical perceptions of the Reformation in England. The Ultramontanists and Cisalpines of another generation would hold views remarkably similar to those of their Exile and Appellant forbears of an earlier period. Remarkably, they would use many of the same arguments and much of the same information as their predecessors.

However, one very interesting development took place in ending this division. Previous to, and during the Reformation, there had existed an intense rivalry between religious priests (belonging to religious orders) and secular or diocesan priests. For centuries they carried on their turf battles. With the elimination of the religious orders in England by 1540, this rivalry became narrowed after 1580 to one between the Jesuits and secular clergy, and persisted for a very long time. Protestants, no matter of what stamp, were unified in attacking both of these groups as Romish and Papist. They were the enemy to be removed. But, as Protestantism dominated and Catholicism became the minority, the Protestants split into multiple groupings: High Church, Low Church, Puritans, Methodists, etc., and the turf battles changed hands. The Catholics were far from done with each other, quite yet, but gradually they set aside their differences and found themselves united in attacking the Protestant majority, no matter what form it took.

Chapter II

THE QUEST FOR CATHOLIC EMANCIPATION

The next major historical work by a Catholic on the English Reformation would not appear until the early 1700s. Events in the seventeenth century conspired to keep Catholics on the defensive, sometimes to the point of struggling to survive. The Gunpowder Plot of 1605 implicated the Society of Jesus unjustly.[1] The ascendancy of Oliver Cromwell, who ruled England from 1645 until his death in 1658, ended any hopes of restoring the Catholic Church in England during the reign of the first Stuart kings of England.[2] The débâcle of the last two Stuart kings, Charles II and James II, and the ensuing Glorious Revolution, wherein the Protestant William of Orange was brought into England (some claim it was an invasion), sealed the Catholics' fate. Once again, a secular priest attempted to deflect blame for the Catholic Church's wrongs onto the Society of Jesus, in the hopes of gaining some relief from the penal laws. Once again, the tool to accomplish this would be history.

Charles Dodd was born Hugh Tootel. It was common for Catholic priests to change their names in order to avoid detection by the government, since the laws against them had stiffened once again in the early 1700s. Dodd also did not want to be detected by the Jesuits. In 1713 he had published an anti-Jesuit tract entitled *The History of Douay College*, under the guise of an Anglican chaplain serving British troops in the area. In this tract, he maintained that Robert Persons had become "banker" to Douai, and had put part of its income aside for the foundation of St. Omer, another continental seminary, and that Douay had become "Fr. Parson's Nursery".[3] Dodd then included the archpriest Blackwell in his assault, saying the latter was "a Priest by his Order, yet a Bishop by his Jurisdiction, and a Jesuit by his Principles".[4] Using Blackwell, Persons thus governed the English Church by proxy. The Jesuits discovered who wrote the tract, and an unpleasant debate ensued. It was with some apprehension, therefore, that they greeted Dodd's more ambitious *Church History of England* when the first of its three volumes appeared in 1737.[5] Dodd renewed his claims against the Jesuits in this book, but this time to answer charges of Catholic disloyalty in connection with the two Jacobite uprisings intent on placing the Stuarts back on the English throne. It did not have much of an impact on the English view of the Reformation – it was expensive and difficult (and possibly dangerous) to obtain. Its place of publication was listed as being in Brussels, but the book was really printed in Wolverhampton, again in order to avoid detection by the authorities. But it provided a comfort and a rallying point for those few diocesan priests living in seclusion in England, who carried on the legacy of their Appellant forebears. And *Dodd's Church History*, as it became known, sufficiently intrigued one English Catholic priest, Mark Tierney, in the 1830s to publish a re-edition. Dodd's history and Tierney's re-edition will be considered in chapter IV.

Proposals for Catholic Relief

Times were changing in the England of the late 1700s. Once Bonnie Prince Charlie's threat was convincingly defeated at the Battle of Culloden in 1745, the penal laws began to be relaxed in application, if not on the books themselves. The Catholic population of England had dwindled to 1 per cent by 1780 and no longer posed the same threat to the government that it once did. The papacy also, largely shorn of its political power throughout the world, was not only less menacing, but appeared to be on the road to obsolescence. Some people thought that the papacy would not long survive. Horace Walpole, writing from Italy in 1769 after Pope Clement XIII had just died, speculated on the election of the "last pope".[6] Eamon Duffy noted more recently, "By the 1780s, every Catholic state in Europe wanted to reduce the Pope to a ceremonial figurehead, and most of them had succeeded".[7]

Not only was the Catholic presence muted both at home and abroad, but Enlightenment ideals of toleration aroused a certain sympathy for the plight of those few English Catholics who still lived in England, and against whom civil disabilities still pressed hardly. Proposals for Catholic relief, once unthinkable, now began to be heard from such eminent statesmen as Edmund Burke and Charles James Fox. By themselves these factors were not sufficient to pass relief legislation as early as 1778, but another seemingly unrelated factor surfaced to give such legislation an urgency it did not previously enjoy: in October 1777 General Burgoyne lost the Battle of Saratoga. The following February, France recognized the United States and concluded a defense treaty, which was tantamount to a declaration of war against Great Britain. The prospect of a prolonged conflict with the American colonies forced the English government to look to the Catholic Highlands for more fighting men. Thus Lord North pursued a quick deal with the Catholic authorities, seeking to lessen the civil disabilities of Catholics in exchange for their enlistment in the Army.

His first overture, made almost immediately after news of Saratoga was heard in England, went unheeded, mainly because the two bishops to whom he appealed (George Hay of Glasgow and the ancient Richard Challoner, who was eighty-seven) did not trust him. Years of living under the penal laws had made them wary of concessions offered by a government which had suddenly become friendly. Moreover, they feared popular reaction to sweeping improvements in the situation of Catholics, a fear which later events would prove correct.[8]

Lord North next appealed to the Catholic laity, in the person of William Sheldon, who was only to eager to wrest negotiations away from the clergy. He arranged a meeting for 2 April 1778 to discuss the proposed relief bill. At this same meeting, a Catholic Committee of five members was formed, and the Cisalpine movement in England was born.

Cisalpinism was an English form of the French Gallicanism and the Austrian Josephism (named after the emperor Joseph II), wherein the national Churches acted independently of Rome to a very large extent. The crown in these countries, acting in conjunction with the national hierarchy, regulated the affairs of the Church without much reference to Rome. The idea was to keep the pope out of one's national and ecclesiastical business. The English version of this – Cisalpinism – agreed with this nationalism in principle. However, since there was no Catholic crown in England, and since the Catholic bishops who resided there were appointed directly by the pope, the laity regarded themselves as the ones who should do the regulating. They emphasized civil obedience, loyalty to the crown, and a disavowal of foreign influence – especially that exercised by the pope. Wilfrid Ward, at the end of the nineteenth century, noted that the "one absorbing desire of the Cisalpines was to convince an intensely prejudiced public that Catholics could be as loyal as and sensible as their fellows, that they were not Jacobites, nor minions of the pope, nor Jesuitical equivocators, nor slaves to superstition".[9]

Cisalpinism (which is best translated as a movement "*this* side of the Alps") began exclusively as a lay movement. At their first historic meeting, every Roman Catholic gentleman of standing had been invited by the Catholic Committee. Edmund Burke gave the address, and the eighty people present approved and signed it.[10] No clergy were present. Sheldon, thinking that clerical interference might doom the bill, strongly opposed "any application to our clergy in temporal matters, the English Catholic Gentlemen being quite able to judge and act for themselves in these affairs". Sir John Throckmorton told Bishop Hay more directly, "We don't want bishops".[11]

On the surface, it appeared that the cisalpine gentlemen had scored a great victory. The Relief Act of 1778 received the royal assent one month after their meeting, and the penal laws began to fall away. The Act of 1700 was repealed. It had imposed life sentences on Catholic clergy and schoolmasters, rewarded any informer £100 for information leading to a conviction, and denied the right of a Catholic to inherit or buy property. But much of the penal legislation remained in place: Catholics were still unable to worship publicly; they were heavily penalized for educating their children in their own religion; they might not be granted commissions in the army or navy; or practise the law in any of its branches. They were still obliged, furthermore, to register their estates, to publish all their family transactions, and to pay a double land-tax. Finally, they were still prohibited from voting and from sitting in either house of Parliament.[12]

In reality, the Cisalpines distorted their importance in the passage of the Act, and stood to lose more than they knew. Aside from the fact that there was already considerable sympathy for Catholic relief within Parliament, the government wanted a Relief Act (because it needed more soldiers) and was going to get it – bishops or no bishops. The Catholic gentlemen were little more than a tool to ease the passage of the Act, providing the government with a group supposedly representative of the Catholic body as a whole, and thus creating the appearance of Catholic approval.

The Catholic gentlemen attempted to perpetuate their "influence" by forming a Second Catholic Committee in 1782 consisting of ten members, and a Third Catholic Committee in 1787, which attempted to appease the bishops by adding three clergymen sympathetic to its cause. In 1792 the Catholic Committee was radically re-organized into a less-structured "club", which quickly devolved into a social body and shed its political program. This Cisalpine Club had forty-two members and lasted until Emancipation in 1829, when it was re-formed into the Emancipation Club, which continued for a further seventeen years. In 1808 a Catholic Board was formed by Charles Butler, a Catholic lawyer who served as secretary and principal spokesman of the various Committees. Its purposes were to monitor anti-Catholic literature, and its membership was an amalgam of laity and clergy, including all four vicars-apostolic.

The vicars were "missionary" bishops in England. They were not bishops-in-ordinary or "normal" bishops, but rather vicars-apostolic assigned by Propaganda Fide to districts, rather than to dioceses.[13] They were the administrators deemed so inconsequential as to be ignored by both the government and the Cisalpines in 1778. But one of the side effects of the Relief Act of 1778 was that these bishops began to gain in stature. Once the conditions were removed which had allowed the Catholic laity to gain so much influence with the likes of Edmund Burke, the laity's influence began to wane in favor of the bishops. When the next round of discussions for further relief began in the 1780s, the bishops were already strong enough to intrude and get their way. By 1803, the Cisalpines, as a political force representing the Catholic Church independent of the bishops, were finished.

In not wanting bishops, the Cisalpines had made a necessary, though fatal mistake. They knew well how bishops operated, and that to invite them would mean abandoning negotiations to them, while all haste and opportunity for relief would be lost. Yet, not to invite them incurred their constant suspicion and hostility. Even though the Committee made a half-hearted attempt to assuage the bishops by adding three clerics to its number in 1788, a year later the Committee was reverting to form in attempting to by-pass the bishops, thus further aggravating them. Joan Connell has asked if the bishops' objections to the Cisalpines did not have more to do with the impropriety of their presuming to dictate to bishops, than with any heretical content of their proposals. She quotes a letter from Bishop Walmseley (Western District) to Charles Butler, in this regard:

> Thus to dictate to us in Ecclesiastical matters, is it not assuming an authority which you have not? Must the Vicars Apostolic learn their Duty from you? Are they obliged to adopt your Verdict or have you a right to give any Verdict at all? Whom did the Founder of his Church speak to, when he said, "Go and teach all nations, he that hears you hears me"?[14]

The Cisalpines subordinated doctrinal matters to the business of emancipation. They needed to avoid theological hair-splitting if a relief bill was to be quickly passed. But this was achieved at the cost of ignoring nearly the whole of papal claims, and this was a serious theological complication. Joseph Berington, a Cisalpine priest, wrote to his friend John Carroll, Catholic Bishop of the United States, to advise him that he should "shut his eyes on the last fourteen centuries, and only consider what was the prerogative of the See of Rome during the Apostolic ages and the years immediately succeeding to them. All that is essential then existed; the rest is abuse and corruption".[15]

Alexander Geddes, a Scottish Catholic priest associated with the

Cisalpine movement, took Berington's sentiment a step further when he wrote:

> The Papal Primacy became when stript of all its usurped appendages and reduced to its primitive simplicity nothing more than a bare primacy of honour, rank and precedence, which is not more dangerous to the liberties of the Christian Church in general, than the primacy of Lyons is to the liberties of the Gallican, or that of Canterbury, is to the liberties of the Anglican Church.[16]

Berington, not to be outdone, added, "The word Roman has been given us to intimate some undue attachment to the See of Rome . . . I am no Papist, nor is my religion Popery."[17] In the 1787 volume of *Gentleman's Magazine*, he would elaborate:

> It is no matter of faith to believe that the Pope is in himself infallible, separated from the Church, even in expounding the faith; by consequence papal decrees, taken exclusively from a General Council or universal acceptance of the Church, oblige none, under pain of heresy, to an interior assent.

> If the Pope should pretend to absolve or dispense with His Majesty's subjects from their allegiance, on account of heresy or schism, such dispensation would be vain and null.[18]

Sir John Throckmorton, Berington's patron, showed the theological naïvete of the Cisalpines by suggesting that the English bishops simply declare themselves bishops-in-ordinary without waiting for Rome's approval. Which is exactly what Elizabeth had done!

This was all too much for the vicars-apostolic. Berington and Geddes were suspended from their priestly duties. Charles Berington, Joseph's cousin, also fell under suspicion and had his episcopal appointment so obstructed that he would die before he took office. This disciplinary action was a sign that the bishops had gained the upper hand. Nor was it only a sign. A substitute Oath of Allegiance, proposed by the Catholic Committee, was strongly condemned by the bishops, who addressed the Committee in the unambiguous words, "To these determinations [i.e. corrections to the proposed oath] we require your submission."[19]

Joseph Berington and the Papacy

The Cisalpines chose history as their tool in mediating the effects of the penal laws because history would explain their plight, perhaps provide clues about how to ease the situation, and would justify the actions they had taken in negotiating directly with the English government. For them, the problems of the sixteenth century had yet to be solved, and they hoped that, by showing those problems in a clear and honest light, they could go some distance in solving the problems of their own day. Their appeal to history is an interesting one because it is double-edged. There is, on the one hand, the attempt to explain the Catholic position to a non-Catholic world – to insist on Catholic loyalty, on the misfortune of the Reformation, and on the inessential quality of the break. On the other hand, there is the need to reflect on their own communion and to question Catholic adherence to outdated and possibly unnecessary "doctrines".

To the Cisalpines, all that stood between English Catholics and emancipation was papal claims. They searched history and judged that the final break with Rome came when Pius V excommunicated Elizabeth and deposed her. Excommunication was one thing, because it involved the spiritual realm; but deposition intruded into the temporal realm, and her Catholics became traitors, at least legally, as long as they adhered to the authority of the pope. Thus, in order to extract themselves from the dilemma of dual (and conflicting) civil allegiance, they needed to distinguish between the pope's spiritual authority, which they recognized, and his temporal authority, which they did not. History would be the means by which they would convince the government, and the people of England, of their loyalty. Once again, their attention would focus almost entirely on the reign of Queen Elizabeth.

John Throckmorton, one of the most impetuous Catholic laymen in the England of the late eighteenth century, asked the priest-philosopher Joseph Berington to produce a work which would expose a foreign ecclesiastical government which prevented its subjects from guaranteeing their good behavior and civic duty to the state.[20] Joseph Berington had become one of the voices of the Cisalpine movement and had already incurred the suspicion of the majority of English bishops with his *State and Behaviour of English Catholics* (1780), which was written to lessen fears that the government and people of England might have about Catholics.

Berington accepted Throckmorton's request with a blend of courage and characteristic recklessness. He decided to publish an expanded re-edition of *The Memoirs of Gregorio Panzani*. The authenticity of these Memoirs had never been proven, and only extracts had previously appeared in print – in Dodd's *Church History*. Berington said that publication of the entire manuscript had been deliberately avoided by Dodd, lest it "might prejudice the evil-disposed", a caution Berington no longer found necessary to observe.[21]

Publication in 1793 was a coup in two ways: first, it meant that

Berington was not going to re-arrange or edit Dodd's volumes, as several authors in succession had tried (and would later try) to do, but that he was going to attempt something entirely new. Secondly, he was introducing an original and largely unknown manuscript into the debate on the subject of Catholic loyalty. He fully intended it an act of defiance and the starting-point for his own historical observations.

Gregorio Panzani was a secret papal agent who had been sent to England from 1634 to 1636 by Pope Urban VIII in the hope of settling the disputes between the religious and secular clergy, and to assess both the expediency of appointing a bishop-in-ordinary (as opposed to a missionary vicar-apostolic) and the lawfulness of taking the Oath of Allegiance. His actual *Memoirs* would serve Berington as a peg to hang his own ideas. The *Memoirs* themselves are only 145 pages long, while Berington's Preface, Introduction, and Afterword run to 262 pages.

The Reformation issues which Berington treated were twofold: the papal actions against Elizabeth, and the role of the regular clergy, i.e. the Jesuits. Berington felt that the central problem in the English Reformation was the pope's temporal power, and especially his deposing power. Because Berington wrote so little about the Henrician Reformation, it is safe to say that he viewed the Reformation in England as essentially an Elizabethan phenomenon, and the problems of his own day to the result of the Elizabethan Settlement. In his earlier book he called Elizabeth's reign "the real era of the Reformation".[22] But already here we see a problem: Berington did not regard Elizabeth's headship of the Church as an issue at all; he does not mention it as being a complication in the taking of the Oath of Allegiance. Elizabeth, in his view, had hardly changed the religion, and what changes she had allowed were sensible and executed in a conciliatory manner. "To conciliate the minds of men," he wrote, "not to divide them, was the goal of this uncommon woman."[23]

Berington echoed the Appellants by noting that the first ten years of Elizabeth's reign saw little persecution, except "what arose from the act of supremacy, the severity of which was lessening".[24] Granted, the Marian bishops had been deprived of their sees, but they had been treated humanely, and only Bishop Bonner was kept in prison – not surprising in light of his role in the Marian persecution. Berington suggests that even those few who refused to take the oath probably did so for reasons which were less than religious: "Few then remained firm to the old cause; and of these few, as many were placed in elevated stations, we may, perhaps, be induced to think that a point of honour, rather than a conviction of duty, influenced their determination."[25]

Elizabeth's moderation was further elucidated, Berington thought, when news of the excommunication helped to instigate the Rising of the

North, to which she responded by punishing only the active participants. No priest was executed until 1577, even though Parliament had given the queen warrant for such action as early as 1571 – this despite the provocative presence in England of fifty missionary priests since 1574. In all of this, Elizabeth appeared to Berington to be the very model of restraint.

The pope, on the other hand, was a model of excess. Berington called Paul IV "the haughty Paul", and referred to the account by the seventeenth-century historian, Peter Heylyn, of the conversation between Edward Carne and the pope, when the latter was informed that Elizabeth had acceded to the throne. The pope told Carne,

> that the kingdom of England was a fief of the holy see; that Elizabeth was a bastard, and had no right to the succession; that he could not annul the decrees of Clement VII and Paul III with regard to her father's marriage; that it was an act of signal audacity in her to have assumed the title of queen, without his participation; that thus she was undeserving of the smallest indulgence . . . [26]

John Lingard, later on, found convincing evidence that this did not happen. It was not welcome evidence, either, as far as Lingard was concerned, because he was of a mind similar to Berington's when it came to papal "pretensions". And, if it did not happen, Lingard could no longer defend her as a victim of the pope's intransigence (see below, p. 69).

Berington saw the deposing power of the pope clearly as a temporal power which had been assumed in a superstitious age. He saw the use of this power, coupled with the petulant attitude of the pope, as fixing Elizabeth's resolve.[27] By way of asserting that Elizabeth's claim to supremacy was justifiable, Berington seriously questioned the primacy of the pope. These two opinions were, in fact, correlative. The Oath of Allegiance could be taken without damage to one's conscience, Berington thought, because there was a benign interpretation of the Oath which rested largely on minimizing of the pope's spiritual authority. Thus, almost imperceptibly, Berington moved from denying the pope's temporal power to questioning the extent (and possibly the existence) of the pope's spiritual power. He wrote:

> To the jurisdiction of the Roman see and to the supremacy of its first pastor I bow with reverence; but neither with that jurisdiction nor with that supremacy, though they are sometimes sullied by the contact, has the court of Rome and its fifteen congregations any proper concern.[28]

In other words, the claims made by popes to temporal and spiritual jurisdiction *outside of Rome* have been the "contrivance of human ambition on the one hand, and of weak concessions [by secular governments] on the other".[29] Even Berington's avoidance of the word "pope", and his insistence on calling him "bishop", are telling. In a letter to John Kirk, a priest friend, Berington sarcastically drew a relation between the theory of the primacy of the pope, and its practice.

> I find, for instance, that from St. Peter to the time of Constantine there is no document to prove, that *any primacy* was exercised *by the Roman Bishop*. On this ground, I state the fact; but during all that period, I do not say, that those bishops were not jure divino, possessed of the primacy. The right to jurisdiction and its exercise are obviously different things.[30]

Is it not suspicious, Berington implied, that a divine right, claimed by later popes as originating with St. Peter, was not exercised by him or his successors for 300 years? Logically, then, Berington saw any resistance to this pretended jurisdiction, "acquired by human means", to be perfectly lawful.[31]

The Oath of Allegiance, or it earliest form called the Oath of Supremacy, was crucial in all of this because Catholic hesitation in the signing the oath, going all the way back to Sir Thomas More and Bishop John Fisher, depended on the notion of papal primacy in spiritual matters. A position like Berington's was antecedent to the removal of obstacles to signing. Berington, in fact, suggested that signing the oath was an easy step:

> Just notions of the *oath of supremacy* are becoming peculiarly important to us, as it alone withholds us from the exercise of our *elective franchise*: and why should we importune government for a further redress of grievances, or complain that we are aggrieved, if the remedy be in our own hands? One bold man, by taking the oath, may dissipate the whole charm of prejudice, and restore us to the most valuable privilege of British citizens.[32]

That one bold man would have to be someone beside Joseph Berington, because he never took the Oath of Allegiance. To be fair, Berington's hesitation here was probably not due to cowardice. He probably had a more prominent person (e.g. a bishop) in mind.

Joseph Berington and the Society of Jesus

Tied in with Berington's treatment of the papacy was his treatment of the Society of Jesus. In his eyes, the Society was responsible, more than any other group or person, for encouraging a lofty opinion of papal power and, as a result, for perpetuating the problems associated with the Oath of Allegiance. He regarded the Jesuits as dangerous apostles of papal prerogatives.[33] He rejected the claim that they were simply trying to maintain Catholics in the faith, saying, "It was not for any *tenet of the Catholic faith* that they were exposed to this persecution".[34] They had provoked Elizabeth and, although she had reacted cruelly in the end, no one could fault her unease at the presence of Jesuits in England and the missionary priests who had been trained by the Jesuits abroad. Proof for this was found by Berington in her relatively mild treatment of the other priests:

> To say, if these men [the Jesuits] had been away, that fewer penal statutes against Catholics would have existed, is a conjecture founded on no light evidence; but to say . . . that, before the close of the reign of Elizabeth, the public odium against us would have ceased, is, perhaps, as obvious a truth as history can reveal. By a proclamation of November 7, 1601, the queen banished the Jesuits and such priests as espoused their principles and party, . . . but to such clergy as would have a true profession of their allegiance, she signified her wish to shew favour and indulgence.[35]

Berington's bête noire in all of this was Robert Persons, the Jesuit who came to England with Edmund Campion in 1580 and later fled to the continent to become the President of the English College in Rome. To Berington, Persons represented, more than anyone else, those tendencies to disloyalty, foreignness, and intrigue: "Devoted to the most extravagant pretensions of the Roman court, . . . his writings, which were numerous, are an exact transcript of his mind, dark, imposing, problematical, seditious."[36]

Such outbursts are common in the *Memoirs of Panzani*, and summarize Berington's grievances against Persons. If one charge stands out, it is that Persons infected the secular clergy with his stratagems of disloyalty. Persons was seen as designing a Jesuit takeover of the Catholic Church in England, first by persuading the pope to allow his chamberlain Cajetan ("calling himself the protector of the English nation") to pass this authority onto Persons himself.[37] It was then a small matter to assume control of the education of the exiled priests and the direction of their missionary efforts in England. Had these missionaries, Berington commented, "returned actuated by a pure zeal for religion, and with sentiments of an enlightened patriotism and of allegiance to their sovereign, they might have practised the duties of their ministry, unheeded and unmolested".[38] The man who prevented this from happening was Persons, with whose name was associated "intrigue, device, stratagem, and all the crooked policy of the Machiavellian school".[39]

The clergy were not free from blame, either. Berington faulted them for fleeing to the continent in the first place, because they thereby excited suspicion and eventuated persecution. The schools they sought on the continent could have been established in England in due time, which action would have avoided the charge of foreign influence. But what was worse than their flight was the spirit of confrontation which they displayed on their return: "Their notions of deposing princes were not just talk, but the 'pabulum' on which that ultramontane spirit fed . . . And they rendered the men who maintained them obnoxious to the state, exposing them to prosecution and imprisonment, and sometimes even death."[40]

The Jesuit Response

Berington did not go unanswered. While non-Catholics naturally applauded the *Memoirs of Panzani*, they also wondered when the ecclesiastical axe would fall on the author. The vicars-apostolic, for their part, were divided about how to respond. Bishop Walmesley, vicar-apostolic for the Western District, wanted penalties imposed on Berington, and Bishop Douglas, vicar-apostolic of the London District, suspended him from his priestly faculties. That they would have gone further is certain, but they were checked by the hesitations of the vicar-apostolic of the Midlands Districts, Thomas Talbot, who wrote:

> Without abetting any wrong opinion Mr. Berington may have broached, and without pretending to exculpate him from censure when he deserves it, I consider him as a man of learning, and a person very regular and even exemplary in the exercise of his missionary functions. He is ready, as he declares, to explain or even to retract what may be deemed amiss in his writings. Why, then, must he be run down like a wild beast?[41]

Chastened by this rebuke, Berington's opponents had to be content to allow Fr. Charles Plowden, an ex-Jesuit (the Society was suppressed at the time), to write a suitable reply.[42] The result was Plowden's *Remarks on a Book Entitled "Memoirs of Gregorio Panzani"* (Liege, 1794). Much like Berington's book, Plowden's was written in the polemical spirit of the day, though Plowden outdid even Berington in the ferocity of his language. The principal accusation that Plowden made was that Berington had tried to lure him into a trap, by drawing him into writing a full-scale history, a task for which he was admittedly unsuited. He made frequent mention of this "trap" and his skill at avoiding it, only to fall headlong into Berington's real trap: he called the *Memoirs of Panzani* a forgery:

I maintain that either this man [Panzani] was a very unfair and partial nego-
tiator, quite undeserving of credit; or that his memoirs are a forgery; or that Mr.
Berington has garbled, curtailed and altered them . . . Panzani tells us the story
of the first archpriest just as if he had been reading Mr. Berington's *Introduction*,
which stands before his memoirs. The truth is, that the *Introduction* and the
memoirs were collected and written by the same man.[43]

According to Plowden, the chief purpose of these *Memoirs* was to
discredit the Society of Jesus, the popes, and the vicars-apostolic, in the
hope of "inducing [the British Catholics] to swallow the oath of
supremacy".[44] Berington was, "in religion a sceptic, and in politics are
sans-culottes".[45] Plowden had no doubt about Queen Elizabeth's intentions:

The Queen's government never intended to indulge catholics in a quiet tolerance
of their religion, in return for their civil allegiance. That profligate government
well knew, that the catholics were faithful by principle and by habit; but their
policy was, not to protect them honourably, as their duty prescribed, but to
wring from them, by art and by force, that very religion, in which they found
the source and motive of their allegiance.[46]

By this reading, the queen, or at least the government, was the
aggressor, and not the pope. Any priests who were sentenced to imprisonment or death were condemned for the sole reason that they had
exercised their priesthood and not for any feeling of disloyalty or act of
treason. The Appellant priests at Wisbech Prison had particularly
disgraced themselves by playing into the hands of the government; their
loyalty was never suspect, yet they "conveyed a reproach of disloyalty
upon all other priests and catholics".[47]

What Plowden did not see, or refused to see, was the contradictory
nature of dual loyalties to pope and queen, which contradiction was not
the fault of the arrested priests, but was the condition set by both princes:
one could not swear simultaneous allegiance. Plowden's failure was in not
recognizing the historical context of the dual loyalties. While the two
loyalties might not have been seen in his own day as intrinsically contradictory, there was much more confusion about them in the sixteenth
century. Besides, the choices which were offered the priests under interrogation were *intentionally* contradictory. The priests sought to avoid this
predicament by silence or evasion. But they surely did not, and could not,
escape its grasp by ignoring it, as Plowden did.

Evaluation of Berington's History

For all that can be said against Berington's version of the Reformation, it marked a small step in the direction of a more scientific and objective history. He was a child of his time, and this meant he inherited the failings and virtues of his predecessors – but did so as a Catholic, and this was an important difference.

In this regard, he borrowed liberally from previous historians, and accepted them as unerring – a flaw very common in the Enlightenment. His book is filled with citations from Heylyn, Collier, Fuller, and Dodd, any of which he considered to be sufficient documentation on a controverted point. But Enlightenment historians, as much as they depended on this method in their writings, began to show a growing unease with mere citation, and began to look for more and better documents to support their arguments. Berington shared in this search, and we have one instance of his impatience with an uncooperative archivist:

> The liberty I requested [to see certain documents] was refused me, from the generous motives . . . of the peevish animal who, lying in the manger, refused to let the patient ox, whom hunger pressed, feed on the food that was natural to him, and unnatural to the snarling tyrant that did but defile it by his presence.[48]

The use he made of Panzani's *Memoirs* was less than disinterested, but it marked a revolutionary small advance for an English Catholic insofar as it showed, in an important way, that the final arbiter in a dispute would be the scholar who could amass the largest number of the most authoritative documents, and not the person who had popular opinion or the prevailing orthodoxy on his side. Furthermore, his use of the *Memoirs* stood up against its critics. Mark Tierney, a Church historian and secular priest, wrote to his friend, John Kirk, also an historian, years later:

> You will recollect that Charles Plowden, who had publicly treated the Memoirs of Panzani as a forgery, . . . acknowledges that he subsequently found the original MS., but adds that both Dodd and Berington had been guilty of suppressions which totally altered the character of the work. This is false . . . I have Dodd's own copy (in his own handwriting) of the translation of the MS. It is the same in all respects as that published by Mr. Berington, and contains every syllable that is to be found in the Latin original.[49]

The production of the *Memoirs of Panzani* may have been a victory of sorts, but Berington displayed faults which harmed his worth as an historian. A persistent one-sidedness pervaded his narrative. While it was helpful to Catholics to hear the "corrective" for past histories, Berington hurt his own case by making no effort to balance the evidence. In his enthusiasm for Elizabeth's moderation, he failed to mention that 800 men were executed by her for their participation in the Rising of the North in 1569, a military operation which resulted in the deaths of only five people.[50] He also overlooked the activity of Elizabeth and her ministers in fomenting mischief and devising a few plots of their own. In this regard, he dismissed the document *Relation*, which had been drawn up by the Jesuits to spell out these intrigues, as "unsupported by any historical facts".[51]

This one-sidedness became especially evident in his discussion of the Oaths of Supremacy and Allegiance. He judged the missionary priests on the basis of his own day, when the question of dual allegiance and the deposing power had become considerably more settled, and when the boundaries between temporal and spiritual power had been more clearly drawn. To Berington, the simple solution to the dilemma in which the missionary priests found themselves was to minimize the authority of the pope and imply an almost unrestricted authority in the English monarch.[52]

The problem with such an easy solution was two-fold. First, the English Catholics of Elizabeth's time did not hold Berington's view of the respective authorities, so that we find Berington in the position of criticizing them not for what they believed and did, but for what they *should* have believed, and did not do. Secondly, Berington did not take note of the revolutionary quality of Elizabeth's claim. He concentrated entirely on the pope's over-extension of power while ignoring Elizabeth's. Catholics could not sign an oath giving Elizabeth spiritual supremacy, no matter how they regarded the pope's right to depose. The boundaries of Elizabeth's and the pope's authority in spiritual matters intruded on each other, and such were the terms they set that reconciliation through oath-taking was not possible. Thus Catholics became disloyal, at least theoretically. Even if they did not accept the pope's right to depose, they still could not take the oath, which did more than deny the pope this power. The queen had made the penalty for refusing to take the oath high treason, and thus she raised the stakes. Until that sanction was dropped, or the oath changed, Catholics (in the eyes of the law) could not be loyal.

Berington made the mistake of assuming that deposition and the oath were concerned with the same thing, and that once the former was disposed of, there could little objection to signing the latter. The only obstacle to signing the oath, in other words, was the pope. Hence Berington's urgency in attacking papal power, and his bewilderment that "one bold man" never came forward to sign the oath (see above, p. 32).

If these had been his only faults, he would probably have escaped censure. But he was unable to resist the indiscreet remark, and this proved his undoing and the virtual end of his public role in the Cisalpine movement. Even by the liberal standards of the eighteenth century, Berington's language went beyond the rules of decorum. He once wrote of his enemy, John Milner, that he was:

> neither a gentleman nor a Christian. Whether the water-nymphs . . . would take him for their chaplain, I know not; sure I am that communities of a better polish and of better principles must be shocked by his intemperate effusions. And what, after all, was the provocation that instigated the fellow to throw about his stink-pots?"[53]

John Milner was probably worse, but he was the spokesman for the bishops and about to become one himself – the vicar-apostolic of the Midland District from 1803 to 1826. When Milner engaged in a pamphlet war in 1799 with an Anglican, Dr. Sturges, Berington impulsively entered the feud on the side of Sturges, with an open letter to *Gentleman's Magazine*. In this letter, Berington took on more than Milner. Among the sentences found to be objectionable by the bishops were these (the italics are Berington's).

> That some religious societies, benevolently fostered in the country, and protected by its laws, in direct opposition to the opinions and policy of that country, should dare to *perpetuate* themselves by admitting new members, [the Catholick] will think deserving a severe animadversion.

> He [the Catholick whose mind is truly English] readily acknowledges, admitting the Roman bishop to be the first pastor of his church, that much of the ecclesiastical, and all of the temporal power, at any time claimed by him, was acquired by human means, and that its exercise was lawfully resisted.

> In the foundation, or continuance, of *monastic institutions*, to so many the source of misery, to some the source of happiness, he feels no interest.

> In tracing the history of *religious persecution*, he is compelled to own, that his church has persecuted, though, theologically speaking, "persecution may not have been a tenet of his faith," and that *intolerance* is the professed doctrine of her decrees.

> To the authors of the Reformation, the extent of which he deplores, he does not indiscriminately ascribe unworthy motives.[54]

The bishops asked Berington to retract these and other statements, and he did so in a fashion which Eamon Duffy described as "the zenith of his recklessness".[55] In the December issue of the same journal, Berington wrote his sarcastic "retraction":

In mentioning . . . some religious *societies*, benevolently fostered in the country, and protected by its laws, if, in direct opposition to the opinions and policy of that country, they aimed to *perpetuate* themselves by admitting new members, I should have *praised* the measure, and not have said it deserved severe animadversion.

Viewing in the Roman bishop the first pastor of my church, I should *not* have acknowledged *that any part* of the power, at any time claimed by him, was acquired by *human means* and was lawfully resisted.

Of *monastic institutions* I should *not* have said, that to *many* they were the source of misery, to *some* the source of happiness; in their foundation and continuance, I should have expressed much interest.

That my church *ever persecuted*, I should not have conceded; and should have gloried in the *intolerance* of her professions.

I should have represented every part of the *Protestant Reformation* as schismatical, and to *all* its authors indiscriminately ascribed unworthy motives.[56]

Bishop Douglass, who had laboured so long and patiently to work out a reconciliation with Berington in 1797, now suspended him again, and Berington was to disappear from the public eye for the rest of his life. He exasperated the Catholic hierarchy because, as critical as he was about the pope and his curia in Rome, he could be amazingly pacific and generous about the English government. In the same article which resulted in his downfall, he wrote:

Not to awaken dormant animosities by contention, not to institute invidious comparisons between the old and present religion of the country, not to justify acts condemned by the legislature, not to vilify characters generally deemed eminent, but on all occasions, to cherish the cause of liberty, civil and religious, cheerfully to obey the laws of the realm, and, in silence, to practise the duties of their religion, is undoubtedly the prudent line of conduct for Catholicks to pursue, while they confidently look forward to days of more tranquility, when they may deserve to be admitted to all rights of British subjects.[57]

Yet, when it came to the Catholic position, Berington could be intolerant, impatient in the extreme, flippant, and dissembling. His entire scholarly life was a series of retractions and relapses. There is even evidence that he seriously contemplated a schism, and abandoned the project only when it became apparent that few Cisalpines would support it, and that it simply would not work.[58] The only gratitude Bishop Douglass received from Berington, after warding off spiteful demands by Milner to humble Berington, was a letter written by Berington to John Kirk a week later. It predicted the imminent extinction of the papacy and added, "The sooner this happens the better."[59]

Charles Butler

At Berington's eclipse, the Cisalpine torch quickly passed to Charles Butler, the lay lawyer who had served as secretary to the Catholic Committees from their very beginning in 1778. Butler (1750–1832) was ascetic and industrious, and in 1819 wrote his *Historical Memoirs respecting the English, Irish, and Scottish Catholics*, which summarized the situation of Roman Catholics in Britain and Ireland from the Reformation onwards. It was an updated version of Berington's *State and Behaviour of English Catholics*, with more emphasis on history. Butler's training as a lawyer taught him to look for legal precedents, which is why he was interested in the history of the Reformation.

Like Berington before him, Butler was primarily concerned with Catholic emancipation, and this coloured his historical narrative. Butler, however, possessed two advantages over Berington in the writing of history: he was not a priest and therefore more able to elude official censure;[60] and he had a lawyer's restraint in controversy, always remaining a gentleman and refusing to brawl with Milner.

He was attracted to the Reformation because it offered a comment on the current difficulties of Catholics, especially those difficulties arising from the various oaths. He hoped to bring Catholics and Protestants closer together, to effect some unity with the Catholic Church itself, but above all to further the cause of emancipation.

He did not say anything new about the Reformation, and indeed he repeated some of the errors found in Berington (e.g. blaming Pope Paul IV for reacting harshly to news of Elizabeth's accession), but he was fairer to both sides than anyone to date. So, while he excused Elizabeth for her misdeeds, and played down her refusal to meet with papal delegates, he at least felt obliged to mention such activity, as well as to enumerate the suffering of the missionary priests, and to call some attention to the role of Elizabeth's ministers in the proceedings.

Still, there was no doubt where his sympathies lay. Most of his energy was taken up cataloguing and criticizing the papal "pretensions" to both spiritual and temporal power. He wrote that the popes had been reproachable, not merely for their unwarranted pretensions to temporal power, "but they had also been long blamed, by the wiser and more respectable part of the church, for their undue exercise, even of their spiritual power".[61]

Butler listed the general offenses of the papacy first, then moved on to the more specific offenses brought about by the popes against the English people. Among the former were: extending immunities to the clergy; exempting regulars from the jurisdiction of the local hierarchy; excessive monetary demands; interfering in diocesan courts; nominating to ecclesiastical benefices in foreign states, contrary to common right; and carrying on superciliously and expensively. In England, where Butler said that the conduct of the Papal See "had always been more reprehensible, than in any other country", these encroachments and the reactions they generated had a time-honoured history:

> Pope Gregory VII demanded of King Henry II homage to the Apostolic See in exchange for the crown. Henry refused.

> Boniface VIII told Edward III to desist from using force in Scotland. Edward refused.

> When William of Glastonbury was consecrated bishop, he had committed to his charge the spiritualities and temporalities of his bishopric. Edward III summoned him, whereupon William submitted and *asked* Edward to bestow on him the temporalities.[62]

Other offenses, curtailed by various kings, were the export of money by religious houses (Edward I); the appointment of men to benefices before they became vacant – known as *provisors* (Edward III); the misuse of Church courts by trying cases which should have been tried in civil courts (Edward III); contempt in paying obedience to papal processes, which was due to the king alone – known as *praemunire* (Richard II and Henry IV). From all of this Butler concluded: "Such were the provisions, by which, when the popes were in the zenith of their authority, our catholic ancestors disclaimed and resisted their claims to temporal power; and even the undue exercise of their spiritual power, within this imperial realm."[63]

Opposition to the popes, in other words, was a long-standing and hallowed tradition in England. The popes had got into the bad habit of giving orders on matters over which they exercised no competent authority, while English rulers had got into the very laudable habit of ignoring those orders or countermanding them in some way. For Butler, these precedents all pointed to the claim by the pope to depose rulers, and to the right of the rulers to resist that claim.

Butler was quite forthright in praising Elizabeth for her lenience, and in placing blame for the enactment of the penal laws on the Bull of Excommunication of Pius V, the Mitigation of Gregory XIII, the policy of Sixtus V in support of the Armada, and the provocative actions of the missionary priests. Yet Butler was convinced, at the same time, that these priests were not traitors, that Catholics could be loyal and did not deserve punishment, and the Elizabeth's ministers were partly to blame for the nature and extent of the persecution.

When it came to the Oaths of Supremacy and Allegiance, Butler's acumen as a lawyer became evident. The confusion over the "temporal power" of the Church, he claimed, began in the Middle Ages, when the state conferred upon Church courts the power to enforce spiritual injunctions. The Church, by usage and custom, assumed that this power was its own by right. Thus, when the supremacy was conferred upon Elizabeth, Butler maintained that it was only a supremacy over that jurisdiction which the clergy, or their courts, (and, by extension, the pope) received from the state. Correspondingly, what was denied the pope was his claim to supremacy over that same temporal power.[64]

The objections to Elizabeth's supremacy, Butler continued, first came from the missionary priests who were trained in foreign seminaries to believe that the pope was entitled, at least indirectly, to temporal power by divine right. After all, did not Persons claim that the deposing power of the pope was an article of faith and binding in conscience under the pain of mortal sin?[65]

Butler's point was sophisticated, but flawed because he used the reign of Elizabeth as his starting-point, instead of the reign of Henry VIII, when the Oath of Supremacy originated. The first opposition to it was voiced, not by missionary priests in the age of Elizabeth, but by Sir Thomas More, Bishop John Fisher, and the Carthusian priors of the Charterhouse, Belleval, and Shene – whose sympathies were anything but Ultramontane, and who preceded the arrival of the first missionary priests by nearly thirty-five years. The Act of Supremacy was repealed by Mary Tudor, but restored by Elizabeth in a slightly revised form – dropping the title "The only supreme head of the Church of England" and substituting "The only supreme governor of the realm, and of all other her highness's dominions and countries, as well in all spiritual or ecclesiastical things or causes as temporal". The point of the change, some have maintained, was that no one would accept the idea of a woman as "Head" of the Church, although a case could be made that the change was made in order to soften the title.

But objections to the accompanying Oath remained the same as to the old Oath and, significantly, none of the Marian bishops subscribed to it – again, a full ten years before the arrival of any missionary priests. Elizabeth, knowing of the previous objections to the Henrician Oath, did not attempt to satisfy those objections or alter the text in any way approaching Butler's understanding of it. Butler avoided this evidence because mention of it would have ruined his case. J. B. Code, in his work on English historiography, noted, "With all the appearance of impartiality, which naturally goes far to create an atmosphere of credibility,

Butler was not above the lawyer's device of eliminating such witnesses as might be contrary to the point he wished to make."[66]

And the point he wished to make was that a benign interpretation of the Oath was possible in 1819, and had been possible in 1559, and that such an interpretation was the key to Catholic emancipation:

> Were it quite clear that the interpretation contended for is the true interpretation of the oath, and quite clear also that the oath was and is thus universally interpreted by the nation, then, the author contends, that there might be strong ground to contend, that it was consistent with Catholic principles to take either the oath of supremacy which was prescribed by Elizabeth, or that, which is used at present.

> He also thinks it highly probable, that, if a legislative interpretation could now be obtained, the interpretation suggested would be adopted.[67]

Butler himself admitted that the actual existence, as opposed to the possibility, of such a benign interpretation in Elizabeth's time was doubtful, and that such an interpretation would ever be attached to it in his own day was equally doubtful.[68] Thus, he was forced back onto Berington's perception of history, which had more to do with what *should* have happened than with what actually did.

So why did Butler expend so much energy on interpreting the oath in a way which it had never been interpreted before and, in all likelihood, never would be interpreted? The answer, admittedly conjectural, can probably be found in Butler's profession as a lawyer. He was concerned that the process of emancipation, which had come to a standstill after the Napoleonic War, would never reach fulfillment until some solution was found to the quandary of divided loyalties, and he believed that he had found a loophole. How Henry or Elizabeth or the Catholic martyrs interpreted the oath was not important – at least, not to the prospects for emancipation in 1819. What mattered was the legislature, which would have to enact an emancipation law, and whether that legislature could now obtain his interpretation. What was simpler, and what actually happened, was for the government to drop its requirement of an oath. What is surprising is that neither Berington nor Butler suggested it as a possibility, though that may have been because the events which led to the sudden removal of the oath seemed far more distant than they really were.

Evaluating Butler's History

Charles Butler was not an historian, and Joseph Berington was even less so. They both came to their histories as polemicists – by way of the contemporary debates on emancipation. Their purpose was not to discover historical truth or accuracy, but instead they wanted to use history to make a modern statement. Because the roots of Catholic disability rested in the Reformation, it seemed to them that the solution rested there as well. Little did they dream that it really rested in the hands of a solitary Irishman named Daniel O'Connell.

While Berington and Butler may have had a similar purpose in writing, they were clearly different in their approaches to history. Berington was more the philosopher and, as a rationalist, condemned those things at the time of the Reformation which the people of his own day condemned in their own: intolerance, autocratic authority, and superstition – judging the past, in other words, on its approximation to or alienation from the Age of Reason. Just as Berington condemned those in his own day who made it impossible to take the oath, he also condemned those during the Reformation who did the same.

Charles Butler's training as a lawyer suited him much better for the writing of history. He saw in it a vast quarry of precedents, and listed past incursions of papal power and the corresponding justifiable acts of resistance by English monarchs, with the understanding that they all pointed to the last great confrontation of that kind: the papal excommunication and deposition of Elizabeth, and the Oath of Supremacy. It was important for Butler to establish, if not a precedent for taking the Oath – since there had been no Oath before – then at least a general precedent of disobedience to the pope and the possibility of taking the Oath, the reality of which had been avoided because of ultramontane interference.

His historical sense was also far superior to Berington's. He did not, for example, condemn those in the past who acted differently than he would have liked. Berington did not condemn those who refused to take the Oath – not, at least, in so many words – but one cannot avoid feeling that he thought them to have been mistaken. Butler does not leave that impression at all, but rather he admitted the historical conditions which caused the refusal. Where he differed from Berington was in saying that times had changed, that a benign view of the oath was now possible owing to historical research, and that, even though Catholics had once died for refusing to take the Oath, they could now take it without any fear of betraying their ancestors or their consciences.

Secondly, he was more willing than any Catholic writer in the past to consider both sides of a controversial story. Much as he disapproved of the pope's diplomatic conduct, he was able to say that the pope conducted himself during Henry's divorce proceedings with "ever so great moderation and temper", a concession Berington would have found it impossible to make. Butler also found that some of the fault for the breach with Rome lay with Henry and, later, Elizabeth; that the dissolution of the monasteries entailed an irreparable tragedy; that the Jesuits were unjustly tortured.

Thirdly, Butler used sources with greater care than did Berington – who, one suspects, used them mostly to antagonize his adversaries. Butler used the best available source and tested it more thoroughly, even if that happened to be a Protestant source, and sometimes precisely because it was a Protestant source. This not only could gain him a more sympathetic hearing among non-Catholics, but was a good debater's trick in scoring points. As J. B. Code pointed out, Butler "had the habit, to which Milner referred more than once, of taking Protestant evidence in preference to Catholic, or of adducing Protestant sources in support of Catholic as if the latter was not sufficient of itself".[69]

John Milner

No treatment of Butler's work would be complete without mention of the reaction it evoked from John Milner. Since 1803, Milner had been vicar-apostolic of the Midlands District, a promotion which was indicative both of Rome's approval of his defense of orthodoxy, and Rome's caution in not granting him too much power. Milner had long coveted the London District as the most suitable forum for his fight with the Catholic Committee, but he was never to obtain it.

In addition to his defense of orthodoxy, Milner is best remembered for his defense of the rights of the clergy against lay interference – be it from the Catholic gentry or Protestant government. He ensured that the Relief Act of 1791 affected all Catholics, and not just the "Protesting Catholic Dissenters" proposed by the Catholic Committee. Since that time, he did not trust the Committee, and he especially did not trust Charles Butler, whom he regarded as "the prime mover in all Catholic affairs".[70] Furthermore, he thought Butler would sell his soul in order to gain emancipation. When Butler was named King's Counsel, the first Catholic to be so named, Milner commented that it was "one of the honours and emoluments achieved at the expense of his conscience".[71]

In a direct response to Butler's *Historical Memoirs*, Milner published *Supplementary Memoirs of the English Catholics* the following year (1820) and accused Butler of writing no more than "a covert apology for the measures in which the author, with a few of his friends, has been engaged, during the thirty years of his direction of Catholic affairs in this country".[72]

In this response, Milner sought to correct the Cisalpine view that Elizabeth had been unnecessarily provoked by the pope and the Jesuits. He claimed that Elizabeth never believed the Catholic martyrs to be guilty of treason, since only one Elizabethan martyr refused to acknowledge her title to the crown, and that Catholics remained loyal to her despite the Marian bishops' refusal to crown her and despite the pope's excommunication. Elizabeth, furthermore, abandoned the ancient faith in order to keep her kingdom intact; she had overreacted to Catholic "threats"; she was hypocritical, arbitrary, and despotic.

In general, Milner suspected Butler of being a closet Protestant – by wondering out loud whether Butler approved of the pope's measures on Henry VIII's divorce, or on any other matter where Butler granted some concession to the non-Catholic position. Milner wrote: "What uninformed reader . . . would not suppose that the learned author meant to vindicate the pretended Reformation? . . . would he not hesitate to pronounce whether the author is, in fact, a Catholic or Protestant."[73]

More specifically, Milner was vexed by Butler's attitude towards the deposing power of the pope. He raised the difficulty of deposing princes under any circumstances, and wrote, "It is hoped . . . [Butler] will answer the following question: Is the deposing doctrine on the score of religion, so impious and damnable in Catholics alone; or is it equally criminal in Protestants?"[74]

It was a good question, but the wrong one, because Butler was asking whether the *pope* had the right to depose another prince; whether the *people of England* did or not, be they Catholic or Protestant, was another matter altogether, and one which Butler wisely avoided. In any event, Milner thought that the pope decidedly did have the right to depose, and based that opinion on grounds which were Ultramontane in the extreme: "Does C. B. mean seriously to charge the illustrious popes of the sixteenth century with not understanding the nature of their divine commission?"[75]

Milner's statements on this subject bear examining because they are so typical of the man. Philip Hughes said of Milner, "He lacked accuracy of exposition and, a still more important defect, he not only failed to realize the inaccuracy, but seemed scarcely to understand how it could matter."[76] What Hughes was talking about is borne out in these telling paragraphs by Milner in defense of the deposition:

First, then do St. Thomas Aquinas, Turrecremata, Bellarmin, and other advocates of this [temporal] power represent the Pope as an universal monarch, who has the right to take and give away the kingdoms of the earth? No. So far from this, they teach that, as Pope, he has no direct power or temporal property whatsoever.

Secondly: has any Pope pretended to depose or otherwise molest any of our sovereigns, under pretence that they were Protestants and persecutors of the Catholic religion, since the reign of Elizabeth? No: and if a bull of deposition was issued against her, it was because she was illegitimate; because she was an apostate; because she was the murderer of her royal guest and sister; because she was a general pirate and firebrand among the sovereigns of Europe. Finally: this very bull was of no serious detriment even to her, as her Catholic subjects were universally faithful to her, and this with the consent of the Pope himself.[77]

The problems with this are many. Factually, Milner placed part of the blame for the papal action on Elizabeth's murder of "her royal guest and sister", Mary Stuart, which occurred in 1587, a full seventeen years after the deposition. But, aside from factual liberties, Milner's argument is a bit diffuse. He begins by saying that Thomas Aquinas, Juan de Torquemada (a well-known theologian and uncle of the more famous Tomas de Torquemada, Spain's Grand Inquisitor), and Robert Bellarmine all opposed the pope's direct right to depose, then says Elizabeth deserved it, and ends by saying it did not matter much, anyway, because the deposition was ignored by Catholics. It seems that, for Milner, any stick was good enough to beat the Cisalpines.

To be more specific, Milner avoided Butler's point altogether by using the qualifier "direct" in reference to the pope's power to depose. Butler had made the point that the pope had no right, direct or indirect, to depose rulers, thus including political censures which might accompany an excommunication. Butler's point was that excommunication was one thing, and deposition another, and that the popes had no right to involve themselves in the business of deposing princes. Milner ignored this distinction and stubbornly refused to recognize the problem.

Secondly, one wonders why Milner cited the three theologians at all. What matters here is not what these theologians thought, but what Pius V thought, or whether Pius V depended on the writings of these theologians on this subject, and of that Milner gave no clue. We know, at least, that one of the theologians (Bellarmine) was not a theological force in Rome until well after 1570, the year he was ordained.

Thirdly, the information that popes had not deposed any ruler since Elizabeth is hardly pertinent. The action against Elizabeth was the issue, and the appeal to later cases is of little moment.

Fourthly, why should the pope depose the queen at all if he did not intend to cause her serious harm by the loss of the allegiance of her people? Milner fell victim to the same conflict of loyalties which trapped the missionary priests under interrogation. He noted that they could not disagree with Pius V's deposition, but, "It was sufficient that they disclaimed obedience to it".[78] Milner assumed, as did the missionaries, that the pope acted legitimately. Yet he approved of their disobedience to his legitimate exercise of authority. Hence Butler's charge remained poignant, i.e. the martyrs' answers in the interrogation were unsatisfactory, unfortunate, and provocative.[79]

In retrospect, it is easy to condemn Milner for his intransigence, yet his case is a stronger one than he makes himself. By contextualizing the excommunication and deposition of Elizabeth by the pope, Milner might have salvaged what to later generations looked like an intolerant and triumphalistic act. Pius V was excommunicating in the only way he knew how, and the only way the Church had done for centuries. The excommunication against Henry VIII, issued by Paul III in 1538 – drawn up but never published – had been even more sweeping. The problem was that the rules had changed and were continuing to change, and the popes were learning that excommunication and deposition could be clearly distinguished. Pius V can hardly be faulted for not learning this lesson soon enough. Milner's mistake was in trying to defend everything the pope had done, simply on the grounds that he was the pope.

Later writers have called Milner the most important English Catholic figure of the period, though one wonders if this appellation is not more the "propaganda of the victors" than representative of actual fact. John Henry Newman said Milner was "the champion of God's ark in an evil time" and the "principal luminary" of the time.[80] Similarly, William Amherst, a Jesuit writing in 1886, called Milner a hero and a "doughty champion", one who "almost single-handed, kept the lists against all comers". His conduct, continued Amherst, "was not merely glorious; it was exemplary. . . . In Milner we see all that a loyal priest could do".[81]

If Milner was indeed "great" in what he accomplished, and the reputation of greatness persists to this day, it is precisely his conduct that reduces or qualifies that greatness.[82] His tone, as Bernard Ward pointed out, "did more to damage his own influence and reputation than he was aware of".[83] William Barry said of Milner:

> [He] was a great man, whether we judge him by the work which he did or by the zeal and energy which he flung into it . . . .It was his misfortune that, in the everlasting hurly-burly of which he became the center, no fellow-bishop, priest, or layman, could persuade him to suspect ever so faintly that he might in some things be mistaken.[84]

Barry is over-kind in not noticing that the "hurly-burly" was mostly brought on by Milner himself, and that persistent efforts were made to accommodate him, to include him in projects and to modify what he was saying. These efforts only seemed to polarize him even more. When Bishop Poynter established a Catholic Bible Society, and invited Milner to join him in the undertaking, Milner refused and boasted to his friend Gandolphy that it was a "proposal which I always resolutely withstood as standing in opposition to the Catholic Rule of Faith and being grounded on that of Protestants".[85]

Among his other faults, Milner was "congenitally unable to understand, or make allowance for, the light and shade of another's opinion".[86] Every argument became for him a personal feud and was pushed to extremes, with frequent threats of eternal damnation for those who opposed him. At times, he appears to have taken the process of damnation into his personal care, as when he directed his clergy to withhold absolution from Butler, even *in extremis*.[87] When the troublesome Scottish cisalpine priest, Alexander Geddes, died without benefit of the sacraments, Milner commented smugly that "God is not mocked".[88]

Not even good intentions were recognized. When the Catholic Committee sought to appease the bishops by appointing three priests to represent the clergy, Milner dismissed the gesture as insincere. The Committee's choice of Bishop Talbot was suspect because, according to Milner, "they could not pass him by, and hoped to hoodwink him".[89] In defending his opinions, Milner even appealed to deathbed statements, which were implausible and unverifiable. A good example is his description of Bishop Talbot's death:

> When . . . the Bishop was chosen a member [of the Committee], he assured the author [Milner], that he accepted the nomination for the sole purpose of restraining the others, and that he had prepared a formal protest against them. Lastly, when he was on his deathbed, he told his spiritual friend, the Rev. Mr. Lindow, that if he recovered, he would write against the Committee.[90]

Two censures were pronounced against Milner – one by the Catholic Board (the successor to the Catholic Committee), and the other by the Vatican. In the first instance, the Catholic Board held a meeting in 1813 in order to dismiss Milner from its membership. Milner appeared at the meeting, against the advice of friends, and defended his recent *Brief Memorial*, which had opposed the *exequator* and veto concessions for emancipation.[91] He was then asked whom he meant by "certain false brethren of the Catholic body", and he pointed to Charles Butler, saying, "Charles Butler there for one". The Board then, in a rambunctious mood, immediately passed a resolution thanking Butler for his services and declaring Milner's charges a gross calumny. A further resolution expelled the bishop, who proceeded to denounce the sixty-five members of the Board for presuming to represent the Catholics of England, since "it does not represent them or any part of them". As his dramatic finale, he said, "You may expel me from the Board, but I thank God, gentlemen, that you cannot exclude me from the kingdom of heaven."[92]

The second censure was far more serious. In 1820 Cardinal Fontana, the Prefect of Propaganda, at the request of the pope, ordered Milner to stop contributing to the *Orthodox Journal* under pain of dismissal from his vicariate. He complied, and the *Orthodox* died quietly within a month, as Milner convinced the editor, William Eusebius Andrews, to shut it down. The *Orthodox* had been founded in 1813 by Andrews and had served as Milner's platform, from which he attacked Butler, John Lingard, and, more importantly, Bishop Poynter. As long as the Prefect of Propaganda was the pro-Jesuit Cardinal Litta, Milner was safe. Once Litta died in 1820 and was replaced by Fontana, Propaganda tired of Milner very quickly.

Milner's stock had fallen considerably before this. In 1819 Butler had considered writing either to Litta or Cardinal Consalvi about Milner's interference, but found "every person, to whom I have mentioned this project, has assured me, that Doctor Milner's character at Rome, is such as makes it unnecessary".[93] The fear was that Milner's fulminating was damaging the prospects of emancipation. Poynter wrote to Gradwell in 1819:

> Mgr. Milner ha provocato il Duca di Norfolk ed I Cattolici, ed offesi [sic] i Membri del Parlamento . . . quasi a tutti una vile e volgare scrittura (poco avanti il dibattimento sul Emancip. Cattol.) che aveva gia [sic] stampata pochi giorni prima nell'Orthodox Journal. Questo papo [sic] ha sortito cattivo effetto.[94]

Given such information, it is difficult to defend the thesis put forward by Philip Hughes that Milner was "the leader of a generation that had all but passed away, bred for times that had, in fact, disappeared . . . .Milner was the last great figure of a great time".[95] If anything, Milner was the first figure of note for a different age. He was the first English Ultramontanist of any stature, the first English bishop of the nineteenth century to have a high theology of the papacy which combined with an air of triumphalism so characteristic of the Ultramontanism of the next one hundred years.

Milner was, in fact, the proto-typical Ultramontanist – the son of a tailor where his predecessors had been gentlemen, an eager controversialist where they had been meek and cautious, the unashamed apologist for clerical rights where they had clung desperately to what little power they had. Hugh Aveling, in his history of the English Catholic Church, claimed that Milner was no triumphalist, but instead "the austere voice of traditional Catholicism".[96] But his voice was much less akin to that of Richard Challoner, the premier English Catholic bishop of the eighteenth century, than it was to those of Cardinals Wiseman and Manning. His achievement was of a kind which was yet to develop fully, which indeed transformed the English Catholic Church into a force in which even Joseph Berington would be mistaken by a later author as "the Pope's vicar-general".[97]

Chapter III

JOHN LINGARD AND THE
CAUSE OF CATHOLICISM

People in the 19th century are too wise for such trash as forms Popery."
(*Gentleman's Magazine* 89 [April 1819], p. 343)

John Lingard was the Cisalpine heir-apparent to Charles Butler. He was a diocesan priest, articulate and subdued, who had the interests of the diocesan clergy and emancipation constantly in mind. He had attracted the notice of the ever-vigilant Milner, but was savvy enough not to be lured into a fight with the bishop. Lingard was no stranger to the penal laws. He was born a Catholic in 1771 and remembered as a youth going to Sunday Mass at night in order to avoid the authorities. All told, he lived for fifty-eight years under various forms of the penal laws, and was anxious to do what he could to bring them finally to an end.

He studied at Douai College, though was forced to leave because of the Napoleonic War. But while he was there, he imbibed the research-based, scientific methods of Claude Fleury (1640–1723), Jean Mabillon (1632–1707) and the Maurists, as well as the Bollandists (Jesuit editors of the *Acta Sanctorum*) and others, all of whom travelled extensively in search of original documents and examined them critically.[1] We know that Lingard read Fleury's *Histoire Ecclesiastique* (1691–1720) and compared it favorably to Edward Gibbon's *Decline and Fall of the Roman Empire* (1776–88).[2] And, in his *Antiquities of the Anglo-Saxon Church* (1806), Lingard referred the reader to Fleury, Mabillon, and the Bollandists.[3] After ordination in 1795, he taught moral and natural philosophy, and helped to establish the Catholic seminary of Ushaw in 1808. His first large-scale attempt at history, *The Antiquities of the Anglo-Saxon Church*, was an undisguised attempt to show the Roman roots of the English Church. While the project was laudable, Lingard admitted that new information was scarce. His book, as a result, was little more than a re-interpretation of previous known documents and histories, and had an edge.[4] However, one reaction it received was telling. The *Quarterly Review* of 1815 responded to Lingard's claim by stating, essentially, that we do not know about these matters, and we do not care about them:

> Here again [in the Anglo-Saxon doctrine of the Real Presence] we are compelled to assert our perfect indifference to the matter in controversy, farther than as a subject of speculation. Englishmen in the nineteenth century will scarcely lend their understandings to the cloudy metaphysics of Paschasius, Radbert, Hincmar, Alcuin and Rabanus Maurus.[5]

In 1811 he moved to the remote parish church of Hornby, near Lancaster, where he remained until the end of his life in 1851. Here he began his great project of continuing the *Antiquities* by writing a history of England which the *Quarterly* could not ignore. He knew that emancipation was near, but when and how it might come about was very uncertain. He did not want to jeopardize the project by writing an inflammatory history, but he also thought a true history might "be read by protestants: under the idea, that the more it is read by them, the less Hume will be in vogue, and consequently the fewer prejudices against us will be imbibed from him."[6]

It was an imposing task that he set himself. In 1819 John Lingard published three volumes of his *History of England*. His would be the first attempt by a Roman Catholic in modern times to write a comprehensive history of England. Five hundred copies of these volumes, concerned with the pre-Reformation period, were sold within eight days. In 1820 and 1823, the volumes on the Reformation were published. When he was finished in 1830, he had published eight quarto volumes, which eventually ran to nine editions (five within his lifetime). Lord Acton, who could be grudging in his praise of Catholic scholarship, wrote, "Lingard's history of England has been of more use to us [Catholics] than any thing that has since been written . . . All educated men were obliged to use it . . . It is to this day a tower of strength to us."[7]

Lingard had two goals in writing a history of this gigantic scope: he wanted to break from Catholic historical writing of the recent past and write something truly comprehensive; and he wanted to break from the histories written during the Enlightenment, especially that history produced by David Hume.

Achieving the former was a relatively simple matter. Previous Catholic histories were narrow in that they subordinated everything to emancipation or to a defense of the Church; they focused almost entirely on the reign of Queen Elizabeth; and they accepted the word of previous historians uncritically. Berington, in his *State and Behaviour of English Catholics*, admitted that his sources were the historians Burnet, Hume, Clarendon, and Dodd, and never once questioned what he drew from them. Furthermore, the use of original documents was, as we have seen, limited and arbitrary.

With Lingard, all of this changed. Not only did he deal with the English Reformation in its entirety, indeed the entire history of England, but he treated manuscripts in a more comprehensive way – their accumulation and evaluation had become the a priori condition without which conclusions could not be reached.

Hume was another matter. He was much read and believed, and regarded the Catholic Church with considerable disdain – equating it with medieval thought, which was for him superstitious, obscurantist, and thoroughly debased. If Lingard was to succeed, he needed to show that Hume was a prejudiced creature of the Enlightenment whose history was no more than an extension of his philosophical beliefs and party prejudices. To do so he had to write a history that was comparable in scope to Hume, but completely different in historical method – otherwise he would simply be matching one philosophy against another. He set himself the task of *not* doing what had been done before. He wrote in the Introduction to the *History of England*:

> They [Hume and Enlightenment writers of history] come before us as philosophers who undertake to teach from the records of history: they are in reality literary empirics who disfigure history to make it accord with their philosophy. Nor do I hesitate to proclaim my belief that no writers have proved more successful in the perversion of historic truth than speculative and philosophic historians.[8]

This meant Hume, of course, despite Lingard's protestations that he was not trying to overthrow Hume. John Allen, writing in the *Edinburgh Review*, stated that Lingard's work was harmed by this transparent preoccupation with Hume: "If a person of note is praised by Hume, he has a good chance of being presented in an odious light by Dr. Lingard; and, if censured by Hume, Dr. Lingard generally contrives to say a word in his commendation."[9] On the surface, at least, Lingard was annoyed with such criticism and defended himself by claiming not to have read Hume at all during the composition of his history, writing to his publisher, "I have on almost every subject forgotten his statements."[10] But his annoyance had more to do with being caught in the act. He wrote to Robert Gradwell, his friend and Rector of the English College in Rome: "For even where I acknowledge the exactions of the Court of Rome, on examination it will be found that my narrative is a refutation of the more exaggerated accounts of Hume, etc., though it is so told as not to appear designed for that purpose."[11]

Lingard, not unlike his contemporaries, saw history as a series of lessons for the present. When he published his first volumes, emancipation was still ten years away, and it no doubt seemed further away to Catholics at the time. Lingard wanted his book to instruct non-Catholics in the political ways of his religion – all the time en route to demolishing Hume – hoping to create a theoretical basis for emancipation. If Protestants could learn from a reputable history that Catholics had always been loyal and that papal pretensions were inessential to faith, then freedom might not be far away. It was a far more subtle and visionary approach than had appeared before. Whether Lingard could actually do it was another matter.

Lingard's "instinct" for obtaining a hearing from a hostile audience would probably never have seen the light of day were it not for his Protestant publisher, Joseph Mawman. When Lingard first began writing, his efforts were first directed at Anglican polemicists like Shute Berrington, the Anglican Bishop of Durham. Mawman told him that this sort of apologetics was foolishness, saying, "After all, what is the use of these pamphlets? Few Protestants read them. If you wish to make an impression, write books that Protestants will read."[12] Thereafter Lingard's goal became a history that Protestants not only would read, but could not ignore, even if they wanted to. In a letter to John Kirk, he expressed this hope:

> Through the work I have made it a rule to tell the truth, whether it made for or against us; to avoid all appearance of controversy, that I might not repel protestant readers . . . In my account of the Reformation I must say much to shock protestant prejudices; and my only chance of being read by them depends on my having the reputation of a temperate writer. The good to be done is by writing a book that protestants will read.[13]

The only way to write a book that would be objective and free of contentious language was to pursue sources ruthlessly, print whatever one found, and let the facts speak for themselves. "My object is truth", Lingard wrote, "and in the pursuit of truth, I have made it a religious duty to consult the original historians. Who would draw from the troubled stream, when he may drink at the fountainhead?"[14]

This sentiment was nothing new, as anyone knows who has read the introductions to previous histories of England, with their protestations of objectivity and fairness. And, as we shall see, the mere discovery and presentation of manuscripts was no guarantee of objectivity. Yet Lingard, partly through circumstance and partly through his own historical instinct, was able to implement that goal in ways which were far beyond the reach of his predecessors.

Fortunately for Lingard, archives were being opened to scholars, and Lingard had the advantage (in this case) of being a priest, which opened to him the Archives of Propaganda Fide and the Vatican in Rome and the Simancas Archives in Valladolid long before they were accessible to other historians.[15] However, this did not solve all of his problems because these archives, especially those of the Vatican, were largely uncatalogued and in a chaotic state.[16] The Vatican Archives were just recently returned from Paris, minus one-third of their contents, and the archives at Propaganda were no better. When Robert Gradwell, his agent in Rome, went to Propaganda he found a "cartload of dusty and rotting papers" on the floor, with letters of Pole, Garnet, and Persons among them. He wrote to Lingard:

> I selected all the valuable papers and carried them carefully to my room, where I filled three drawers with them . . . Unfortunately two of my drawers did not lock. A superannuated servant had used these valuable treasures as waste paper before I found it out. Of about 120 papers, scarcely thirty valuable ones remain.[17]

If this was not bad enough, Lingard faced the very real possibility that entry to the various archives could be arbitrarily and suddenly denied, or their use so curtailed as to present considerable obstacles to authentic research. The irascible Bishop Milner tried to have the Vatican Archives closed to Lingard, considering his danger to the faith, and Cardinal Litta refused him entry on the grounds that he was a "notorious Jansenist".[18]

The Vatican Archives were by no means the only archives to which these limitations applied. Lingard used the Simancas Archives – by way of an agent – as early as 1820, nearly twenty-five years before anyone but a Spaniard could gain access. Even here Lingard had frustrations, and detailed them in a letter to his publisher:

> I should observe to you that in quoting the records of Simancas, I do not mention the number, or the page, etc., as in quoting other documents. This arises from the jealousy of the Spaniards, or rather the standing orders of the place. The officials will not allow my friend to take any notes. He can only read them, and write down what he remembers, when he leaves.[19]

At times, Lingard's friend had to be satisfied with transcribing the contents of a document which had been read by someone else. Hardly the stuff of exacting research, but in 1820 these appalling conditions were almost welcomed because they could provide an author with the materials to fashion a completely new approach to history.

Lingard's History of England

As in nearly all histories to this date, Lingard's saw the reign of Elizabeth as the decisive focus of the Reformation. Yet Lingard attributed to Henry VIII an importance in the process of reform that he had not been given before. Without Henry the Reformation picture would not be complete, and, besides, Henry provided an interesting lesson in the relationship between sovereign and pope. Henry was not an innocent victim. His gradual separation from Rome had less to do with the pope's intransigence than with Henry's own passion. Lingard sought to demonstrate that Henry's interest in Anne Boleyn, which began on 18 June 1525 and became public at Greenwich on 5 May 1527, predated his pangs of conscience.[20] There was no question of Henry's real motive. Lingard wrote:

> His increasing passion for the daughter of lady Boleyn, induced him to reconsider the subject [of his marriage to Catherine of Aragon]: and in the company of his confidants he affected to fear, that he was living in a state of incest with the relict of his brother.

> [Henry] ventured to ask the opinions of the most eminent canonists and divines: who easily discovered the real wish of their sovereign through the thin disguise with which he affected to cover it, the scruples of a timorous conscience, and the danger of a disputed succession.[21]

Lingard looked to another, more subtle, reason to show Henry's real motive. Later sexual behavior and increasing impetuosity were convincing enough, but Henry's desperate maneuvering for the divorce was even more damning. Any excuse would serve Henry to be rid of his first wife. At first, Sacred Scripture was searched, then abandoned when it was found to be ambiguous. Next, the original dispensation was examined; it appeared to be lacking in three particulars: the dispensation had not been sufficiently ample, it had been obtained under false pretenses, and it had been solicited without Henry's consent.[22]

Behind these legal objections to the pope's authority was an ironical desire on Henry's part to grant the pope even more power, if necessary, than he already claimed. Henry sent two agents (Sir Francis Bryan and Peter Vannes) to Rome in order to inquire secretly from canon lawyers their opinions on three questions: (1) whether, if a wife were to make a vow of chastity and enter a convent, the pope could authorize the husband to marry again: (2) whether, if the husband were to enter into a religious order, and might induce his wife to do the same, he might be released from his vow afterwards, and thus free to marry: (3) and whether, for reasons of state, the pope could license a prince to have, like the ancient patriarchs, two wives, of whom one only should be publicly acknowledged and enjoy the honours of royalty.[23]

The pope appears, at least in the beginning of Henry's divorce proceedings, to have recognized this and is presented by Lingard as a sympathetic figure. Having been caught between the two forces of Henry and Charles V, Queen Catherine's nephew, the pope wisely sought delay in making a final decision, hoping that something would happen to make such a decision unnecessary. Campeggio, the papal representative to Henry, was the perfect choice to bring about such a delay because he was favored by the English and, what might seem an irrelevance, was ridden with gout, an illness which covered the real reasons for delay. Lingard had discovered that:

> The legate was instructed to proceed by slow journey; to endeavour to reconcile the parties; to advise the queen to enter a monastery; to conduct the trial with due caution, and according to the established forms; and at all events to abstain from pronouncing judgment till he had consulted the apostolic see.[24]

In a later edition of his history, Lingard explicitly approved of this tactic:

> Though his holiness was willing to do anything in his power to afford satisfaction to Henry, yet in a cause which had given rise to so many scandalous remarks, and in which one imprudent step might throw all Europe into a flame, it was necessary for him to proceed with due reflection and caution.[25]

But Lingard did not excuse the pope's conduct throughout. After the executions of John Fisher and Thomas More, the pope reacted hastily: "Paul [III] had hitherto followed the cautious policy of his predecessor, but his prudence was now denominated cowardice: and a bull against Henry was extorted from him by the violence of his counselors."[26] The tragedy, as Lingard saw it, was that the pope only recognized the obsolescence of his former power when this attempt to revive it failed. Even though Paul III wrote out the vindictive excommunication of Henry VIII, he dared not publish it because of the state of Europe at the time:

> When he reflected that Charles and Francis, the only princes who could attempt to carry the bull into execution, were, from their rivalry of each other, more eager to court the friendship, than to risk the enmity of the king of England, he repented of his precipitancy. To publish the bull could only irritate Henry, and bring the papal authority into contempt and derision.[27]

Thus Paul III was spared from an embarrassment which would fall to a later pope. Pius V looked on his predecessor's (Paul IV's) caution in not condemning Elizabeth as, Lingard commented, "dereliction of duty".[28] While Paul IV (1555–59) was an octogenarian and, Lingard thought, "adopted opinions with the credulity . . . of old age", at least he did not enact any irrevocable or regrettable measures. Pius V, on the other hand, excommunicated Elizabeth, deprived her of her crown, and absolved her subjects of their loyalty to her. Lingard noted: "If the pontiff promised himself any particular benefit from the measure, the result must have disappointed his expectations. . . . All [Catholics] agreed that it was in their regard an imprudent and cruel expedient, which afforded their enemies a pretence to brand them with the name of traitors.[29]

When it came to the reign of Elizabeth, Lingard shed new light on an old problem. He praised Elizabeth as the greatest of English rulers who had brought about domestic tranquility, successful resistance to Spain, and an increase of power and wealth. Yet he also noticed that she was dishonest, indecisive, vain, despotic, and immoral – though Lingard was restrained about the last. If anything, Elizabeth served as a check on a Parliament now bent on destroying the Catholic Church. In 1563 Parliament passed a series of laws denying Church preferment, university membership, and public office to anyone who had refused to take the Oath of Supremacy; soon after the ban was extended to membership in the House of Commons, and participation in the legal and teaching professions. According to Lingard, Elizabeth was "appalled at the prospect before her" and requested lenience and caution in the application of the new laws:

> Thus, by the humanity of policy of Elizabeth, were the catholics allowed to breathe from their terrors: but the sword was still suspended over their heads by a single hair, which she could break at her pleasure, whenever she might be instigated by the suggestion of her enemies, or provoked by the real or imputed misconduct of individuals of their communion.[30]

The queen was also responsible for ensuring that these laws fell short of applying to the House of Lords, on the grounds "that the queen's majesty was otherwise sufficiently assured of the faith and loyalty of the temporal lords of her high court of parliament".[31]

This lenience began to erode as circumstances and papal action combined to force Elizabeth to choose sides. While she herself was indifferent to religious matters, the greatest threat to her rule seemed to her to come from the Catholic side. Pope Paul IV declared that she had no "hereditary" right to the crown and had insulted her ministers when he was told by them of her accession.[32] Mary Stuart, who had several times stated her claim to the English throne, appeared in England not ten years after Elizabeth had become queen.[33] Not surprisingly, Elizabeth's ministers "urged their mistress to put down a religion which proclaimed her a bastard, and to support the reformed doctrines, which alone could give stability to her throne".[34]

After 1580 Elizabeth also had to contend with the presence in England of missionary priests, most of whom were Jesuits or Jesuit-trained. While Lingard thought these men to be innocent of the charges which were eventually brought against them – conspiracy to murder the queen, to overthrow the government, and to withdraw subjects from their loyalty – he also found their hesitation in denying the pope's claim to be able to depose princes to be "very problematical".[35] Privately, Lingard was harsher on the missionaries and "exiles" (those who had been sent abroad after a first capture or who, like Robert Persons, had fled to escape capture) than he was in print. He said in a letter to E. Price that the dissembling of the missionaries during interrogation "furnished a very plausible pretext for the first murderous laws against us".[36] In a letter to Robert Gradwell, he suspects that the *Admonition to the Nobility and People of England* (1587), supposedly written by the secular priest William Allen, was really the work of the Jesuits. He calls it "perhaps the most virulent libel ever written".[37] In it Elizabeth was accused of being a bastard, the daughter of an incestuous relationship,[38] of intruding by force, of being a heretic, of usurping the title of Head of the Church ("a thing in a woman unheard of"), of violating her coronation oath, of abolishing the Catholic religion, of destroying the ancient nobility, etc.[39] In the same letter to Gradwell, Lingard commented, "After such a publication, I am not surprised at any thing Elizabeth might do."[40]

In this case, Lingard's prejudice against the Society of Jesus simply got the better of him. So certain was he that Dr. Allen, in other ways a moderate man, could not possibly have written the *Admonition*, that Lingard went to great trouble to clear Allen's name. His initial criticism of the document was based on solid historical grounds: the style of the *Admonition* was unlike anything Allen had written before; the signature "the Cardinal" was uncharacteristic of the way Allen or any other cardinal signed documents; it is dated from the "Palace of St. Peter's", a name which the Vatican Palace was never called; Allen was not in Rome until 1591, a full three years after the document appeared; all of Allen's other works had been translated into Latin, and the *Admonition* had not; and finally, the secular priests of the time claimed it had been under the scrutiny of Persons, whose evasions when faced with the charge seemed to acknowledge his involvement.[41]

While this was a good evaluation of the evidence, Lingard fell short of clearing Allen. The piece of the puzzle that remained missing was a disclaimer from Allen; he must certainly have known of the document, and have denied it if he was not the author. But all we have from Allen is silence, and Lingard was forced to admit, albeit grudgingly, that Allen, if he did not actually write the *Admonition*, "adopted the tract for his own, and thus became answerable for its contents".[42] This was a defeat which Lingard did not take easily, and he leaves one with the feeling that, despite this evidence, he still did not believe Allen to be responsible. Immediately after admitting Allen to be "answerable", Lingard added that another history of the Reformation (Strype's) contains contrary evidence, namely a conciliatory letter from Allen to the queen.[43]

Evaluating Lingard's *History of England*

As soon as Lingard's Reformation volumes appeared, John Allen wrote in the *Edinburgh Review* in 1825 to warn his readers that Lingard's *History* was replete with bias, and that the author's "passions are warmed whenever the honor of his Church is at stake".[44] At the same time, the *Eclectic Review*, far more contentiously, found Lingard's treatment of Anne Boleyn "rancorous", and this was "but a specimen (and by no means the worst) of the spirit in which Dr. Lingard's volumes are written".[45] And Thomas Babington Macaulay was mocking in his reference to Lingard as an advocate. After first calling Lingard an "advocate", Macaulay stated that the only possible good to come from such a history was that it would balance advocates who were equally wrong on the other side:

> This is at present the state of history. The poet laureate [Robert Southey] appears for the Church of England, Lingard for the Church of Rome . . . In the midst of these disputes, however, history proper, if we may use the term, is disappearing. The high, grave, impartial summing up of Thucydides is nowhere to be found.[46]

Needless to say, Thucydides could be cited by the "other side" as well. Patrick McMahon's 1842 article in the Catholic *Dublin Review* was typical:

> As Greece had her Thucydides, and Rome her Tacitus, so England will have her Lingard . . . This work is the best history of any country that it has ever been our fortune to peruse; and that it is our deliberate conviction, that a combination of all the literary men in the universe could not produce a better . . .[47]

Catholic critics tended to defend Lingard because of his Catholicism and cite his objectivity and commanding use of documents. Mark Tierney, an historian and friend of Lingard, wrote that Lingard had let the documents tell the story:

> Lingard . . . came to pursue a different course from that of his predecessors. They had appeared as advocates – *he* was an unimpassioned narrator; they had avowedly argued for a victory – *he* simply stated the case that was before him; they had drawn their own conclusions, and exhibited their own views – *he* allowed the narrative to tell its own tale, and to make its own impression, and to suggest the inferences that would naturally arise from it.[48]

This would remain a constant theme in Catholic praise of Lingard. As the nineteenth century wore on, Cardinal Wiseman called Lingard "the only impartial historian of our country".[49] As late as 1950 Shane Leslie said that Lingard was "simply a transcriber of records", and in 1969 Donald Shea wrote an adoring book entitled, *The English Ranke: John Lingard.*[50] Most recently, Edwin Jones has written a book praising Lingard's methods and findings. "It is hardly too much, then", Jones concludes, "to claim for John Lingard, the title of the 'greatest' historian of the second millennium, as Bede was of the first."[51] Norman Davies has also commented that Lingard was a

> historical pioneer in two important aspects. For one thing, he was a true scholar's scholar, who based his judgements on the close critical study of documents. For another, he conducted research in French, Italian, and Spanish archives, thereby putting British sources into dynamic juxtaposition with foreign ones.[52]

Other modern scholars are not so certain of Lingard's achievement. Several modern critics have found his work to be too highly-charged with the emancipation debate of the early 1800's, and too manipulative of the reading public. Rosemary O'Day, in *The Debate on the English Reformation* (1986), gives Lingard a thorough and measured treatment, but contends that Lingard's motives in writing about the English Reformation were *primarily* political, i.e. to bring about Catholic Emancipation. This criticism, of course, begs the question whether Lingard's history is accurate or not, but it also implies that Lingard, with such political motivation, could not help but be misled by historical events or give them an inaccurate interpretation. John Kenyon complained in *The History Men* (1984) that Lingard was less than honest: "There is something repugnant in his willingness initially to pander to Protestant prejudice, then alter his work in subsequent editions, when the 'enemy' was off his guard."[53]

Thus, the main arguments against Lingard's account of the English Reformation can be grouped under two headings: that Lingard's motives were so political as to preclude the writing of accurate history, and that Lingard was consciously deceptive in his presentation – i.e. the *real* Lingard emerged in later editions only after he had established his reputation. These two arguments come together because of Lingard's Roman Catholicism, which dictated how he would approach the Emancipation debate and how (cautiously) he would approach his original audience. And these criticisms fail as a result – not because such arguments are not without validity, but because their obsession with Lingard's religion causes them to miss the point. Lingard made mistakes, and sometimes very big mistakes, but he did not make them because he was a Roman Catholic.[54]

But was it good history? Was Lingard so prejudiced by his religious belief and swayed by the controversies of his day that his historical judgment suffered to a serious degree? Was he deceitful in making his opinions more pointed after gaining a hearing?

Let us begin by taking Lingard's treatment of Anne Boleyn. The British public had accepted the opinions of Gilbert Burnet (1643–1715) and Hume, who had both affirmed that Anne had kept her chastity until her marriage to Henry in November of 1532, a respectable ten months before the birth of Elizabeth. Lingard maintained that the marriage had not occurred until late January of 1533, when Anne was already pregnant.

This sent Lingard's critics scrambling to defend the good names of Henry VIII and Anne Boleyn. The *Quarterly Review* objected strenuously to this charge – on the slender and pious grounds that charity demanded more respect for Anne's integrity – and Lingard brushed this aside in his *Vindication of Certain Passages in the fourth and fifth volumes of the History of England* with more documentation.[55] Sharon Turner produced a biography of Henry VIII in 1828 which attempted to salvage the reputations of both Henry and Anne, but did not succeed.[56] Rosemary O'Day curiously calls Lingard's attack on Anne Boleyn "character-assassination" on one page, and later says that "it was extremely difficult to overturn Lingard's measured case against Anne Boleyn".[57] As O'Day points out:

[Turner] tried to [retrieve the situation] by diverting attention away from the embarrassment of Anne herself . . . But Turner was forced to deal with Anne's own tragic history. And there is not doubt that she was a severe embarrassment. As Lingard pointed out in the first edition of his *History*, even her daughter had made no attempt to clear her name, preferring rather to forget that there ever had been such a person as Anne Boleyn – as far as Elizabeth I was concerned, she was her father's and not her mother's daughter. She preferred to forget that she was a chip off the old block, when that block was located on Tower Green.[58]

But there are problems with Lingard's treatment of Anne Boleyn which partially sustain the charges of character assassination made by O'Day and of "rancour" made by the *Eclectic Review*. Previous to Lingard, Anne Boleyn's reputation either rose or fell on that of her daughter Elizabeth. Lingard's contribution in this case is that he separated the two and examined the life of Anne Boleyn on its own merits and demerits, distinct from anything that Elizabeth may have been or become. This tended to soften criticism of Anne, but made what criticism remained more cogent. Lingard recognized that religion had colored previous accounts of Anne's character, and had made an accurate understanding of her role somewhat elusive:

> The question [of Anne's guilt or innocence] soon became one of religious feeling, rather than of historical disquisition . . . As her marriage with Henry led to the separation from the communion with Rome, the catholic writers were eager to condemn, the protestant to exculpate her memory.[59]

Lingard also recognized that a contradictory cycle of praise and blame had fastened on the life of Anne, and began as early as the reigns of Henry VIII and Elizabeth. "To have expressed a doubt of [Anne's] guilt", he wrote, "during the reign of Henry, or of her innocence during that of Elizabeth, would have been deemed proof of disaffection".[60] But Lingard overstepped when he made the suggestion that Anne must have done *something* to provoke the charge of adultery. Only her guilt in this regard, he reasoned, would explain Henry's "insatiable hatred" towards her.

Lingard admitted that he could not support his argument with documentation, yet he was intrigued enough by Anne's cruel death to include his opinion about it in his history. He claimed that a divorce would have been sufficient in Anne's case, but that Henry was not satisfied with this punishment and "must have been impelled by some more powerful motive to exercise against her such extraordinary, and, in one supposition, such superfluous rigour".[61] That motive, Lingard reasoned, would have to be Anne's infidelity.

There are other explanations. Anne was executed in 1536, at a time when opposition to Henry was systematically being rooted out. Examples abound of those who were faithful subjects and even renowned for their virtue, but who opposed the king in one or two particulars – sometimes even tacitly. Their deaths were overly dramatic – such as the hanging of the Observant Friars (1535) in their religious habits – as a warning to others, but also as a way of stating that they had done something significantly wrong, even if they had not. The cruelty of the punishment was, in some sense, a way of justifying the verdict on the victims. If the eighty-year old abbot of Glastonbury, who had signed the Oath of Supremacy and had sent money for the defeat of the Northern Uprisings, could be dragged to his place of execution, then hanged, drawn, and quartered, Anne Boleyn could conceivably have been treated unfairly. Lingard's error is in not offering another explanation, or suggesting that there is one. For one pledged to objectivity, this must be seen as a shortcoming.[62]

Lingard also errs in this case in that the same logic, which brought him to suspect Anne, is not applied to the deaths of More and Fisher. There is no comparable mention that they must have done *something* to provoke Henry to such superfluous cruelty. Interestingly, there is such mention in the *Eclectic Review*. It claimed that since the refusal to take the Oath of Supremacy had not been made high treason by the statute, and hence "could not alone have made them liable to the loss of life", these men must have done something else to deserve death, though the reviewer does not suggest what.[63]

Similarly, Lingard applied this double-standard to the deaths of Catherine of Aragon and Anne Boleyn. He related the genuine grief of Henry at the former and his utter joy at the death of the latter as indicative of their respective virtues. So great is Lingard's preoccupation with the contrast, most of which is inaccurate to begin with, that he could be fairly laid open to the charge of gloating.[64] There is as much here to condemn Henry as Anne, and what finally undermines Lingard's case is his handling of Henry's "grief" at the death of Jane Seymour: "His grief for her loss, *if he were capable of feeling such grief,* seemed to be absorbed in his joy for the birth of a son."[65] One wonders where this leaves Henry's supposed grief at the death of Catherine of Aragon.

Lingard's presentation of the reign of Mary Tudor, however, lends itself to the charge that Lingard favored Catholic figures beyond the legitimate bounds of the available evidence. He extended to Mary a sympathy which is not shown to other sovereigns. If Mary was cruel in her punishment of heretics, it was not her fault but rather her "misfortune . . . that she was not more enlightened than the wisest of her contemporaries".[66] While sound historical criticism will contextualize past events, comparing them to contemporary events or tendencies, Lingard here used this device to draw attention away from Mary's persecution, and thereby lessen her guilt. While he did not ignore the Marian persecution, as did Catholic historians both before and after, and indeed criticized it as "barbarous", he failed to note that several of Mary's contemporaries – from Philip II to Cardinal Pole to the pope – urged her not to persecute on the grounds of heresy. Furthermore, Lingard implied that Mary learned the craft from Protestants:

> I am inclined to believe that the queen herself . . . had imbibed the same intolerant opinion, which Cranmer and Ridley laboured to instil into the young mind of Edward: "that as Moses ordered blasphemers to be put to death, so it was the duty of the Christian prince, and more so one, who bore the title of defender of the faith, to eradicate the cockle from the field of God's church, to cut out the gangrene, that it might not spread to sounder parts". In this principle both parties seem to have agreed.[67]

The word "imbibed" is a very loose word to use in this regard, and Lingard is guilty of using it to create the subtle inference that Mary's intolerance was somehow dependent on Protestant intolerance. Again, Lingard failed to notice evidence that Catholic intolerance toward heretics antedated the Reformation and could have been as responsible, if not more so, for Mary's actions than any recent purge by Protestants.

But Lingard is never quite so easily categorized and he occasionally defended the name of a non-Catholic (e.g. Elizabeth), or another Catholic (e.g. Fr. William Allen), at the expense of a Catholic party.

There are several yardsticks by which Lingard's history of the English Reformation can be measured. The first is to examine his various editions. The charge is that, once the first edition was published and favorably reviewed, the real Lingard emerged. Subsequent editions, according to this view, bear his outspoken Catholicism, his deceit, and his misperception of history.

There is no question that in his desire to be read by Protestants, he may have taken his conciliatory approach too far. When his publisher saw the manuscript of the fifth volume – on the reign of Elizabeth – he balked at printing something so contrary to the generally accepted view of the queen, and worried that sales would be affected so seriously as to jeopardize the entire project. Lingard wrote to reassure him in words that betray to what lengths he was willing to go to obtain a hearing:

> You observed in a note some time ago that Elizabeth did not appear a very amiable character. I can assure you, I have not set down ought in malice, nor am I conscious that I have ever exaggerated. On the contrary, I have been careful to soften down what might have appeared too harsh to prejudicial minds: and not to let any severe expressions escape, that I may not be thought a partial writer. I should be sorry to say anything that may hurt the sale of the book, and on that account have been particularly guarded in the conclusion, where I touch upon her character. However, if there be any expression which you may think likely to prove prejudicial, I shall be ready to change it.[68]

When this same publisher suggested that the fifth volume include a "dissertation on the consequences of the Reformation", Lingard was the one to hesitate: "Were I to write such a dissertation *ex professo* and to say what I think, I should probably displease the majority of my readers, both protestants and catholics, and rather injure than promote the sale of the book."[69]

This gives some credence to the charge that Lingard subordinated truth and his real feelings to the sale of the book. And there is a worse charge – that Lingard did this deliberately and fully aware that once his audience was gained, he would reveal what he really thought. This is supported by the fact that Lingard did, in fact, add material to his later editions and commented more explicitly on material he had previously let speak for itself.

It is significant that the first noticeable changes appeared after emancipation – in the fourth edition published between 1837 and 1839, and in the editions thereafter. Lingard details the amount of new information available to him in the Preface to the sixth edition, which he wrote at the end of 1849 (and would be the last he had a hand in revising), though certainly many of these sources were included by him in the all-important fourth edition, published between 1837–39, where most of the important editorial changes occur. The first volume of the State Papers was published in 1830, including "the correspondence of Henry with his ministers of state, his ambassadors, envoys and agents, public and secret; with his commanders, military and naval; with his bishops and with his council".[70] Over the years four more volumes were added and various older collections were printed by the Secretary to the Records Commission, Charles Purton Cooper.[71] Lingard singled out the work of Agnes Strickland, whose gossipy but immensely informative *Lives of the Queens of England* was of special assistance.[72] Mark Tierney, for whom Lingard had an affection and high professional regard, had produced a three-volume sourcebook between 1839–43, which no doubt assisted Lingard in his final editing, although mention of Tierney was accidentally omitted by the publisher.[73]

Not only did Lingard have access to new information, but the atmosphere of caution which had characterized Catholic behaviour before emancipation was rapidly disappearing, and a newer atmosphere of aggressiveness was taking over. It is safe to say that Lingard joined in the jubilation. He had also gained confidence as a historian and had been praised by Protestants and Catholics alike as an important critical scholar. The combination of these factors led him to be more outspoken than he had been previously. But, before we can reach any conclusions about his true intentions in altering the text of his history, it is important to examine some of the actual changes he made.

To begin, Henry VIII was accused by Lingard in later editions of deserting Mary Boleyn, Anne's older sister and Henry's mistress, whereas there was no mention of this in the first edition.[74] Nor was anything said in the first edition about the character of Henry's monastic visitators, except that their instructions "breathed a spirit of piety and reformation . . . so that to men, not intrusted with the secret, the object of Henry appeared not the abolition, but the support and improvement of the monastic institute".[75] The later Lingard added this note:

> The visitors themselves were not men of high standing or reputation in the church. They were clerical adventurers of very equivocal character, who . . . had pledged themselves to effect . . . the extinction of the establishments they should visit. They proceeded at first to the lesser houses only. There they endeavoured by intimidation to extort from the inmates surrender of their property to the king; and, when intimidation failed, were careful to collect all such defamatory reports and information as might afterwards serve to justify the suppression of the refractory brotherhood.[76]

These additions are harmless enough, but they do not get to the heart of the monastic problem. As David Knowles would point out more than a century later, the character of the visitors was really irrelevant to the state of the monasteries. Any comprehensive defense of the monasteries would have to mention the visitors' characters, but to base any defense of late medieval monastic life on their bad reputations was a logical mistake. The fact is that Lingard accepted the *Comperta* (the reports compiled by Cromwell's visitors) at face value, and concluded that the monks had become "men of little reputation . . . a degenerate, time-serving lot".[77] But he mentions none of this in his history. Rather, he followed his own advice that, when it came to English monasteries, "the less stirred up the better".[78] Later evidence from Aidan Gasquet and David Knowles in this regard shows not only that Lingard's anti-monastic bent had gotten the better of him, but that failure to report the evidence puts him in a bad light. But any conclusion cannot point simply to Lingard's Roman Catholicism as the reason for omission. Admittedly, he believed that the monasteries were corrupt or, at best, of little use, and he no doubt withheld a review of the already well-known (though seriously inaccurate) details of the *Comperta* because such a review would only damage "his" side; yet, he had no sympathy with the monasteries to begin with. Why bother detailing the sins of an institution which he found to be indefensible and inessential to the Catholic faith in England? To omit what he knew of the monasteries was reprehensible, because it was to omit a serious reason why the Reformation was supposedly popular and wholesome, but he omitted such mention for larger than confessional reasons. If Geoffrey Elton could dismiss the work of David Knowles (who had largely removed the corruption of the monasteries as a reason for the

English Reformation) as not focusing sufficiently on the larger picture (i.e. social renewal), presumably Lingard can be forgiven for agreeing with Elton.[79]

The reign of Elizabeth is also dealt with more harshly in Lingard's later editions, where Lingard was more apt to dwell on her illegitimacy,[80] the sins of her ministers,[81] and the invalidity of Anglican Orders.[82] Lingard did not change his mind on any of these matters, but there is a significant shift of emphasis from a Lingard mildly sympathetic to the queen to a Lingard openly hostile.

The reason for this shift can be explained by the discovery that the pope did not respond harshly to the news of Elizabeth's accession. This discovery, if true, threw her subsequent activity into a completely different light. No longer could she be defended as a victim of the pope's intransigence. Thus Lingard's qualified support for the queen evaporated in his later editions, not because he consciously altered his views after he had duped his audience, but because he found new evidence. Given Lingard's low opinion of the papacy, it was probably unwelcome evidence at that. Seen in this light, Lingard's letters to his publisher, offering adjustments in the work, are far less alarming than his critics suppose, since the proposed adjustments involved expression far more than they did factual content.

There is other evidence in Lingard's favor. First of all, he remained concerned about Protestant sensibilities long after he had gained his hearing, and long after emancipation. When the title "Westminster" was proposed for the about-to-be formed Catholic diocese in London, Lingard recoiled on the sole grounds that such a title would offend Protestants unnecessarily, and suspected that it had been chosen partially with that end in mind. In addition, he found triumphalistic expressions, such as the wearing of religious habits in public, to be provocative and deserving of the abuse they attracted. If Lingard's true colors were displayed after the success of his history, they were the colors of moderation (when this was becoming unpopular among Catholics) and integrity.

Secondly, Lingard did not significantly alter those statements which he had introduced, supposedly, to please the Protestants. Not only do the hostile remarks about the Jesuits remain, so do the criticisms of the various popes. On the pre-Reformation subject of Joan of Arc, he had removed his comment from the first edition that Joan was the victim of "an enthusiasm which, while it deluded yet moved and elevated the mind of this young and interesting female", but still maintained of Joan's childhood as late as the sixth edition that "in those day dreams the young enthusiast learned to invest with visible forms the creation of her own fancy". Furthermore, he said of her trial that "an impartial observer would have pitied and respected the mental delusion with which she was afflicted".[83]

However much Lingard was moved by a desire to be read by Protestants, he did not compromise his text to the extent that his critics have charged. One modern Lingard scholar has even suggested that this desire had a positive effect on Lingard, in that he benefited from "audience reaction". Edwin Jones writes, "The fact is that finding himself opposed to a conventional framework of thought, the historian can gain a positive benefit from being faced with an unsympathetic, critical, or even hostile audience."[84] All Lingard wanted was a hearing. He was not trying to prove that the Catholic Church was the true Church, nor was he trying to proselytize. He simply wanted to present a side of history that people had not seen before, in the hopes that such exposure would lead people to a better understanding of Catholics and, eventually, to emancipation.[85] To focus on Lingard's religion or politics is to do him a disservice as a historian, if it is not to misread him completely. The theme which runs throughout Lingard's history is not the correctness of Catholicism, or even the wisdom of Emancipation, but the correctness of toleration. Everywhere he praises or condemns historical figures on the basis of their proximity to tolerance. Mary Tudor was castigated by Lingard, not because such a severe critique would please the Protestants, but because she was intolerant. He wrote that the executions during her reign were "horrors" and inexcusable not only because of their manifest brutality, but also because they were productive of sham conformity, hypocrisy, and perjury.[86] He continued:

> After every allowance it will be found that, in the space of four years, almost two hundred persons perished in the flames for religious opinion; a number at the contemplation of which the mind is struck with horror, and learns to bless the legislation of a more tolerant age, in which dissent from established forms, though in some countries still punished with civil disabilities, is no where liable to the penalties of death.[87]

Conversely, those who promoted toleration were praised by Lingard. The chaplain to Philip II, Alphonso de Castro, was commended by Lingard because he attacked the Marian persecution in a court sermon.[88] Any ruler who counseled moderation attracted Lingard's positive notice, including Mary Tudor and Elizabeth because their reigns began with such gentleness. A few popes received his approval as well – Clement VII who cautiously stalled the divorce proceedings of Henry, and Paul IV who did *not* react effusively to the news of Elizabeth's accession.

If a generalization could be made about Lingard's view of the papacy, it is that he saw the papacy as tending too often toward intolerance.

Power, once accumulated, was difficult to disperse. Temporal powers and privileges had come to the popes in the Middle Ages, and the later popes seemed chary of letting go of these powers, even though a new age had demanded a change. He noted, "The servant of the servants of God became the sovereign of the sovereigns, and assumed the right of judging them in his court, and of transferring their crowns as he thought proper."[89] Problems arose precisely because the popes had clung to a system which no longer worked, in the hopes of preserving their power. And this bred intolerance.

There was a message for the English government in this, namely that Catholics could criticize their own Church for its history of intolerance, but might also find the present English government guilty of similar intolerance as long as emancipation was delayed. Emancipation must come, irrespective of the truth or untruth of Catholicism, because toleration was inherently good and a virtue to be practiced.

The message to his own Church was vaguer since Lingard did not specify in what way it could be applied, especially in the debate over the Papal States. He probably meant it as a warning that, as Acton would later remark, "power corrupts", and the pope should not claim too much nor say too much in the exercise of that power. Furthermore, Lingard's message was an assurance that, in days when the pope's temporal possessions and authority were everywhere being threatened, their loss would not involve the spiritual claims of the Church or the pope.

As much as Lingard felt that a reduction of papal "pretensions" would be salutary for the papacy and for Church-State relations, he did not disparage the papacy as such, and he regarded one pope with some affection. It is thought by some that Pope Leo XII wanted to give Lingard a cardinal's hat. In October 1826 Leo held a consistory in which he alluded to one of his appointees *in petto* as a scholar whose writings were drawn from original sources and who had done great service to the Church.[90] That Leo thought highly of Lingard could not be questioned, for during the Holy Year of 1825 he had given Lingard a gold medal and asked when the *History of England* would be completed.[91] But whether Leo meant Lingard for the cardinalate is another matter. Cardinal Wiseman later recalled that the pope intended the honor for Lamennais, whom he was known to call "the last Father of the Church".[92]

One thing is certain – Lingard thought the pope meant the honor for him and was thrilled by the thought. He wrote to John Walker in high spirits, calling Leo "the greatest pontiff that Rome has seen since the days of St. Peter", and added:

Why so? Because he is the only one who has ever had the sagacity to discover the transcendent merit of J.L. He patronized my work, he defended my character against the slanders of Padre Ventura and the fanatics, he made me a cardinal in petto, he described me in a consistory as not one of the servile *pecus* of historians, but one who offered the world *historiam ex ipsis haustam fontibus*. Are not all these feathers in his cap, jewels in his tiara?[93]

Another yardstick to measure Lingard's achievement is that of the contemporary revisionism of the English Reformation. How well do Lingard's conclusions stand up against the most recent research and findings about the Reformation? In many ways, this is an unfair question due the obvious fact that a detailed comparison of Lingard's Reformation to the Revisionist Reformation is a major project in itself, and to the equally obvious fact that 150 years of research and scholarly debate have been done since Lingard and that new archival and source material are available to scholars that were unheard of to Lingard. Also, the writing of history has evolved from an evaluation of state papers and letters, parliamentary actions, and decisions made by leaders, to an examination to local records – gleaned from parish rosters, warden's reports, liturgical practices, sermons, etc. Having said that, it is still instructive to see that Lingard's opinions stand the test of time. While no one reads Lingard's contemporaries (Hume, Gibbon, Hallam, Macaulay, etc.) for anything but literary style or historiographical curiosity, Lingard's history remains cogent. As Edwin Jones points out, "I know of no other historian who has anticipated in such detail and over such a wide area, the radically advanced work of 'revisionist' historians, a century and half later . . . Every one of the particular historical interpretations about which he himself was criticized by his conemporaries such as Macaulay and Henry Hallam, has been decided in Lingard's favour in the light of the most recent scholarship."[94]

To take one example, Lingard's treatment of Henry VIII generally supports J. J. Scarisbrick's assessment of the king as someone who was increasingly driven by a lust for power, pleasure, money. But mostly power. There is close agreement with Scarisbrick about the divorce and the fact that Henry would stop at nothing to obtain it. Related to this is Lingard's perception that it was Henry, and not his ministers, who determined policy. This would find support in Peter Gwyn's thesis that Wolsey was a faithful and skillful servant doing his master's bidding. Policies and actions are described by Lingard as though Henry VIII, rather than Wolsey, were the one setting the direction. While Lingard might be more censorious than Gwyn of Wolsey's personal failings and personality defects, he is in general agreement about Wolsey's subservient and loyal role in governmental policy and practice.

Even on details he matches many of Gwyn's conclusions. In the case of Archbishop Warham, whose sudden removal from the Chancellor's position cast suspicion on Wolsey who replaced him, Lingard is in agreement with Gwyn, who thinks that Warham was worn out and was happy to pass the reins to the capable Wolsey.[95] In the case of the Duke of Buckingham, who was executed for treason, Wolsey has been blamed in the past as attempting to eliminate an innocent rival. Lingard, like Gwyn, felt that Buckingham himself was his own worst enemy.[96]

There are times when Lingard is at variance with the revisionists, as when he agrees with Hume (and nearly everyone else at the time) that Wolsey hungered after the papacy and was bitterly disappointed when he did not win the election. Both Scarisbrick and Gwyn agree on evidence from the relevant state papers that Wolsey did not seek the papacy, but not so much because he did not covet the office as that he knew he could not be elected.[97]

But, generally speaking, Lingard's findings are remarkably in keeping with the conclusions reached by Scarisbrick, Gwyn, and Eamon Duffy in his landmark *The Stripping of the Altars.*

A further yardstick is to examine the version of the English Reformation that held the field when Lingard began to write, how that history was affected by Lingard, and what measures were taken to respond to Lingard, once he had written his history. There can be no question that David Hume's *History of England* was the latest word, and it was a version which was not favorable to the Catholic Church. No opportunity was missed to "bash" the monasteries, the hierarchic Church, the Middle Ages. What strikes the reader of Hume, besides his patent anti-Catholicism, is his heavy dependence on previous historians. He cited Burnet most of all, then Strype, Stowe, Fuller, etc. Lingard had, indeed, done a great deed. Evidence of this can be seen in the extent to which Lingard's opponents retreated. The *Eclectic Review*, much as it disliked Lingard's work, made a few concessions which betrayed the strength of Lingard's assault. The first example was a virtual disavowal of Henry VIII and other ministers whose effectiveness in bringing about the Reformation had long been mistaken for their virtue in doing so:

> The cause of the Reformation cannot be identified with Henry, for, though he rejected the tyranny of Rome, he retained the absurdities of Popery; nor with Cranmer, for he was deficient in firmness and decision; nor with Cromwell; since, although he gave an enlightened protestation to the professors of the new doctrine, it is yet doubtful how far he had himself embraced them.[98]

The second example was an admission that some of the reformers were guilty of misdeeds:

We ought not . . . to be surprised that some of the Reformers . . . degraded themselves, and betrayed their cause, by retaining a portion of that spirit of persecution which they had imbibed from their "working mother", the Church of Rome.[99]

Lingard had backed the *Eclectic* into a corner, whence it lashed out almost desperately, preaching that the righteousness of the Reformation could never be affected by the immorality of its promoters: "[Our antagonists] prove . . . only that a higher power than man's was dictating events; they carry us onward from the instrument to the operator, – from ignorant and powerless man, to almighty and omniscient God."[100]

Such statements could not long survive in a world of critical history, and Lingard's achievement is that he introduced that new world to England. He had rendered previous history obsolete by raising the level of historical debate from one of ideology to one of documentation and interpretation. Prior to Lingard all that was needed to discredit a historical work was to discredit the philosophy that was behind it. Now, that was no longer sufficient. If a critic was going to attack his history, it was necessary to attack the factual evidence of the work rather than the religious belief of the author. This was a momentous change, and it meant that thereafter the best historians would be those who amassed the best documents.

Lingard was not without his flaws, as we have seen. He mistook the reproduction of a manuscript for the exhibition of its truth, and did not comprehend the degree to which an author could still color a seemingly objective collection of texts – by the very selection he made, by the order in which he put them, by the editorial comments he added about them, by the weight he placed on them. Lingard was more a product of the Enlightenment and Roman Catholicism than he admitted or realized. But this is a far cry from the calculating political advocate and religious apologete. He was a great historian first and foremost, his achievement was described by Norman Davies as "Colossal",[101] and both the political and religious fortunes of his fellow-Catholics improved as a result.

Historical writing has changed considerably since Lingard took pen to paper. Evidence from the bottom up has become far more important than it ever was in Lingard's time. But nothing which has been recently discovered has overturned the conclusions reached by Lingard. And the extent to which historical writing changed is largely a result of Lingard's work. What Lingard found was a history of the Reformation which was truly revolutionary. The history and the historiography of the English Reformation, quite frankly, would never be the same.

Chapter IV

THE JESUITS AND
MARK TIERNEY

isalpine historical writing did not end with Lingard and emancipation. There was to be one significant aftershock in the work of
the secular priest Mark Tierney (1795–1862). His concern would
not be over the issue of Catholic loyalty, but over the one Cisalpine
concern which remained: the power of the Jesuits. Emancipation, instead
of putting this issue to rest, as it had done in the case of Catholic loyalty,
brought it to a crisis.

Strictly speaking, the connection between emancipation and the
restoration of the Jesuits in England was coincidental. The Jesuits, as a
religious order, had been restored by the pope in 1814. However, the
English bishops had voted not to restore them to England, for fear that
their presence would, among other things, jeopardize the ongoing negotiations for emancipation. Bishop Collinridge, the Vicar-Apostolic of the
Western District and a Franciscan friar, had long opposed the founding
of any new missions in his district by the regular clergy. But in 1828 he
changed his mind, and petitioned Rome for a full restoration of the Society
of Jesus. In January 1829 the decree for this restoration arrived just as
Parliament was discussing the Emancipation Bill. The timing could not
have been worse, and Parliament reacted by including clauses in the Bill
which required all "Jesuits and Members of Other Religious Orders,
Communities, or Societies of the Church of Rome, bound by Monastic or
Religious vows", to register – this, in the hope that such a registration
would lead to their gradual extinction.[1] No novices could be accepted, nor
any new members enter from outside the country.

This provision appeared to be a sham, and Irish Liberator, Daniel
O'Connell, was so certain that it would never be enforced, that he claimed
he could drive a coach and horses through its clauses. But the Jesuits were

nervous about it, and took the precaution of admitting *all* of their student-candidates at Stonyhurst as novices in the Society before the provision was passed.[2] Other religious orders were nervous about the proposed bill as well. The English Dominican provincial, John Ambrose Woods, protested to Robert Peel and the Duke of Wellington, who responded that they did not think forcing resident religious to register with a magistrate was a harsh measure at all.[3]

The English government did not have a monopoly on suspecting the religious. The same suspicion had a long history with the Catholic Church itself – in the often vicious rivalry between secular and regular clergy in England. Recently it had been fed by the general Enlightenment distrust of monasticism. Joseph Berington wanted to get rid of all religious orders, on the grounds that they promoted a group, rather than an individual, spirit.[4] He condemned this esprit de corps and "all behaviour dictated by that spirit, and the individuals that it sways . . . Men of party, unblushingly do, what, when taken out of that influence, they would reject with horror".[5]

Lingard shared this distrust of religious orders. His letters are replete with a dogged hostility towards the regular clergy in general, whom he thought difficult to regulate.[6] When the Jesuit Provincial (Cobb) was announced as the preacher for the opening of Southwark Cathedral, Lingard remembered that this same man had preached a sermon in Preston on how the Blessed Mother had delivered Jesus standing up, in the presence of a cow (not an ox), which had been purchased by St. Joseph specifically for the purpose of giving milk.[7] Lingard's comment, however, was more than just a swipe at Cobb:

> I explain it thus: regulars are obliged daily to spend much time in mental prayer; a new idea strikes them. They pursue it and become habituated to it, unconscious of its indelicacy and absurdity, and at length detail it to others as a great discovery in the economy of religion.[8]

Lingard's disapproval of the Jesuits was more specific. When a new calendar of English martyrs was proposed, Lingard reacted: "Not a Jesuit is omitted; and few secular priests, in proportion to the number, are admitted. Can there by any trick in this?"[9]

The vicars-apostolic, with the exception of Milner, shared in this feeling and fretted about the regulars, and especially about the Jesuits, and their ability to circumvent the wishes of bishops. Bishop Poynter was more vigilant than most in watching for Jesuit incursions, and once wrote that the Jesuits were "labouring to raise in our English mission an *imperium in imperio*".[10] The vicars felt that the Jesuits, if restored as a religious order, would conspire with Milner and the Irish bishops, who had already connived at several projects, and prove to be contentious and difficult to control. There was a distinct fear that the Jesuits would try to "take over" as they had done during the Reformation. Any weakness or confusion of jurisdiction was exploited by them to their advantage.

Especially annoying was their control of the English colleges abroad, particularly the English College in Rome, which had become a virtual recruiting ground for the Society. When the Jesuits were suppressed in 1773, the College was taken from their hands. The seculars, led by John Lingard, were determined not to allow them to return, even if they were to be restored as a religious order. After 1814, when the Society was restored, one crisis led quickly to another. When Cardinal Consalvi died in 1824, Lingard fretted that the Jesuits would take advantage of his absence to intrude once again in the running of the College. Even as late as 1840, when there was talk that Nicholas Wiseman, the current rector of the College, would be appointed bishop and return to England, Lingard feared another Jesuit move to regain control.

Robert Gradwell, Lingard's friend and Wiseman's predecessor as rector, fought as hard as Lingard to keep the English College in secular hands. He had discovered a bundle of papers written by Jesuits which, he said in a long letter to Lingard, were "evidence against their honesty and fair play; and prove the Fathers were either rogues or enthusiasts". Gradwell said that he had "not room to characterise these papers, but they exhibit such scenes of rascality, such intrepid lying, such mean and wicked policy under the garb of Religion, as really shock the reader".[11] The Jesuits were arguing against appointing ordinary bishops, and used a whole host of reasons, claiming such an appointment would displease the king, then that the bishop in question would be useless and be a tyrant over the society, and finally that no secular priest in England was fit or capable for the job.[12]

Much of the fear of restoring the Jesuits had to do with the immediate business of emancipation. The government did not trust Jesuits and often singled them out in documents under a separate title – such as "bishops, priests, and Jesuits".[13] Any appeal for relief from the existing penal laws would have to be couched in terms which excluded the Jesuits. There restoration in 1814 caused one secular priest to write to Bishop Bramston, "The hope of emancipation may never be realised because we must be forced to have, what is obnoxious to the state, and what is not wanted in the Country – Jesuits".[14] And Gradwell, not long after, warned Cardinal Consalvi of the political dangers of re-establishing the Jesuits in England:

[Re-establishment] is a subject of considerable moment both in a political and religious light. The political reasons which had considerable weight in April last are rather increased than diminished by the election of a new Parliament; to whom the British Catholics will apply for relief with increased confidence.[15]

The Jesuit "menace" re-appeared in 1838 when Rome gave permission to the regulars to establish missions without reference to the bishops or secular clergy. This was unwise. The bishops were justifiably angry that this had been done without their consultation. The secular clergy, for its part, petitioned Rome in 1840 – requesting that regulars no longer be selected as bishops in England. Mark Tierney, who was a major leader in this agitation, went so far as to suggest to Bishop Poynter that bishops should be elected by the secular clergy, just as every religious order elected its superiors. He wrote, "Election is the great security against abuse, the great pledge of the subject's attachment to the authority under which he lives".[16]

Tierney was a recognized historian who had been appointed chaplain to the Duke of Norfolk in 1824, an important post which he held until his death in 1862. He was elected a fellow of the Society of Antiquaries in 1833 and of the Royal Society in 1841, largely on the merits of his work on the history and antiquities of Arundel. He also served as Canon-Penitentiary of Southwark Cathedral from 1852–62. His major work, the re-edition of Charles Dodd's *Church History of England*, was an attempt to carry the anti-Jesuit crusade into the arena of history. While valuable for its wealth of complete original documents, the project was doomed from the start.

The choice of Dodd's book was a curious one. It was already one hundred years old in 1837 when Tierney began the re-edition. It was outdated in several regards: new and better documents had come to light, the very writing of history had undergone a revolution – thanks to John Lingard – and there was little in Dodd that could not be found in Lingard. But even Lingard felt that a re-edition was warranted because Dodd's book was, as he called it, the only consecutive history of the Catholic Church ever to be written (an odd claim since the book began with the year 1500), it had been regarded as an authoritative source book, and it had become scarce and expensive. A re-edition would save time – sparing the editor the effort of writing an entirely new book – and the original would serve as a starting-point for a continuation.[17]

Several attempts had already been made to resurrect Dodd, the latest by John Kirk, another secular priest, who admitted that the work was beyond him. In a letter to Joseph Berington, which appeared in the *Catholic Miscellany* of 1826, Kirk explained what he had collected for a continuation of Dodd, how he had organized the material, and how problems had crept in to delay any publication. Kirk was a sensitive man and balked at continuing a history which, as it became increasingly evident to him, would only re-excite the bitter feelings created by the original Dodd.[18]

The first Dodd was Charles Dodd, born with the unfortunate name Hugh Tootel. The name change, however, probably had more to do with his being a Catholic priest, among whom aliases were commonplace until the early 1800s. Dodd went to great lengths to make his book appear scholarly, including a bibliography divided into three major sections: Catholic historians, Protestant historians, and manuscripts. He supported his statement with numerous quotations and references, a method which, while praiseworthy, had its practical defects. For one thing, Dodd had to work in secret because of the penal laws, and had difficulty both in obtaining original documents and then in re-checking them. In addition, Dodd often "loaded" his Protestant references with Puritan authors, which rendered the history less objective than appeared on the surface. Tierney was well aware of these and other shortcomings, and mentioned them in the "Advertisement" to the new edition:

> With all his excellencies, Dodd is sometimes defective, and frequently incorrect. With him, dates and names are too often mistaken, or confounded; transactions of stirring interest, or of lasting importance, are occasionally dispatched with the indifference of a passing allusion; and occurrences, that scarcely merit a casual notice, are swollen into consequence . . . [19]

One can readily see that any re-edition of Dodd was going to cause just as much concern to the Jesuits as the original publication, and a more reckless man than John Kirk would be needed to pursue the project. Tierney interrupted the Kirk–Berington exchange with a letter of his own, suggesting to Kirk that his work was being needlessly prolonged because it was slavishly following Dodd's original outline, which was unwieldy, and because Kirk had transcribed too much unnecessary material – hurting himself by not trusting to a secretary. Above all, Tierney wrote, one should not worry about the opposition of the Jesuits: "Such opposition can originate only with that body whose name you have concealed behind a blank".[20] Tierney went on to give Kirk a lecture on references: if there is "no colouring of your own", the only way of attacking the text is to produce better manuscripts, which will either invalidate Dodd's (or Kirk's) or explain them. Either way, the product will be better.

But Tierney did not let matters lie there. He told Kirk that a re-edition was urgent precisely because it *was* provocative. Tierney was certain that a re-edition would be assailed only by a party, "whose intrigues have been worse than tempest in the land, and whose spirit, still unchanged, is ready to cry out against the unveiling of its mysteries".[21] That party was the

Society of Jesus, of course, and Tierney was confident that a new *Dodd's Church History* would do the English secular clergy a great favor by exposing the Society which had "so constantly endeavoured to accomplish their pernicious purposes".[22]

And so, Kirk, probably anxious to be rid of the work, passed his collection of manuscripts, as well as the entire project, onto the eager Tierney. Tierney's first task was to re-order Dodd's volumes, which were a confused tangle of narrative and biography, and set about skillfully combining the narrative passages into a coherent unit, relegating biographical notices to later volumes (which were never published), and the mass of additional documentation to footnotes and appendices. So dense was the collection of manuscripts that Lingard worried that it would injure the sale of the book.[23]

This pile of documents and the re-edition of Dodd served another purpose besides scholarship: they were a wall for Tierney to hide behind. An original work would have made him vulnerable to attack; better to reproduce an old work and deflect whatever criticism might come to the original. In controverted statements, Tierney could claim that it was Dodd, and not he, who was the irritable Jesuit-baiter. When he was charged in 1840 by two members of the Bodenham family with indulging anti-Jesuit prejudices, he replied, "I can challenge Mr. Bodenham and his son together to discover one word in any passage bearing on the subject, that breathes but respect and veneration for the Society."[24]

The Jesuits, at least, felt that they had found some passages which breathed less than respect and veneration, and they refused to send Tierney any more manuscripts. Fr. Lythgoe, the Jesuit superior, wrote to Tierney:

> My attention has . . . been called to certain passages in your new Edition of Dodd, particularly in Vol. IV [concerned largely with the reign of James I], which as it seems to me, cannot be well reconciled with your declaration made to Fr. James Brownbill, in your letter to him dated April 27, 1837, that you would not avail yourself of the Confidence reposed in you for any purpose "of which the Society should have reason to complain".[25]

The Jesuits had lent manuscripts to Tierney on the conditions that he would compile a fair history and also return the manuscripts.[26] In the latter case he was certainly delinquent, and the Jesuits stopped co-operating with him as much because he did not return documents as for his anti-Jesuit slant.[27]

In a way, Tierney's use of Dodd was reminiscent of Berington's use of Panzani, i.e. an excuse to air his own ideas. Just as Berington had brought out an anti-Jesuit warhorse, so had Tierney. The state of the art had

changed: as we have seen, Berington made a great deal over a single document, blanketing it with a lengthy introduction and afterword, neither of
which had much to do with the original Panzani. Tierney, on the other
hand, restricted his comments to footnotes (many of them lengthy), which
were scholarly and critical, and supplemented Dodd with a massive collection of documents.[28]

Part of the reason for doing this was to prove that Dodd was instinctively right, even if his collection of authentic documents was meager by
modern standards; partly to supply historians with those documents
which had never before seen the light of day; and partly because he
believed that, with such a massive array of documents, as he told Kirk,
"there can be no views, no colouring of your own".[29] He failed to see, as
Kirk had seen, that the very publication of *Dodd's Church History* was a
red flag.

When there is no change in, or addition to, the original text, we may
presume that Tierney agreed with the original Dodd, as when the pope
was treated benignly. Dodd, for example, wrote that to accuse the pope
of collusion with Emperor Charles V in the matter of Catherine of Aragon
was to go too far:

> Doubtless, the pope had several politic considerations, as well as those of
> religion, not to comply with king Henry; but to make a declaration, that he kept
> off merely upon a temporal view, is a mismanagement that discerning pope can
> never be thought guilty of.[30]

That is weak, left to stand without supporting evidence, but Tierney
let it stand without comment. Neither did Tierney question Pope
Clement's power to pronounce against Henry VIII, though there were
doubts raised against his prudence:

> [I] shall mention what a certain author observes, from St. Augustin [sic], that
> the prelates of the church ought to be cautious in their censures, where there is
> danger of schism. That Clement VII. usurped not a power which did not belong
> to him, and that he offended not against justice, in the sentence he pronounced
> against Henry VIII., all must acknowledge, who own his supremacy in matters
> of religion.[31]

While Tierney's silence on these texts can be seen fairly as tacit
approval, even more important are Tierney's explicit comments on other
texts. Often, Tierney underlined Dodd when he agreed with him, or qualified him when he disagreed. For example, when Dodd stated that
Elizabeth reacted violently only after the pope had excommunicated and
deposed her, Tierney added: "At first, she sought a revocation of the
sentence: afterwards, finding that her efforts were unsuccessful, she

resolved to adapt other measures, and, if possible, to cut off all communication between her catholic subjects and the See of Rome."[32]

For Tierney, the pope played a greater part in the Rising of the North than Dodd was willing to admit. When the original Dodd excused Northumberland of working independently of the pope before the excommunication was published – the result of "personal sentiment" – Tierney disagreed:

> The absence of all concert between Rome and the insurgents is by no means certain. During the summer [of 1569], Dr. Nicholas Morton, a near-relative both of the Nortons and of the Markenfields [both conspirators with Northumberland] . . . had arrived from Rome, in the character of an apostolic penitentiary. His ostensible purpose was, to impart spiritual faculties to the catholic clergy: but he mixed continually with the discontented leaders in the north; he assisted in arranging their plans and animating their courage; and though he could not announced the publication of the bull of deposition, which was not yet signed, it is more than probable that he informed them of the measures, already taken to prepare such an instrument.[33]

Tierney also implicated the pope in the Armada, whereas Dodd had claimed that "neither the English Catholic, nor the see of Rome, did any way concern themselves".[34] Tierney pointed out that the pope had made William Allen a cardinal in time for the expedition, drew up a bill of deposition, ordered Allen to prepare a statement on his arrival in England, and collected a million crowns "ready to be paid, as soon as the invading army should have landed in England".[35]

Dodd's history, while it did not excuse Elizabeth from all blame in the matter of the Reformation, almost always deflected criticism of her to other targets: her ministers, the pope, and the Jesuits. The reader would be hard pressed to find a single instance in Dodd where Elizabeth is accused directly. Elizabeth reacted strongly to the Rising in the North, for example, only after the pope had issued his sentence of excommunication and deposition; Mary Queen of Scots was executed because Elizabeth's ministers (notably Walsingham) had concocted a Catholic plot in order to prevent her marriage to the Catholic Duke of Anjou; the missionary priests were executed because they compromised their loyalty.

This last concern is the heart of *Dodd's Church History*, and the principal reason why Tierney wanted to see it in print once again. Tierney underlined the dilemma of the thirteen people interrogated with Edmund Campion, who had all professed their loyalty to the queen, but had also asserted, "either directly or my implication, the power of the pope to deprive her".[36] The principal offenders were the exiles who persisted in interfering in the political affairs of England. These fugitives had continued to make treasonable statements from the safety of the continent, endangering those Catholics who were still within reach of the government's resentment.[37]

Not only had the Jesuits intruded where they did not belong, but they jeopardized the lives of the missionary priests who were placed in an impossible predicament. What is worse, they compromised the loyalty of those English Catholics in general. These innocent Catholics had served in Elizabeth's army and in her cabinet, until the meddling of the Jesuits cast them all as rebels.[38]

Robert Persons represented all that was negative about the Jesuits, which was to Tierney no more than an elite club of usurpers who could appeal over the heads of local churches, come and go as it pleased, move in on all the best territory, and generally try to take control. Tierney quoted a letter from Persons to the pope, after students at the English College in Rome had petitioned for the removal of the Jesuits. In this letter, Persons assured the pope that the Society of Jesus "was essential to the existence of religion in this country . . . Were the fathers to be removed . . . the salt would be taken from the earth, and the sun would be blotted from the heavens of the English church".[39]

Neither Rome nor the English bishops were in the mood for Tierney's opinion. The Roman court, besieged at this time by republicans who were threatening the territory of the Papal States, was prickly about any criticism of its temporal powers, and more so if such criticism came from Catholic historians. It was a nervous time and Rome did not suffer internal dissent gladly. As a result, there was no reason to stifle the growing Jesuit anger over Tierney's work. And thus Tierney went under.

The only people capable of saving him were the bishops, and they found him as much a nuisance as they did the Society of Jesus. And more easily got rid of. Tierney had not helped his cause by leading the opposition to Bishop Wiseman, nor did Tierney's re-stirring of the religious/secular waters impress the bishops, who still found themselves in the middle of that debate. The bishops were therefore just as anxious as Rome and the Jesuits to see Tierney's work halted. The fifth volume, published in 1843, would be the final one.

How, exactly, the work was halted has yet to be documented. An obituary in the *Gentleman's Magazine* mentioned that Tierney was forced to abandon the Dodd project because of paralysis in one hand.[40] But there are numerous samples of Tierney's handwriting – some of them running to great length – as late as 1857, more than a decade after he laid aside *Dodd's Church History*. Joseph Gillow, in his *Dictionary of English Catholics*, claimed that pressure from the Jesuits caused Tierney to quit, an observation which is supported by circumstantial evidence. Lingard wrote to Tierney in 1846, asking, "Are you labouring at your great work? Is the next volume almost ready for press?"[41] And Lingard repeated this question in almost every extant letter to Tierney as late as 1848. He would not have done this had he known Tierney was disabled. Tierney, for his part, would have informed Lingard of a paralysis, but might not have thought Jesuit pressure would be permanent, and so entertained thoughts of continuing the project, once the pressure eased. He certainly mentioned Jesuit interference in the sale of the book, and wrote bitterly to the pro-Jesuit George Oliver that the Jesuit provincial (Lythgoe) was trying to ruin his project:[42]

> Mr. Lythgoe is himself the very person who, from the very first moment that he heard I was engaged on my present work, set himself studiously, but of course secretly, to create a feeling against it, and as far as he could to injure its sale. This *I can prove*.

> In earlier life, I expressed myself strongly on the conduct of the Jesuits. I afterwards, felt that I had spoken *harshly*, and I told you so. I told you more – I told you that I wished to be able to prove that I had spoken *unsoundly* as well as harshly: – but, I grieve to say it, the treatment which I have experienced, and the conducts which I have witnessed have more and more convinced me that however *harsh* my censure, my judgement was not erroneous.[43]

All things considered, however, Tierney's worst enemy was himself. Had his temperament been more conciliatory, the work may have proceeded despite the opposition. Two instances of his extraordinary pettiness may explain the censure far better than any anti-Jesuitism.

The first case involved the Bodenhams, mentioned above. The younger Bodenham, apparently a friend of Tierney, had visited him Arundel and mentioned to a Jesuit friend the nature of the conversation which took place there. Word of this got back to Tierney, who was incensed that he had been mentioned as having anti-Jesuit feelings, and that private hospitality had been the means by which this slander was derived. He wrote Bodenham and demanded an apology and retraction, noting, "I have never spoken ... with *any* asperity, or *any* hostile feeling whatever, against any body or society, whether of Jesuit or others."[44]

Bodenham promptly apologized for any misunderstanding he may have inadvertently caused, which left Tierney unsatisfied. He pressed Bodenham for illustrations, and Bodenham responded by recalling two incidents at Arundel which, he felt, justified his estimate of Tierney as having anti-Jesuit feelings. One was that Tierney had waved in the direction of some Jesuit manuscripts lent him by Stonyhurst, and said if they were published they would irretrievably ruin the Society in public estimation. The other was a reference Tierney made to some dishonourable transactions the Jesuits had been accused of, and remarked, "It was just like them".[45]

Tierney never denied these stories, but continued to pursue the younger Bodenham so relentlessly that Bodenham's father intervened and requested a halt to the exchange. Tierney persisted, and the older Bodenham became embroiled in the argument to such an extent that he threatened to publish pertinent parts of the correspondence. Tierney rejoined by threatening to publish the entire correspondence, which he eventually did (privately), thus providing further evidence of his almost blind confidence in printed documents. Given the nature of the letters, it is almost beyond belief that he thought a publication of the entire correspondence would benefit his cause.

Why Tierney was in such a state of pique is not easy to explain, since the evidence against him was so overwhelming. There was no secret about his anti-Jesuit leanings, and Bodenham, in only stating the obvious, must have been more than a little bewildered at the reaction. One plausible answer is that pressure was already mounting on Tierney to discontinue *Dodd's Church History*, and he was on the defensive. He may have also suspected Bodenham of a design to discredit his position as a detached historian, and thereby jeopardize the work.

Tierney was intemperate in controversy. He had been admonished once by Lingard for his language, and his friend John Jones asked him to moderate his attack on the Jesuits, writing, "An old friend . . . observed that unless the religious, and the Jesuits in particular, are handled very tenderly, I should ruin my Hastings concern [?] and make enemies of those I ought to have as friends."[46]

The second case is even more revealing. Tierney was offended when Cardinal Wiseman, writing in his *Recollections of the Last Four Popes*, mentioned that John Lingard was not the one intended for Pope Leo XII's *in petto* nomination to the cardinalate – rather, it was meant for Lamennais. Tierney replied to this with a long article charging Wiseman with malice: "Every engine is set in motion, and every office in Rome is ransacked, in order to obtain evidence which may assist in depriving the historian of the supposed honour."[47] He called Wiseman "my assailant" and wrote further: "He is not driven to the painful necessity of either establishing his innocence, or retiring from the office which he holds."[48]

Wiseman, of course, did not find it necessary to do either, and the controversy shows little more than Tierney's peevishness and the distorted view he held of his own power in effecting events.[49] Wiseman had always held Lingard in high regard, and had even solicited his advice on the matter of Anglican Orders, so there is no reason to suspect Wiseman of an ulterior motive.[50] And Tierney mentioned no such motive. Bernard Ward, who made the most complete statement about this controversy, said that both sides had a good case. Ward put Tierney's first:

> In the controversy of pamphlets, however much we may regret the tone in which Tierney wrote, it much be admitted that he scored more than one point against his opponent. His accurate historical mind fastened on several loose expressions in the Cardinal's writings, and more than once he convicted him of grave inaccuracy.[51]

But Ward balanced this by pointing out that Wiseman's intimate knowledge of Roman affairs and politics forced the observer to take his interpretation of events seriously.[52]

Tierney, it appears, was a victim of his own zealousness. There always had to be a controversy, the controversy always had to become a personal feud, and there always had to be a melodramatic expression of innocence and demand for apology, followed by a tiresome marshalling of the facts. In this, as in his use of Dodd, he was reminiscent of Joseph Berington. Both had strong feelings and could not keep those feelings out of their work. Both saw matters in black-and-white, winner-and-loser categories. No compromise was possible or even desirable.

What Tierney never learned was that the presentation of history was possibly as important as its truth. It was a lesson Lingard had learned in walking his tightrope between Catholic and Protestant criticism. Some compromises were necessary, and Lingard realized when they had to be made. Therein lay his supreme common sense. What was important was the publication of the whole work; specific instances of de-emphasis could be corrected later. Tactfulness was a property which was needed by the historian, and those who recognized that need were the first to benefit. Lingard and Tierney agreed on virtually every issue concerning the English Catholic Church; yet Lingard, because of his political sophistication, was respected as a wise counselor, while Tierney was labeled a firebrand.

Tierney was not a bad historian, but he suffered from a naïveté about the nature of history, and about the nature of the Church. The Jesuits were not necessarily innocent victims, and Tierney's case against them was at least an arguable one. But it was all overdone, at the wrong time, and in the wrong way. Tierney wanted a duel, with history as the weapon, and no doubt felt cheated when he learned that the choice was not his.

But, even worse, he was fighting a battle which had been decided several years before. To look on the English Reformation primarily in terms of the penal laws and the denial of Catholic civil liberties, was to outdate himself pathetically. Wider issues, both theological and historical, had arisen which pointed more directly to the real substance of the English

Reformation, and Tierney was blind to these or unaware of their impact on historical studies. The Catholic community had come of age and was no longer going to concern itself solely with intramural quarrels, but would instead find larger theological contexts to engage, namely those of continuity and authority.

Chapter V

THE RESTORATION OF THE MIDDLE AGES AND MONASTICISM

After the passing of Catholic Emancipation in 1829 the nature and tone of Catholic historical writing changed dramatically. Preoccupation with the state and with political freedom, expressed discreetly in terms of conciliation and self-criticism, gave way to an aggressive assault on the state religion, the Church of England. Several factors combined to bring about this "sea-change". One was emancipation itself. Elation following the Act of 1829 was natural. Catholics viewed the Act as a victory and not merely a concession made by a tolerant government. Rather, emancipation had been forced on the government by political pressure. The Jesuit William Amherst wrote in 1886, "All the world knows that the Emancipation Act of 1829 was passed, as Wellington and Peel both avowed, to prevent a civil war in Ireland."[1]

This spirit of triumph was productive of a good amount of irresponsibility. The strictures which had previously urged a certain caution were gone, and with them the moderating force of "audience reaction". Catholics had survived the catacombs, and were in little mood for further self-criticism and fault-finding with their own. They were relieved, optimistic, and ready to settle old scores. The Church of England, which had been perhaps too sure of itself, having held the field uncontested for so long, found itself suddenly exposed as part of the protection of the state was removed.

Emancipation caused a crisis within the Church of England itself. Now that Catholics, non-believers, and even Jews were permitted to sit in Parliament and make decisions about the administration and beliefs of Anglicanism, conservative members of that Church revolted. That a governing body so composed could presume to suppress several bishoprics in Ireland, to appoint a German Lutheran to be the Church of

England's bishop in Jerusalem, and eventually to decide on the orthodoxy of an Anglican divine (Gorham), was simply unconscionable.

Thus in 1833 the Oxford Movement began, with the intent to question the direction the Church of England was taking. Not only did it seem to the Oxford "conspirators", as they were called, that the Established Church was becoming dangerously subordinated to the state, but this Church was also, in the process, disassociating itself from the Church of the earliest Christians. John Henry Newman found that he was compelled to become a Roman Catholic, not because he wanted to be in communion with the pope, but because of "the visible fact that the modern Roman Communion was the heir and image of the primitive Church".[2] The Reformation became the battleground. The Tractarians (or Puseyites) who led this movement found their strength in antiquity. Their translations of and commentaries on the Fathers of the Church quickly became problematical, as the Fathers seemed to them increasingly to come in conflict with the claims of the Reformers. The closer the Tractarians came to the early Church, the further they went from the Reformation. They saw the Reformation as a barrier which had prevented the spirit of this Early Church, with all its institutions and liturgy, from becoming an essential part of the reformed Church. Their conclusion was that the Reformation, far from reforming the ancient Church, had cast it aside and set up something new in its place. This realization led William George Ward, while still a member of the Church of England, to call the Reformation "that miserable event", and add, "I know no single movement in the Church, except Arianism in the fourth century, which seems to me so wholly destitute of all claims on our sympathy and regard, as the English Reformation."[3] The worry about appearing too much like the early heretics also bothered Newman, who wrote in his *Apologia*: "My stronghold was Antiquity; now, here, in the middle of the fifth century, I found, as it seemed to me, Christendom of the sixteenth and nineteenth centuries reflected. I saw my face in that mirror, and I was a Monophysite."[4]

Theologically, of course, Newman was no such thing. Monophysites (or Docetists) believed that Jesus Christ only *seemed* to be a human being, and they were condemned by the Council of Chalcedon. But Newman's difficulty lay in his awareness that the same Church which had condemned the Monophysites had also condemned the Church of England. He wrote, "Whatever line of early history I look into, I see as in a glass reflected our own Church in the heretical party, and the Roman Church in the Catholic. This is an appalling fact – which, do what I will, I cannot shake off."[5]

Interestingly, Newman and most of the Tractarian converts to

Catholicism had little to say about the Reformation in a systematic or comprehensive way, yet the Reformation was central to their theology and their upset with the government. Only those who remained within the Church of England produced this kind of history, by way of defending their own adherence to Anglicanism, properly understood. William Palmer was one such, and held that "the Romish party, at the instigation of foreign emissaries, separated itself, and fell from the Catholic Church of England".[6] This may have been the classic apology for the Church of England, but it no longer satisfied Newman. Neither did Dr. Hook's claim, i.e. the Church of England was not founded in the sixteenth century, but had simply reformed the Catholic Church and watched as the Romish wing separated itself from the main body.[7] Newman held on for awhile, interpreting the Thirty-Nine Articles rather acrobatically in a Catholic sense, but soon admitted that his Via Media – positing the Church of England as a middle position between the evangelicalism of Calvinists and the authoritarianism of Rome – ingenious as it was, existed only as a paper Church.

Catholics were, perhaps, even more eager than the Tractarians to drive a wedge between the Reformation and the Early Church, and entered the debate in 1838 with Wiseman's article on apostolic succession.[8] By 1845, significant defections to Catholicism, Newman's among them, raised the temperature as converted Anglicans now began to attack their former Church. The debate about the Reformation thus became more concerned about religion than about politics. And it was clear to the Catholics of the nineteenth century that people of the sixteenth century fell into one of two camps: Catholic or "Anglican". The shade of Anglicanism did not matter, be it puritanical, Low Church, or High Church, or Anglo-Catholic. It was all, as far as Catholics were concerned, outside the one true Church. It did not matter if they paraded in vestments and mitres with incense, or met in meeting halls.[9] Events, especially taking place during the reign of Elizabeth – the enforcement of the Oath of Supremacy and Thirty-Nine Articles, combined with Elizabeth's excommunication, had clearly marked the boundaries. Richard Simpson, a convert to Catholicism from the Church of England, concluded in his biography of Edmund Campion that "the torture-chamber was one of the institutions on which *Anglicanism* seemed to rely most securely".[10]

The assault on the Church of England was broad-based and continued unabated well into the middle of the twentieth century.[11] It concerned topics ranging from art, the monasteries, and medieval liturgy, to politics and the papacy. It sought, at one and the same time, to rehabilitate characters of the Reformation such as Cardinal Wolsey and Mary Tudor, and to attack others such as Cranmer and Elizabeth. It spanned the intellectualism of Lord Acton and the emotionalism of Robert Hugh Benson. Organization of this diverse material provides more than enough challenges, but inclusion of the material is crucial to an understanding of the Catholicism of this period.

If any age was disparaged by the Reformation, it was the medieval period. There the reformers found the sum total of a corrupt Church – adrift in theology and religious practice. Ever since Thomas Cromwell had re-interpreted the canonical and historical acts of the Middle Ages in order to justify his re-structuring of English society, the prevailing Protestant view was that the medieval Church was thoroughly debased and had forfeited all claim to being the Church founded by Jesus Christ.

Monasticism bore the brunt of this anti-medieval sentiment. While Jesuits exported their brand of oppression, monks built walls around theirs. To the Rationalists, monks erred not only by believing in a God, which was bad enough, but by closing themselves against the world so that they could neither see nor hear the truth. Monasteries stood as metaphorical monuments to ignorance. Voltaire's notion that monks could not possibly be happy was borne not so much from factual evidence, but from ideological arrogance. And most historians of the period shared this prejudice.

Cracks in this negative view of the Middle Ages began to appear in the late eighteenth century, with the dawn of the Romantic Revival, which was led in Britain by Sir Walter Scott. At first the interest in the medieval period was areligious – the sheer beauty of ruined monasteries led to a revival of Gothic architecture, and even to the building of "sham ruins". Horace Walpole had sparked interest in Gothic architecture by transforming a small villa in Twickenham, which he purchased in 1747, into a Gothic castle of sorts. But Catholics could not be kept out of this revival for long. Even Robin Hood and his merry men included a friar. The ubiquitous John Milner wrote an introduction and one of four essays in the first popular book on Gothic architecture, published in 1802, and then designed the first Gothic church of the revival, St. Peter's Chapel in Winchester. While the chapel was not an architectural success (Kenneth Clark wrote of it, "Unfortunately, St. Peter's Chapel still stands"), the book displayed some "real architectural learning".[12]

Hugh Aveling viewed Milner's chapel not as an expression of medieval romanticism, but as fulfilling a more devious purpose. It is, he wrote, a "typically restrained hint that the Catholics might not possess the old English churches, but that the English past was theirs by right".[13] If this is true, the hint would not remain typically restrained for long.

Kenelm Digby began the process of spelling out the nature of the loss due to the Reformation in his book, *The Broad Stone of Honour* (1822), which drew a relationship between chivalry and the Catholic Church, and showed how chivalry had declined as a result of the Reformation.[14] Digby was not a Catholic when he wrote the book, but became one three years later.

Augustus Welby Pugin

It was left to another convert, Augustus Welby Pugin, to draw out the full implications of this incipient Gothic enthusiasm. Born in 1812, Pugin had become a Catholic 1834, well in advance of his Oxford counterparts. By 1840 he was building seventeen Catholic churches. More than anyone else, he embodied both the best and the worst of the Gothic Revival. His *Contrasts*, published in 1840, not only established his reputation, but underlined the uncompromising quality of his work. Bernard Ward later said of his work, "To call it an attack on Protestantism would be ridiculously understating the terms of contempt which he poured forth on the Anglican Establishment."[15]

Pugin identified good art with good religion. "Everything grand, edifying, and noble in art", he wrote, "is the result of feelings produced by the Catholic religion on the human mind".[16] Pugin's logic led him, first of all, to assume that the Middle Ages were the zenith of religion, and then to deduce that pointed architecture, which was the expression of that religion, was the zenith of art. That the two – religion and architecture – had become perfected at the same time was no accident, but rather an indication of the intimate relation between religion and art. He wrote: "When Christianity had overspread the whole of western Europe, and infused her salutary and ennobling influence in the hearts of the converted nations, art arose purified and glorious; . . . Exalted by the grandeur of the Christian mysteries, ennobled by its sublime virtues, it reached a point of excellence far beyond anything it had previously attained."[17]

Attendant on this achievement of medieval building was a gradual decline due to the decay of religion.

> Christian art was the natural result of the progress of Catholic feeling and
> devotion; and its decay was consequent on that of the faith itself; and all
> revived classic buildings, whether erected in Catholic or Protestant countries,

are evidences of a lamentable departure from true Catholic principles and feelings . . . [18]

These sentiments from the *Contrasts* were defended in a later book
entitled *The Apology for the Contrasts*, in which he listed the results of
the Reformation as being the destruction of art, irreverence toward
religion, contempt of ecclesiastical persons and authority, and a
"complete loss of all the nobler perception of mankind". Furthermore,
"the degraded state of the arts in this country is purely owing to the
absence of Catholic feeling among its professors", etc.[19] Even contemporary efforts to restore Gothic buildings were carried out by Protestants in
ineffectual ways. When he saw what the architect James Wyatt
(1746–1813) had done to "restore" Hereford Cathedral, Pugin wrote,
"The villain Wyatt had been there, the west front was his. Need I say
more? . . . This monster of architectural depravity – this pest of cathedral
architecture – had been here: need I say more?"[20]

The book *Contrasts* took its name from a series of architectural drawings contrasting medieval art with "pagan" (Renaissance and
neo-classical) art. The drawings (see the contrasted altars on pages 92–3)
were executed in such a way as to leave the reader in no doubt about
which art form was superior. Kenneth Clark noted that, in this book,
Pugin made the Gothic appear "rich and solid", while the neo-classical
looked "Skimped and preposterous". Clark continued, "The central
doctrine of the *Contrasts* . . . is the direct connection between art and
morality. Good men build good buildings."[21]

Pugin placed the blame for the destruction of Christian architecture
(which to him was co-equal to Gothic architecture) squarely on the
Reformation, an event which represented paganism and the destructive
principle. Because Pugin's focus was entirely on the destruction of
medieval buildings, his attention was directed back to the time of Henry
VIII. He devoted one chapter to "The Pillage and Destruction of the
Churches under Henry VIII". As for Edward VI and Elizabeth, they were
less to blame since the former only completed the destruction by ruining
the interiors of the buildings which remained, while the latter merely
approved of what was a *fait accompli*.

Focusing as he did on Henry, Pugin introduced an entirely new theme
to the Reformation debate: namely, the conclusiveness of the Henrician
Reformation. The destruction of the monasteries and Gothic architecture
was, for Pugin, both symbolic and effective of this Reformation, and the
roles of both Edward VI and Elizabeth diminished as a result.

One particular theme which Pugin emphasized was the influence of
avarice in the dissolution of the monasteries. Henry destroyed them

primarily out of greed, and Edward – owing to the greed of his ministers – completed what his father had left undone. Matters of genuine reform were secondary at best, and were more probably rationalizations for what had been done. The only churches which were left standing were preserved not for aesthetic reasons, but for utilitarian ones: their preservation secured lands and incomes which would otherwise have been impossible to claim.[22] Proof of this can be found in the reformers' use of popish titles, such as dean, canon, and prebend – "because good incomes were attached to them".[23]

Pugin's reflections on the Reformation are as interesting for what they do not say as for what they say. It is important to note that he did not defend the state of the monasteries at the time of the dissolution. Pugin thought, along with almost everyone else at the time, that the monasteries had become degenerate. What was wrong with the Reformation was not its expulsion of bad monks, but its wanton destruction of good art. He was led to attack the Church of England because it had provided the theology which defended – in fact, encouraged – this sort of destruction. He and his fellow Romantics were not interested in religious life as such, only in its outward expressions: Gregorian chant, Gothic vestments and buildings. Consequently his defense of the monasteries did not concern their inner life, but rather the loss of their inessential ambience. Whether the monks came or went seemed rather unimportant to Pugin, as long as they kept up the singing and the buildings.

Aidan Gasquet

It is not until we come to Aidan Gasquet (1846–1929), himself a Benedictine monk, that we find a historian who defended the monasteries on their own merits. Previously, Catholics had defended them obliquely, because their loss symbolized the loss of the ancient Faith or because they were dissolved by avaricious men. No one had ever bothered to question whether the dissolution was justified on its own merits. Only with Gasquet do we begin to get an insight into the inner lives of the monks; only with him do we begin to get a true idea of what, besides property, was really lost. For Gasquet, like Pugin, the dissolution was *the* event which summarized the Reformation. For both it was a calamity. But Gasquet was the first important Catholic in the nineteenth century to think it was undeserved.

Catholics came to this realization late in the day. When Pugin died, Gasquet was six years old. Gasquet was prior of Downside Abbey in 1885 when he resigned due to ill health. After moving to London to live as an invalid with his mother, he began to read Tudor history. As his health improved, he began to research Tudor monasticism at the British Museum – influenced in this, no doubt, by Edmund Bishop, who claimed to have "pulled Gasquet out of his coffin".[24]

Bishop's claim was probably true, but Gasquet had friends besides Bishop. Cardinal Manning became his staunch, and unlikely, patron. Manning disliked the religious, but he protected Gasquet when his unsympathetic superior began to pressure Gasquet into returning to parish work. Gasquet's brief autobiography explains why Manning's decision was so remarkable, given his prejudices against monks and the Middle Ages, and reveals, perhaps, one reason why Manning has come to be regarded as so outstanding a churchman. Gasquet had told Manning that he wanted to examine the state of the religious houses – especially in regards to their moral character – and that Manning "held firmly" that the tradition of the moral decrepitude of the monasteries was "probably true". Manning agreed with Lingard, who had left the bishops thinking that "the less stirred up the better".[25] But after Manning had read Gasquet's first volume on the dissolution of the English monasteries, he admitted that he had been wrong about the medieval Church, an admission he did not often make.

What Gasquet had attempted to overturn was the prevailing judgment that the monks of the sixteenth century had been corrupt and the monasteries in a decayed state. This judgment had been brilliantly espoused by James Anthony Froude in his *History of England*, published between 1856–70. While Froude's volumes gave expression to, rather than being formative of, the popular prejudice against Catholicism, it was nevertheless a monumental statement, and to leave it unanswered was to consent to its conclusions.[26]

Froude's thesis was that Henry VIII, far more than Edward VI or Elizabeth, was crucial to the Reformation process in England. Furthermore, Henry was a more sympathetic character than had been believed: he was less cruel, less selfish, less sensual. The dissolution of the monasteries was necessary because the monasteries had become both centers of immorality and garrisons of Rome. Their spoils went to education and national defense. The visitors were "as upright and plain-dealing as they were assuredly able and efficient".[27]

In defending the monks from this attack, Gasquet conceived his own attack on the Church of England. If Froude was wrong, then it was quite possible that the Church of England was wrong as well. Gasquet did not equate the English Reformation with the dissolution of the monasteries, but he did recognize that there was more to the dissolution than just monasteries. The dissolution was a considerable part of Henry's reform program; the reform could not have gone on without the dissolution; and the reform was given a certain direction and a certain finality because of the dissolution. If this essential part of the reform could be discredited, the entire program might fall as well.[28]

For Gasquet, the dissolution was the very body, the matter, of the Reformation, and he sought only to show that this dissolution was effected by evil men for evil purposes using evil means, and allow readers to draw their own conclusions about the spiritual state of things. His thesis was straightforward: the monastic houses were dissolved on the grounds that they were corrupt, and these grounds amounted to no more than an enormous and elaborate lie – concocted deliberately to hide the real reasons of greed and power. It is a faulty thesis for its very straight-forwardness, because the dissolution was a complicated amalgam of several forces, a great part of which may very well have been those forces of greed and power. In exposing these for what they were, Gasquet provided a great service to students of Reformation history; but in providing a comprehensive discussion of the reasons for the dissolution and the Reformation, his conclusions are painfully inadequate.

Gasquet saw two somewhat distant and disconnected events as preparing the way for the dissolution: the Black Death and the feud between the Houses of Lancaster and York. The Black Death was not merely a drastic loss of population, which was catastrophic enough; it meant the loss of an entire economic and political system.[29] Permanent retainers disappeared from farms, to be replaced by fewer people who leased the land. A great deal of farmland was turned into pasture. As a result, fewer people owed their allegiance to landowners, and those who still did owed little more than the rent. And so, the principal de-centralizing forces within England – the gentry and the monastic houses – began to lose their influence on the people. Their place was taken by an emerging group of nobility, not tied to the land, who depended more and more on the king and royal policy for their advancement. Therefore, the power of the king increased, while the prestige of his traditional rivals decreased.

The Church in England never recovered from the Black Death. Numbers of clerics shrank so rapidly and institutions were so slow to adapt to the changed climate, that some cataclysm was inevitable. Gasquet mentioned some of this – absenteeism, plurality of benefices, small religious communities with large holdings, an uneducated clergy – but trod rather lightly on them. That the monastic houses could not, in the two hundred years following the Black Death, find a solution to reduced numbers and the ongoing accumulation of land and wealth, may point to the necessity of outside interference in these affairs. Gasquet did not consider the point. Nowhere did he try to assess the wealth of the monasteries which may have given rise to a simmering resentment; he said only that the wealth of the monasteries was better distributed than the same wealth in the hands of the state.

He was perhaps correct in that judgment, but for someone who was attempting to delineate the reasons for the dissolution, it was quite off the mark to argue that this wealth was subsequently spent very poorly, since it was not known then how or by whom the wealth would subsequently be spent. And it is impossible for the historian to disregard this wealth altogether.

The effects of the Black Death were abetted by the feud, about one hundred years after the plague first hit England, between the Houses of Lancaster and York. This feud did not decrease the population in any spectacular way, but it took its toll by so wearying the people and exhausting the nobility that any future internal struggle was unthinkable. To a generation which had a personal knowledge of this feud, or knew about it from parents, retreat and compromise at any cost seemed preferable to a repetition of hostilities. The Wars of the Roses, according to Gasquet, produced a generation which betrayed "a willingness to hazard everything rather than recur to such a period of distress and bloodshed".[30] The unstated consequence was that the Reformation succeeded in England, *not* because the people were strong and dynamic, but because they were exhausted, submissive, and pliant. The Reformation could not possibly have come from such a people; it had to originate from some other source. That other source was the English government.

There had been precedents for "thinning-out" the monasteries. Wolsey had carried out a less ambitious dissolution in his early years as chancellor. Monasteries had been dissolved in the past because they were "alien" monasteries – i.e. their revenues went to motherhouses outside the country – or because they had very low numbers. As Henry found himself more in need of money, this activity increased. The line between reforming a religious house and gathering its money could often be blurry. Was Wolsey acting out of motives of reform, of appeasing his master, or both? Gasquet thought that Wolsey and Henry were planning extensive suppressions as early as 1521, when two houses were suppressed with the approval of Bishop John Fisher of Rochester. The note from the king to the Bishop of Salisbury, in whose diocese the suppressions were to take place, was an omen. It claimed that the suppressions would put an end to the "enormities, misgovernances, and slanderous living" of the convents involved. However extensive this early dissolution would have become in the ordinary course of events – and it could have been considerable when we realize what little regard the reform-minded Bishop Fisher and Cardinal Pole had for the monks – it is almost certain that Wolsey did not envision the complete eradication of the religious houses of England. His fault, rather, was in creating a mechanism by which that destruction could come about.

What Wolsey did was to combine in himself the sort of temporal and spiritual power which could easily lead to enormous irresponsibility. For the first time, Gasquet commented, supreme secular power and spiritual power resided in one man. It was a dangerous precedent, and mattered little whether these powers were held by a churchman or the king. The effect of the combined temporal and spiritual authority began to be felt by the monasteries in the matter of the divorce. For Gasquet, the divorce was not one incident along the inevitable road to Reformation; it was the one crucial act which led to everything else. Here Gasquet called on James Gairdner for support: "[What] we call *the* Reformation in England . . . was the result of Henry VIII's quarrel with the Court of Rome on the subject of his divorce, and the *same* results could not possibly have come about in any other way."[31]

The monasteries stood in the way of the divorce, if not by their active campaigning against it, then by their unease. Monasteries were independent of Henry's usually compliant bishops; they housed the best and most popular preachers; they were less easy to intimidate with threats.[32] They presented Henry with the only serious opposition *en bloc* to his power, to his desire for a divorce, and to his eventual demand for supreme headship of the Church. Knowing what we know about the psychology of Tudor princes, their feelings of inferiority and of sensitivity to criticism of their usurped rule, the monasteries had to go – regardless of their wealth. Sir Thomas More and Bishop John Fisher had gone, irrespective of their financial prospects, and the monasteries would go as well. The fact that they owned so much property and wealth only hastened the day.

Whether Gasquet was correct in his high estimate of the divorce is debateable. J. J. Scarisbrick has argued that Henry was heading in the direction of spiritual supremacy quite apart from the divorce. He wrote:

> The Royal Supremacy . . . grew from the divorce campaign, but was distinct from it. Had there been no divorce, or had [Pope] Clement yielded, there would probably still have been a clash between the clerical estate and a prince who, in the name of reform, was beginning to claim new spiritual jurisdiction.[33]

But Gasquet was accurate at least in recognizing that the divorce question caused the immediate dissolution of at least one religious house – that of the Observant Franciscans in Greenwich. In addition, he correctly noticed that the aggrandizement of temporal and spiritual power, in which the divorce played a significant part, made the destruction of the monasteries easier.[34]

How guilty were the monks of corruption? Their vice was given as an important reason for the dissolution, and in Gasquet's day was still pictured by historians and seen by the popular mind in that light. Gasquet suspected that monastic vice was no more than an excuse used by evil men to further their own selfish ends. But how to prove that point was difficult. There was very little direct evidence that religious houses were observant, and it was a difficult position to prove in the best of circumstances. Vice is always much more visible and easier to chronicle than virtue. Gasquet, therefore, relied heavily on indirect evidence: the character of Cromwell's monastic visitors, their motives, and their methods. Another route sent Gasquet looking for logical flaws in the charges of vice: Why had some clearly observant houses fallen? Why was the dissolution not popular? Why were the greater houses left till later?

A wealth of information was available to Gasquet which had not been available before. As David Knowles pointed out, Gasquet was "the first to explore methodically the whole of the relevant Cromwell papers, but also the accounts and particulars and pensions of the Court of Augmentations, and the pension list of Cardinal Pole".[35]

Gasquet was in no doubt that the character of the visitors invalidated their reports. He wrote, "It is absolutely upon the testimony of these men, unsupported by other evidence, that the monks have been condemned". Richard Layton, the most important of the visitors, was the worst:

> His letters, which are the most numerous and the most full of detail, abound in the most filthy accusations, general and particular. They manifest the prurient imaginations of one, who was familiar with vice in its worst forms. His letters, on the face of them, are the outpourings of a thoroughly brutal and depraved nature; even still, they actually soil the hand that touches them. He tells his stories in a way to allow no doubt that evil was for him a zest, and that he believes his master will appreciate and approve.[36]

Layton had a notable lack of principle, the most celebrated instance of which was his report about Abbot Whiting of Glastonbury. After his first visit to Glastonbury, Layton reported that all was in good order and that Whiting was a virtuous man. Cromwell replied sharply that Layton's job was not to find virtue in the monasteries, but vice. Layton apologized, writing of the Abbot of Glastonbury, "[He] appeareth not, neither then nor now, to have known God, nor his prince, nor any part of a good Christian man's religion, [his monks] were all false, feigned, flattering hypocritical knaves."[37]

The visitors, however, were only imitating their master, whom they unscrupulously strove to serve and whose style they copied. The record of Cromwell's degenerate life began, for Gasquet's purposes at least, with his theft of Wolsey's royal license for legatine powers – at one stroke depriving Wolsey of any legal defense against the *praemunire* charges, and ensuring Cromwell's own survival.[38] His career, moreover, was one of unabashed debauchery. Quoting Maitland, Gasquet underlined his opinion:

> He was the great patron of ribaldry, and the protector of the ribalds, of the low jester, the filthy ballad-monger, the ale-house singers, and "hypocritical mockers in feasts", in short, of all the blasphemous mocking and scoffing which disgraced the protestant party at the time of the reformation.[39]

In addition to this, Cromwell was a free spender who accepted bribes as easily and often as he offered them, making liberal use of monastic lands or the lands confiscated from recalcitrant gentry to reward himself and his lackeys. The evidence found by Gasquet was as stunning as it was unknown, and it was his tendency to pass this evidence on without sifting the contradictions. Thus, in his haste to convict Cromwell of un-Reformation-like sentiments, he proposed that Cromwell was both an infidel *and* a closet Catholic, positions which Gasquet placed side-by-side without explanation. As evidence that Cromwell was an infidel, Gasquet drew once again on Maitland:

> That Cromwell had before that time [1 November 1529] avowed infidel principles is beyond a doubt. Cardinal Pole asserts that he openly told him that he considered vice and virtue were but names, fit indeed to amuse the leisure of the learned in their colleges, but pernicious to the man who seeks to rise in the courts of princes.[40]

Yet, in spite of this, there were Cromwell's Catholic leanings to be considered. He had, for example, been "caught" by Cavendish saying Our Lady Matins to the point of tears.[41] In his will of July 1529, he left twenty shillings to five orders of friars within London to pray for his soul for three years.[42] Even more pertinent was Cromwell's speech from the scaffold in 1540:

> And now I pray that be here to bear me record, I die in the catholic faith, not doubting in any article of my faith; no, nor doubting in any sacrament of the church. . . . But I confess, that like as God, by his holy spirit, doth instruct us in truth – so the devil is ready to seduce us – and I have been seduced.[43]

Many years later, Hilaire Belloc would look at this same evidence, but make an attempt to reconcile the seeming contradiction. He thought that

Cromwell was indifferent to religion or at least "let his sense of religion sink out of his consciousness", until he was faced with certain death, at which time his act of contrition was genuine.[44] Scarisbrick provided a third alternative by claiming that Cromwell was merely defending himself against the lies of his enemies, among them Bishop Gardiner and the Duke of Norfolk, who were denouncing him as an extreme Calvinist. He was possibly groveling as well, in a desperate attempt at pardon; but his denial of association with any extreme sect was certainly justified, however short it may have fallen of an assertion of a resurrected Catholicism.[45]

What were the motives behind the visitation? For Gasquet, the only word to describe them was "robbery". The visitors were Machiavellian opportunists who cooperated with Cromwell in reporting evil in the hopes of furthering their own political and financial prospects. In other words, they were robbers, and robbers make good liars. In this regard Gasquet quoted Edmund Burke, writing on the French Revolution: "I rather suspect that vices are feigned or exaggerated when profit is looked for in the punishment. An enemy is a bad witness, a robber is worse."[46] Gasquet applied this to the dissolution in a similar statement: "The fact that the avowed object of the visitors was plunder, and that the charges made against the religious were only means to attain that end, will be to most minds the most conclusive evidence of the untrustworthiness of their testimony."[47]

"The truth is," Gasquet concluded, "that money was the object, which Henry and his ministers had in view."[48] Henry was desperately short of money due to his indulgence in foreign wars as well as his personal habits of gambling and lavishness. Even cooks who pleased his palate could be given estates.[49] His visitors were called by Gasquet, "our English Ahab commissioned to slander the Naboth whose fair vineyard he coveted".[50] What was not passed on to the king was set aside for the visitors themselves, or for those whom Cromwell wished to reward. One register, in Cromwell's hand, read:

> Item to remember Warran for one monastery,
> Mr. Gostwyke for a monastery,
> John Freeman for Spalding,
> Mr. Kingmill for Wherwell,
> *myself* for Launde.[51]

Further evidence that the dissolution was carried out principally for financial gain was drawn from a number of sources, among them the haste with which the monasteries were visited and their wealth carried away – leaving the monks no time to put into effect any recommended reforms, or to correct abuses. The sudden destruction of two rigidly observant

THE RESTORATION OF THE MIDDLE AGES AND MONASTICISM

houses was also telling, as was the division of lesser houses from greater houses, based on income rather than vice or virtue. Finally, the pensioning of monks from houses reported to be irreformably immoral was taken by Gasquet as a sign that somebody was lying, and it wasn't the monks. While these latter arguments did not point directly to a financial concern, they helped to eliminate the motive of reform from the process of dissolution. Gasquet then implied that the only conceivable alternative was financial.

The manner in which the visitations were conducted gave support to the financial thesis – again, indirectly, by exposing the fraudulent way in which evidence was gathered. Intimidation was a common ploy used against the religious; and evidence counted only when it weighed against the monasteries. Silence or contrary reports (favourable to a particular house) were discounted as a conspiracy to conceal. No attempt was made to measure the value of negative reports or the veracity of certain witnesses.[52]

Cromwell's attempt to model his visitation on that of former episcopal visitations was for appearances only – more an attempt to give credibility to his findings than to be fair. Episcopal visits, according to Gasquet, were qualitatively different from the Cromwellian version. The former tended to temporal and spiritual issues, included an "injunction" or summary which estimated the worth of complaints, and made suggestions about the better ordering of the house and the correction of individual offenders. It was a solemn occasion. Cromwell's visitors, on the other hand, gave it the atmosphere of a police raid. The only temporal matter attended to was the financial value of the house. Future spoliation was intended, not reform. The difference was best exemplified in the diocese of Norwich, where the bishop made regular visits to the monasteries in his diocese between 1514–32, and was scrupulous in noting and correcting faults. Often he registered "All is well" in places where, just a few years later, the visitors found unspeakable crime.[53] The royal visitations, in other words, were charades.

Evaluating Gasquet's History

Contemporary reviews of Gasquet's work were glowing. James Gairdner was overwhelmed by Gasquet's achievement and said that Gasquet had dispelled the charges against the monks forever, and that non-Catholics would "be forced to hold the same view [as Gasquet] if they are honest men".[54] Cardinal Manning made a similar misjudgment when he wrote in his review of the first volume that Gasquet had "made history tell its own tale". He continued, "[The last] excellence of the book is the disappearance of the author. The History speaks for itself in clear, simple, and good English."[55]

But flaws appeared which were typical of Catholic historical writing at the time. One was defensiveness. Maisie Ward, in her history of the period, cited a twentieth-century Jesuit, who explained to her that Jesuit teaching in the nineteenth century was too concerned with combating the reformers. Those Catholic doctrines which had been denied by them were the ones which were particularly stressed. Ward commented, "Theology came to be looked on rather as a weapon against the heretic than as food for the Catholic mind and soul".[56]

People who were not Jesuits, like Gasquet, fell into this pattern as well. Even though he tried to break away from a defensiveness, he succeeded only partially, and too often became the apologist, descending to advocacy, one-sidedness, and polemic. He even admitted to advocacy, though he insisted there was a reason for it:

> If I have insisted more on the facts which tell in favour of the monasteries than on those which tell against them, it is because the latter are well known and have been repeated, improved on and emphasized for three centuries and a half, whilst that there is anything to say on the other hand for the monks, has been little recognized even by those who would be naturally predisposed in their favour.[57]

One lawyer's device used by Gasquet was to quote non-Catholic historians to support his case, whenever possible. Thus he quoted Maitland, Gairdner, Rogers, and even Froude – precisely because they were non-Catholic. This gave his word more authority, especially when, taken by itself, his word might have been taken as prejudice. The reader, however, cannot avoid feeling that Gasquet was building a legal brief rather than a historical argument. If he could cite Thorold Rogers on the contribution of the monks, there would be little need to say more:

> The monks were men of letters in the Middle Ages, the historians, the jurists, the philosophers, the physicians, the students of nature, the founders of schools, authors of chronicles, teachers of agriculture, fairly indulgent landlords, and advocates of genuine dealing towards the peasantry.[58]

This advocacy sparked a serious disagreement between himself and Lord Acton, who had invited Gasquet to write a chapter of the *Cambridge Modern History*. Acton had a high regard for Gasquet's historical work and was disappointed at what Gasquet submitted – what would eventually become *The Eve of the Reformation*. In proposing the project, Acton had written that no one would be able to tell "without examining the list of authors, where the Bishop of Oxford [William Stubbs] laid down his pen, and whether Fairbairn or Gasquet, Lieberman or Harrison took it up".[59] David Knowles thought that Acton, in so writing, had rated Gasquet as the equal of Stubbs and Lieberman, but the sense of Acton's letter is more a hope of what the history would achieve. To mention Gasquet in this company, Acton showed not so much what he thought of Gasquet, as what he wanted Gasquet (and the others) to accomplish. Acton's letter to Gasquet was stern; he noted that Gasquet sometimes adapted an attitude of contention and argument, and pleaded with him "to make your points clear without thinking of contradiction or of people who have written otherwise".[60]

Gasquet replied that a Protestant or Catholic view of history was as repugnant to him as it was to Acton, but that the truth could nevertheless favour one side or the other. But David Knowles saw Gasquet's problem as tending towards a one-sidedness. Gasquet, wrote Knowles, "started with a conviction or a fact, and went to other documents to find confirmation".[61] This one-sidedness was manifest in Gasquet's work on the Reformation in any number of ways. In one instance, Gasquet cited the lack of popular anti-papal literature before the Reformation as evidence that the pope was well-respected; then, illogically, he made the collolary that the absence of Reform literature implied a lack of sympathy for Reformation ideas. In reaching this conclusion, he failed to discuss the existence of pre-Reformation popular literature in general, which might have given the discussion a certain context against which the amount of anti-papal or pre-Reformation literature could have been measured. In a later book, *Edward VI and the Book of Common Prayer*, Gasquet took similar information – this time a lack of pro-Catholic literature – and came to the opposite conclusion, namely that Edward's government was censoring popular literature and interfering with the true feelings of the people.[62]

Gasquet could use similar evidence in contradictory ways. When the monks, under intimidation by zealous visitors, confessed to monastic vice, Gasquet dismissed their testimony as invalid. Yet, when the monks, under similar threats following the Pilgrimage of Grace, testified to their non-involvement, Gasquet found this evidence sufficient proof of their innocence. At times, Gasquet ignored evidence which told against anything he may have believed or written. One characteristic example involved the historian James Gairdner, a friend of Gasquet, who produced documents which disproved Gasquet's contention that the last abbot of Colchester (Abbot Marshall) was a martyr. Gasquet refused to budge on the matter. "Instead", wrote David Knowles, "he persisted to the end in a *suppressio veri* which in the circumstances (Abbot Marshall was being considered for canonization) carried with it more than a trace of *suggestio falsi.*"[63]

Gairdner was involved in another disagreement when he corrected Gasquet's statement that John Morton, the Archbishop of Canterbury, had made "vague charges" against Abbot Wallingford. Gairdner claimed that the charges were "very specific and particularly abominable", whereby Wallingford "had promoted a married woman to be head of a nunnery and allowed his monks to carry on intrigues with her, and turn the nunnery into a brothel".[64]

More extensive was Gasquet's insistence on defending all of the monasteries as a unit, just as they had been attacked as a unit. Those who had argued against the monasteries proceeded from particular instances of corruption (or allegation) to a general condemnation, and they were answered by Gasquet in kind. This served him well in debate, but as history it fell sadly short of the ideal. Some monasteries were in a pitiable state at the time of the Reformation, and Gasquet was painfully incapable of admitting it.

It must be said, however, that Gasquet could arrive at conclusions which were unusually perceptive, although unwarranted by the evidence that he found or used. Thus, in the matter of the visitors' character, Gasquet relied on *ad hominem* arguments, when he could have criticized the visitors' reports themselves. These reports, taken uncritically, were regarded as a staggering indictment of the monks. John Lingard was shocked when he read them, and concluded that the monks had become, by the time of the Reformation, "men of little reputation . . . a degenerate, time-serving lot".[65] David Knowles was similarly dismayed when he read them, and admitted that he was quite prepared to believe "that the decay which episcopal visitors had long been deploring and exposing had spread at last to almost every member of the monastic body".[66]

What changed David Knowles's mind, in fact, was a careful examination of these very reports, which consisted of the *Comperta* (the accumulated reports of Cromwell's agents) and the reports of the Court of Augmentations, which served as the tax-collecting body in Henry's England. When Knowles compared the different reports, he found that they disagreed significantly, despite the fact that the Augmentations people were unlikely to criticize the reports of the visitors, as they were both working for the same government. The incidence of homosexuality in the monasteries, for example, was found by Knowles to be surprisingly low, while that of fornication and adultery were lower than Cromwell's figures suggested (though higher than Gasquet was willing to admit). The figures given for nuns' pregnancies are also misleading, but only when one compares the two reports. The visitors include the names of nuns who have been pregnant, but the Augmentations reports mention their ages and give other details which almost nullify the visitors' reports. Women were often sent to a nunnery *because* they were pregnant, and the visitors made no distinction between past and present culpability. Taken as a whole, Knowles found that the Augmentations reports were "surprisingly and almost unanimously favourable to the monks".[67]

What is to the point here is that Gasquet changed his mind without very much textual criticism of the *Comperta*. He simply did not trust the *Comperta* because they were compiled by vicious men, and not because they were intrinsically misleading. He also greatly underestimated the value of the reports of Augmentations which he, like Gairdner, thought were composed by "country gentlemen" who would have been friendly to the monks. It was here that Gasquet had a stronger hand than he played, since Augmentations appointments were official and their reports an essential counterweight to the *Comperta*. But Gasquet had made up his mind without employing essential historical balances, and revealed in the process his prejudice.

Another device used by Gasquet in favour of the monks was exaggeration. His book *The Eve of the Reformation* suggests that the Renaissance developed largely from monastic scholarship. The revival of Greek studies had begun in Canterbury with the monks Selling and Hadley, who taught Linacre (also a cleric), who in turn taught More and Erasmus. The monastic houses of Reading, Ramsay, Canterbury, and Glastonbury were well known for their scholarship. Gasquet mentioned all of this, not only to emphasize the difference between the Renaissance, which was conservative, and the New Learning, which was innovative, but also to assert the destructiveness of the Reformation, which effectively brought the Renaissance and serious scholarship to an end. All monastic studies ended overnight, the number of Oxford graduates (many of them monks) fell dramatically, Greek studies disappeared, libraries were destroyed or dispersed, foreign education (hitherto held in high regard) fell into disrepute.[68]

Knowles felt that this emphasis on the monks' role in learning was overdone. William Selling, the Benedictine prior of Christ Church in Canterbury, was a good example. He may have taught Linacre as a boy, but Linacre "learnt most of what he knew at Oxford and Florence". Selling, according to Knowles, "had the fortune to be the patron of Linacre, and to introduce Greek to Canterbury, but he holds no important place in the development of the Renaissance".[69]

Another exaggeration was Gasquet's estimate of the social damage due to the Reformation. According to him, the Reformation stopped the upward movement of the lower classes by depriving them of education and advancement in the Church; it also increased the number of the poor and made them more destitute than ever. What was worse, this catastrophe was planned: "However satisfactory it might be to believe that this robbery of the poor and sick by the Crown was accidental and unpremeditated, the historian is bound by the evidence to hold that the pillage was fully premeditated and deliberately and consciously carried out."[70]

The removal of the nation's largest (and arguably the only) charitable organization, combined as it was with the turning out of 8,000 religious into the world, along with the release of 80,000 others who were dependent on the monasteries, resulted in an economic crisis of grave proportions. Knowles concluded that the plight of the religious was exaggerated by Gasquet, and that the number 80,000 was "stupendous".[71]

Gasquet also suffered from several lapses of logic in his account of the dissolution which were convenient for strengthening his case. He attempted, for example, to make more of government policies and documents than was actually there. In one case, he saw the division of the monasteries into lesser and greater houses as an admission on the part of the government that the greater houses, which were not to be suppressed, were in fact observant. The more likely explanation, not even proposed by Gasquet as a possibility, was that Cromwell needed a strategy to carry out the dissolution in an orderly way. If the government stated something as propaganda, such as Cromwell's Preamble to the Act of Dissolution, Gasquet took it at face value and used it as pertinent evidence.

Another example of this illogic is Gasquet's accusation that the government, in pensioning off monks who were allegedly immoral, was guilty of duplicity – i.e. the government never thought they were immoral in the first place. This is taking the evidence too far. A simpler explanation is that the government was in a hurry and did not have the time to separate sheep from goats, although it claimed it was doing so on paper.[72]

Gasquet could reach conclusions which simply did not follow from his argument. His tendency was to think that, having destroyed a lesser argument, he had destroyed the greater one as well. By clearing the reputation of one monastic house, by his way of thinking, he had cleared them all. Likewise for the visitors: if one could be shown to be dishonest, all would be suspect, and their reports untrue. The Black Book of legend, which supposedly convinced Parliament to pass the Act of Dissolution, could be shown never to have existed, then the things it alleged could be implied never to have existed. That is why Gasquet never examined the *Comperta* in any detail. He did not have to. He simply attacked the authors and was done with it.

Later critics focused on Gasquet's inaccuracy in terms of factual detail, a problem which grew markedly after 1900, when Gasquet assumed several administrative duties for the Benedictine Order and the Church in general, and when the restraining hand of Edmund Bishop was withdrawn.[73] G. G. Coulton, an inveterate Catholic-baiter, attributed Gasquet's penchant for inaccuracy, which Knowles said "almost amounted to genius", to a deliberate policy of untruth, which was not surprising in light of the fact that Gasquet was a Roman Catholic priest.[74]

Modern criticism of Gasquet is also directed at Knowles, and consists of the complaint that neither author showed any sympathy for the reformers themselves. Geoffrey Elton writes, "Of late, the inwardness of the Dissolution has always been studied from the point of view of the monks; surprising things might emerge if that of the reformers were substituted and the matter considered in the light of social renewal."[75]

This focus on the monks, continues Elton, leads to "rash moralising about greed and acquisitiveness".[76] Elton's point of reference is very similar to Froude's – the social renewal and political revolution made possible by the dissolution – and therefore his criticism of Gasquet has less to do with particular judgments made by Gasquet than with his entire approach. All of Gasquet's judgments are unbalanced from the start because he makes too much of religion in the process of dissolution. As a result, Cromwell comes across in Gasquet's pages as a villain, since he was the one who effected the dissolution. The danger, according to Elton, is in seeing the dissolution as the most important thing Cromwell did. If Elton is correct in defending Cromwell as a political genius whose revolutionary program encompassed much more than the dissolution, then Cromwell has a case.[77] At least he has a better case than Gasquet granted him.

Going along with this, Gasquet failed to examine the ideological foundation of the dissolution, an affair no doubt carried out by ambitious men for materialistic reasons, but certainly thought out and approved theologically by men of quite a different stamp.[78] It would have been fair to disagree with these "reformers", and even to question the extent to which they influenced events, but Gasquet took no notice of them. His concern was with what happened, and what happened (immediately at least) was the result of grasping and hypocritical acts. It was as though he had condemned the destruction caused by the French Revolution without ever considering the ideological consent given to the destruction. The dissolution of the monasteries was seen by Gasquet as evil because it was carried out by evil men – what he failed to mention was that it was approved of by some very good men who had nothing material to gain.

All things considered, however, there is still a lot to be said in Gasquet's favour. For one thing, his powers of research were considerable, and he had a knack for introducing crucial documents into his argument. And he had one advantage over other historians: an insight into monastic life by one who had lived it. Furthermore, many of his conclusions were later held (and are still held) by scholars who were better historians than he. David Knowles listed five of the most important of these conclusions: that the monks had been blamed too severely in the past;[79] that the dissolution was carried out far too hastily to be aimed at religious reform;[80] that money was the main object of the dissolution;[81] that the notorious Black Book of legend never existed;[82] and that the Pilgrimage of Grace, the northern revolt of 1536–37, was primarily religious.[83] If, in fact, "no one believes Cromwell's case against the monasteries any more", as one historian related to me, then it is due to the pioneering work of Aidan Gasquet.

Furthermore, Gasquet had a gift for making unconventional historical connections and for seeing beyond the immediate period or merely "historical" aspects of the topic he was addressing. Thus he could look to the Black Death and the Wars of the Roses and see remote causes of the dissolution. He could also, like Pugin before him, see in the pulling down of rood screens and choir stalls a disturbing omen: the Reformation was based on a destructive principle. The destruction of art, architecture, scholarship, and religious life was replaced by a void. On the dissolution of St. Peter's in Gloucester, he could be eloquent:

> Having existed for more than eight centuries under different forms, in poverty and in wealth, in meanness and in magnificence, in misfortune and in success, it finally succumbed to the royal will; the day came, and that a drear winter day, when its last Mass was sung, its last censer waved, its last congregation bent in rapt and lowly adoration before the altar there, and doubtless as the last tones of that day's evensong died away in the vaulted roof, there were not wanting those who lingered in the solemn stillness of the old massive pile, and who, as the lights disappeared one by one, felt that for them there was now a void which could never be filled, because their old abbey, with its beautiful services, its frequent means of grace, its hospitality to strangers and its loving care for God's poor, had passed away like an early morning dream, and was gone forever.[84]

This was Gasquet's well-known "tear-stained" touch, yet David Knowles thought there was something to it. He wrote a half-century later, "Visible beauty of form and line and hue is as nothing in comparison with the eternal beauty of things unseen, but those who wantonly destroy the one will not readily be supposed to value the other."[85]

Here we also have a sample of Gasquet's prose style, which could be quite evocative. One tribute to its power is that it still annoys. Both A. G. Dickens and Geoffrey Elton had to go out of their way to defend the good name of Cromwell.[86] But Gasquet did more than annoy. He took the Puginesque thesis – that the heart of the Reformation was found in the destruction of the monasteries – and made it historically respectable. He ensured that scholars would concern themselves less with the peripheral issues and results of the Reformation and more with its central issues. In defending the good name of the monasteries, Gasquet forced historians not only to change their opinion about the state of the monasteries, but forced theologians to take a sterner look at the Church of England, and this may well have been his deeper purpose.

As we have seen, Gasquet did not consider the theology of the reformers who encouraged or acquiesced in the dissolution. To an extent, he did not have to. If one of the major reasons given in the sixteenth century for the need of Reformation was the complete degeneracy of the monastic institution, and if that reason was shown to be largely a false one, then where did that leave the theologians? If the monks were not corrupt, or not nearly as corrupt as had been thought, then what was the Reformation reforming, anyway?

Thus, while Gasquet did not attack the Church of England directly, he stripped away one great argument behind which it had traditionally taken refuge. In so doing, he served to expose the real business of the Reformation, which had more to do with authority and liturgy. It is not surprising that the next Catholic assault on the Church of England would come in these areas, and it is not surprising that Aidan Gasquet should have a hand in it.

Elton said that Gasquet's work was "best ignored", and Rosemary O'Day took Elton at his word and did just that, not mentioning or alluding to Gasquet once in her work on the Reformation debate.[87] But Gasquet had struck a nerve, notwithstanding, and despite their concerted efforts, future historians of the Reformation cannot ignore him. Without a doubt he transformed popular opinion and forced the scholarly world to re-examine its prejudices. If he had his faults, he guaranteed that future historians would have fewer.

Chapter VI

ARCHBISHOP CRANMER AND THE ANGLICAN LITURGY

Towards the end of the nineteenth century the amount of Catholic historical writing increased dramatically as Catholics felt the need to reflect on their past and defend their present. Two topics engaged Catholic historians at this time: the claims of the papacy, and the truth or falsehood of the Church of England. The two concerns had authority as their centerpiece. The papacy had seen its political authority eroded because of Italian revolutionaries, and the Church of England had experienced internal tensions between High Church and Low Church ideologies. The Reformation, and especially the figure of Archbishop Cranmer, shed light on both issues, and won the attention of a small army of Catholic writers. Because of their number and varied worth, we will examine the topics (rather than the historians) in order.

When the Reformation debate began to focus on Henry VIII in the mid-nineteenth century, largely due to the writings of Lingard, Froude and Gasquet, the stakes were increased. While Froude made the case for Henry's good name, A. F. Pollard (a non-Catholic) claimed that the Henrician Reformation was the essence of the Reformation, and was essentially political and not doctrinal – on the grounds that it was about power. He wrote that the Reformation was "not in essence doctrinal", but "an episode in the eternal dispute between Church and State".[1] The problems with this were twofold: first, Pollard assumed that the "eternal dispute" about power was exclusively political and, secondly, that doctrinal concerns did not complicate the English Reformation in an essential way.

The first problem is as old as Constantine. Over the centuries, several popes and theologians detailed the distinction between political and spiritual power. For the most part, they can be kept distinct, but even Pope

Leo I, in the fifth century, recognized that jurisdictions crossed at times: popes were members of the state and under the authority of the king or emperor; emperors were members of the Church and thus under the pope. One question which European rulers and popes wrestled with over the centuries was "Who has primacy: the secular ruler or the pope?" In the East it was settled by Constantine in favor of the secular ruler, but in the West popes were successful in claiming the primary authority for themselves, or at least establishing the theoretical (and theological) foundation for their claim. Rulers from Charlemagne to Napoleon might ignore this claim, or try to neutralize it, but the claim remained. For a historian to ignore this claim, and the complications that accompany the claim, is to ignore what really happened in the Reformation. I will save a discussion of this issue for the following chapter.

A prior concern is that of theological or doctrinal matters which, while they may not have caused the Reformation to occur, ensured that it would endure in a particular form. And that form has been far more difficult to disentangle than any political change brought about by the Reformation. Catholics could be given back their freedom and, in a sense, have their political status returned to normal, but Church of England remained in place. Thus, the theological climate had changed permanently, and Catholics began to wonder why. Their attention turned from the politicians of the sixteenth century to its reformers. Politicians had battled with Rome only by accident. Henry broke with the Roman Church because of power and passion, Cromwell because of power and greed, Elizabeth because of her desire for political stability. For them the break with Rome was an unfortunate, but inessential part of their design. Had the Church not stood in the way, in all likelihood, it would have remained untouched. But the reforming theologians broke with Rome out of necessity, and made the destruction of that Church, as it was then constituted, the very heart of their program.

The one English reformer who personified that destruction was Thomas Cranmer, the Archbishop of Canterbury. He had fashioned the break with Rome and then had acted to bring the break about. He symbolized the Church of England for many Catholics, who realized that to attack Cranmer was to attack the Church of England. His weaknesses were its weaknesses.

Catholic opinion about Cranmer remained constant throughout the period we are considering. Not one Catholic historian, no matter what his political or theological bent, over the course of nearly 400 years, said one good word about Cranmer, other than to praise his prose style. One of the defects cited most often was his dissembling – a good example was his declaring Catherine's marriage invalid, then later dissolving the marriage between Henry and Anne Boleyn. John Lingard was one of the first to mention this in strong terms:

> It must have been a most unwelcome and painful task. He [Cranmer] had examined the marriage [of Henry and Anne] juridically; and had pronounced it good and valid; and had confirmed it by his authority as metropolitan and judge. But to hesitate might have cost him his head. He acceded to the proposal [of annulment] with all the zeal of a proselyte.[2]

For Lingard, Cranmer was a type of bishop who made of dissembling a way of life. Those Henrician bishops who, like Cranmer, subscribed to the new doctrines, were required to put on a façade of being Catholic. Lingard wrote of them: "[They] submitted with equal weakness to teach doctrines which they disapproved, to practise a worship which they deemed idolatrous or superstitious, and to consign to the stake for the open profession of tenets which . . . they themselves believed."[3] More than a century later, Hilaire Belloc would agree with Lingard's assessment in his brief portrait of the Archbishop. According to Belloc, Cranmer was a weak cleric, a "time-server and a coward", who was "crapulous and would do anything he was told". Furthermore, Cranmer "showed little intelligence or foresight, was devoid of all initiative, accepted through fear the various tasks thrust upon him, was always subservient, and by nature hypocritical and wavering".[4]

Belloc also agreed with Lingard's judgment that Cranmer's treatment of Anne Boleyn, once she was threatened, was a "betrayal". But Belloc saw more to condemn than had Lingard, namely Cranmer's pattern of "gentle deceptiveness", applied first to the Maid of Kent, then Anne Boleyn, and later Catherine Howard, feigning sympathy for them, while turning informer. Belloc's claim that Cranmer "wormed out of her by feigned friendship some sort of admission of guilt" is simply not accurate.[5]

Such was Belloc's revulsion of Cranmer, that he turned it into book length.[6] The note of dissembling is prominent throughout the book. The fact that Cranmer had so often escaped from almost certain death – first, in the case of Anne Boleyn, then in the downfall of Cromwell, and for a time during the reign of Mary Tudor – led Belloc to suspect him of cowardice and deceit. Cranmer never groveled more than at the trial of Lambert in 1538, when Henry VIII presided and forced the bishops to defend the doctrine of the Eucharist.[7] In 1540 Cranmer voted for the Six Articles on all three readings, thus again defending the doctrine of the Real Presence, communion in one kind, and celibacy as the law of God.[8] Even worse, John Frith was condemned by Cranmer and burned for denying what Cranmer himself denied.[9]

Philip Hughes also made lengthy comments on Cranmer's "legerdemain". He mentioned that Cranmer had already taken a wife while he was pledged to celibacy, but this was not nearly as serious as his taking an oath to the pope after he had sworn in front of witnesses that he did not mean to honour any such oath.[10] Hughes remarked sarcastically that the "chief of the English reformers" was "about to begin his lifework of bringing back religion to the primitive holiness in which Jesus Christ had founded it" by lying on oath.[11]

Even defenders of Cranmer have had difficulty with his dissembling. Maria Dowling wrote, "Cranmer made a courageous attempt to save [Anne Boleyn], telling Henry of his amazement at the guilt imputed to her, but carefully hedging his bets in an attempt, so to speak, to save the child [Elizabeth] if not the mother."[12] Dowling cited a letter from Cranmer to Henry, written in May 1536, in which Cranmer wrote, "If she proved culpable, there is not one that loveth God and his gospel that ever will favour her . . . for then there was never creature in our time that hath so much slandered the gospel."[13] On the surface, this makes Cranmer look like he was playing both sides of a very dangerous game, in order to save his own life, or the evangelical direction of the Reformation, and Catholics were not slow to pounce on the ambiguous message of the letter. But Diarmaid MacCulloch, in his magisterial study of Cranmer, called the letter "a model of pastoral wisdom and courage", whereby Cranmer was stating his own disbelief at Anne's guilt while allowing for the possibility of her guilt.[14]

It is small wonder that Catholics rejoiced in Cranmer's own death by burning. Martin Haile (whose real name was Maria Hallé) wrote that Cranmer was a traitor as well as a heretic, and deserved all he got.[15] Mary Jean Stone, a frequent contributor to the *Dublin Review*, agreed and added that Cranmer "had proved himself to be so base a dissembler, that no confidence could be placed in any of his recantations even if he had stuck to them".[16] She added, "He suffered according to the notions of the day, according to his own principles in dealing with others, and for causes which he had himself once considered sufficient for death".[17] Interestingly, Belloc did not agree with this, and thought that Cranmer had suffered unfairly. There had always been an implied "contract" that a heretic who had recanted would be spared. Cranmer had recanted and relapsed several times, but the fault was not entirely his. "It seems to me unjust," wrote Belloc, "to have accepted these numerous recantations and to have obviously favoured their repetition and increasing emphasis, if they [Mary and her ministers] had not intended to spare him."[18]

Edmund Bishop and the *Book of Common Prayer*

The principal complaint against Cranmer, however, was more substantial – namely, that he had changed the liturgy into something the Catholic Church had never seen before. A Catholic convert and liturgical historian, Edmund Bishop (1846–1917), was behind this charge and had Aidan Gasquet as a collaborator. Bishop had earned an international reputation in liturgical studies for his discovery, transcription, and annotation of some three hundred papal letters of the fifth to the eleventh centuries. He converted to Catholicism in 1867, and attempted to become a monk at Downside, but ill health prevented him from persevering.

He and Gasquet combined to produce *Edward VI and the Book of Common Prayer* in 1890. Gasquet was accused of serving as no more than a secretary for Bishop, taking down dictation as Bishop strode up and down the room. Gasquet denied this and later wrote, "There is not a single portion of the whole, not a single line of the whole book, which is not his as much as it is mine." Bishop's biographer, Nigel Abercrombie, supports Gasquet in this, but adds, "All the discovery and creative part of it was Bishop's." [19] The two made a complementary pair. Gasquet, with his facility in style, was able to communicate what Bishop would have found difficult to put down on paper. Bishop, according to Gasquet, was "like having a living Ecclesiastical Encyclopedia always to refer to". [20] Without either man, *Edward VI* would not have been written.

The book was concerned with one thing: the continuity of Cranmer's *Book of Common Prayer* with the ancient liturgy. Its conclusion was equally straightforward: there was no continuity. From first to last, in intention and realization, the *Book of Common Prayer* (or *Prayer Book*) was innovatory and revolutionary (bad words to a liturgist) and "displaced the traditional liturgy of England". [21]

Edward VI began by listing questions to be answered: What position did the first *Prayer Book* hold in regard to the ancient service books or to contemporary documents? Was it conservative or innovatory? To what degree was it conservative? How did it arise? What were its sources? The authors added the disclaimer that no *judgment* about the *Prayer Book* would be attempted, but only a statement of fact about the *Prayer Book's* ancestry.

When Henry VIII was still on the throne, some attempts were being made to revise the liturgy. As early as 1535 Cardinal Quignones in Spain had published a breviary which proved so popular that it promised to become the common breviary of the West. Bishop and Gasquet wasted no time in showing the difference between this breviary and Cranmer's *Book of Common Prayer*. The revised breviary of Quignones was used as a starting-point for the *Book of Common Prayer*, thanks probably to the influence of Bishop Tunstall, who wanted to maintain as much contact with Rome as possible. But the conservative features of the breviary were abandoned early on. What Cranmer had produced, as a result, was a revolution in two respects:

> Local and diocesan usage of every sort was swept away and an absolute uniformity was prescribed for the whole realm, – a thing unheard of in the ancient Catholic church in England no less than in France and Germany . . . Secondly, a book was introduced, the form and disposition of which was unlike any hitherto in use for public worship in England.[22]

The old breviary had a superabundance of variety; Cranmer's ran to the opposite extreme. Every church was to have the exact same service, which was "as nearly as possible the same for every day throughout the year".[23] But the heart of the matter was not uniformity, but conformity. Was the *Prayer Book*, the authors asked, "to be ranked with the ancient liturgies of the Christian church or with the group of church services created by the Reformation of the sixteenth century?"[24]

Two Reformation liturgies are discussed in *Edward VI*: the Lutheran liturgy, which removed the sacrificial aspect of the Roman Mass while retaining a belief in the Real Presence, and the "Reformed" liturgy, which removed as far as was possible "every trace of the ancient Mass".[25] In Luther's Mass, gone was the Confiteor, the Offertory, that "abominable canon", and the Postcommunion. The Anglican Service of 1549 conformed to this "Mass" almost exactly, a resemblance which could not have been accidental. Furthermore, the *Prayer Book* of 1549 and Luther's book correspond almost identically in their baptismal and confirmation liturgies.[26] The removal of the Offertory was crucial: "The ancient ritual oblation, with the whole of which the idea of sacrifice was so intimately associated, was just wept away . . . This ritual oblation had a place in all liturgies."[27] Furthermore, the chasuble was made optional because it was a sacrificial vestment.

The difference between the first and second *Prayer Books* could be said simply to be the difference between Lutheranism and Calvinism. The first *Book of Common Prayer* was published in 1549, the second in 1552. The Catholic party had opposed the first book on various grounds, and Bishop Stephen Gardiner, meaning to embarrass Cranmer, cleverly gave the first book a Catholic interpretation, using Cranmer's own teaching on communion from his Lutheran catechism. Consequently, the second book left no room for ambiguity. Whatever Gardiner had found acceptable was removed.

Bishop and Gasquet regarded the progressive changes in the books as calculated. Cranmer had become a Calvinist by 1548 and had begun to regard the *Prayer Book* as a "temporary stage in the development of the Reformation".[28] A damaging letter from Martin Bucer and Paul Fagius to colleagues in Strasbourg was cited as evidence that Cranmer knew exactly what he was doing. Bucer and Fagius assured their Protestant friends that Cranmer was not making concessions to Romish practices, but was retaining certain ceremonies and articles (e.g. vestments and candles) only for a time, and would jettison them all when the people would be "won over".[29]

The overall tone of *Edward VI* is accusatory. The authors concluded that Cranmer was changing the nature of the Mass deliberately, deceitfully, and progressively. Even during his Lutheran days, he exhibited Calvinist tendencies, as in his Lutheran catechism, when he left out certain words thought necessary by Luther. In one case, in reference to the Eucharist, he omitted the following: "When He calls and names a thing which was not before, then at once that very thing comes into being as He names it." Bishop and Gasquet found this omission suspicious, as they did Cranmer's subtle changes to the text. Where the Lutheran text read, "When He takes bread and says: 'this is my body', then immediately there is the body of our Lord"; Cranmer changed this to "When Christ takes bread and saith: 'Take, eat, this is my body', we ought not to doubt but we eat His very body." The difference between them is more significant that at first appears: it is the difference between the presence of the Lord made through an act of consecration (Lutheran) and one made through an act of communion (Anglican). It is the difference, in other words, "between those who held . . . the real presence and those who held the real absence".[30]

It is no surprise, then, to hear the authors join in the chorus of those who accused Cranmer of having a "shifting mind", and then make the suggestion that Cranmer was a weak character.[31] Where the Anglican Canon Dixon had previously written of Cranmer's loyalty in desiring to renew his episcopal commission under Edward VI, and Lingard had mentioned Cranmer's need to do this because of his low theology of priesthood, Bishop and Gasquet claimed that Cranmer did so because he was forced to do so by law – that of 6 February 1547, when the Privy Council required such submission from all bishops.[32]

This accusation was not pertinent to anything except to heap more abuse on Cranmer. Not only was he deceitful, he was a coward as well and blew with the wind. As a contrast, the authors presented Bishops Tunstall and Gardiner, who objected to the above submission, and the rest of the "Catholic party" of bishops, who stood firm against the *Prayer Book*. Not only were their objections important, but the way in which their objections were overcome (i.e. imprisonment) was significant. When the second *Prayer Book* came to a vote in 1552, four of the Catholic party had been deprived of their sees, and Tunstall was already in prison. Only four remained to oppose the changes. Without the use of force, there would have been no approval.

The unpopularity of the new order of prayer went beyond the Catholic party of bishops, and included priests and people as well. In a letter to Bishop Scory in 1583 or 1584, the canons of Hereford complained that very few people were coming to pray, now that all the candles had been removed and superstition overcome.[33]

Edward VI concluded by saying it was not Henry VIII, but the *Book of Common Prayer* which had "swept away ruthlessly the ancient and popular practices of religion and substituted others that were strange, bare and novel".[34] This had to be done by force. The clergy were more easily coerced than the bishops because Cranmer had obtained sole power of granting permission to preach (1548). He used this licensing power to get rid of or silence the opposition. In one incident, treated as symbolic by Bishop and Gasquet, a preacher licensed by Cranmer came to Christchurch in Hampshire to mock the Eucharist as an idol. "In the circumstances," asked the authors, "what could the Catholic clergy, powerless to prevent one sent with authority from speaking, do, but leave the church as they actually did?"[35]

For the most part, the clergy was simply ignored. Parliament approved the first *Prayer Book* without ever having submitted it to Convocation for approval. Finally, the clergy was asked for approval only as an after-thought, when it became apparent that its approval could help overcome popular opposition.[36]

Anglican Orders

Interestingly, Bishop and Gasquet hardly mention the validity of ordination in the Church of England, otherwise known as Anglican Orders. When later events events pushed the subject into the spotlight, Bishop was quite proud of the fact that *Edward VI* had largely avoided the issue, thus relieving him and Gasquet of the charge of special pleading. Bishop was one of the first to see the ordination controversy coming and, knowing how it would ultimately end, begged Lord Halifax not to raise it. Halifax proceeded regardless, partly out of a false optimism for the prospects of reunion with Rome. He was encouraged in this by the Frenchman Abbé Portal, who had little idea what the Church of England was like, and by his own sheltered opinion that the Church of England consisted exclusively of High Church types like himself, eager for reconciliation.

Gasquet reacted swiftly once the matter was brought up. He wanted Anglican Orders condemned unequivocally, leaving no room for further confusion. He saw the French Abbé as the villain. Gasquet wrote, "Unless he is disowned and sat-upon we shall have grave difficulties ahead." What was needed was a "practical decision on the Ang. Orders question".[37]

Gasquet was not the first Catholic historian to feel strongly about the Anglican Orders question. Lingard and Tierney had both addressed it in different ways at mid-century, when Anglican pique at Rome's requirement of absolute re-ordination of convert clerics, as opposed to their conditional re-ordination, had caused a flurry of debate. At that time Lingard advised Cardinal Wiseman to avoid placing too much emphasis on the defect of form (i.e. the words themselves in the Anglican Ordinal were insufficient to convey ordination), thinking that, for both canonical and historical reasons, the defective-form argument by itself could be refuted. Instead, he urged Wiseman to focus on the more general grounds that the Church of England was in the most complete sense a schismatic church.[38] He wrote to Wiseman that form was not a difficulty, but that "I would rather dispute their claim of succession".[39] Mark Tierney saw defect of form as decisive, and sufficient to nullify ordinations within the Church of England. It hinged on Cranmer's phrasing, which omitted all mention of sacrifice. Tierney wrote:

> The question is, not as to what the [consecrating] Bishops *intend* or profess to convey, but what the Ordinal itself actually *enables* them to convey . . . In every ancient form of ordination, in the East no less than in the West, the power of offering *Sacrifice* was invariably expressed: . . . In the Ordinal of Edward every allusion to this peculiar Sacerdotal function is omitted . . . *purposely* to exclude the Sacrificial Office.[40]

Furthermore, Tierney felt that the "intention" of the ordaining prelate or ordinand was insufficient to overcome a defect of form. He wrote that the proper intention "can neither impart validity where [proper form] is wanting, nor enable an imperfect form to convey a power which it was specially framed to descry".[41]

When the controversy arose again in the 1880s, Lingard's approach was adopted. Gasquet, who was asked to serve on the papal commission to decide the issue, was motivated by the larger issue of the Anglican liturgy, and saw Anglican Orders in the context of a more general break with the past. His task was to apply the principles of *Edward VI* to the issue and arrive at a predictable result: Anglican Orders were null and void on the general grounds that the whole spirit and wording of the new liturgy deliberately excluded the notion of sacrifice.[42] Edmund Bishop's thoughts on the matter were important, since he was, to a great degree, the brains behind Gasquet's operation. A forthright letter to a lay friend reveals Bishop's candid feelings on the subject. Bishop thought that the *Book of Common Prayer*, including its Ordinal, had been drawn up on purpose to abolish the sacrifice of the Mass, and that Cranmer's beliefs were clearly Calvinist. But Bishop's most original contribution to the debate was his pointing out that Rome, since Mary Tudor's reign to the present, "has consistently refused to recognise these protestant Orders in England, and has always, then and ever since, acted in practical conformity with this *negative* opinion".[43]

The document which was produced as a result of these opinions, *Apostolicae Curae* (1896), declared Anglican Orders invalid. It read suspiciously like Gasquet throughout:

> Hence not only is there in the whole Ordinal no clear mention of sacrifice, of consecration, or priesthood, of the power to consecrate and offer sacrifice, but, as We have already indicated, every trace of these and similar things remaining in such prayers of the Catholic rite as were not completely rejected, was purposely removed and obliterated.[44]

What stands out in *Apostolicae Curae* is not the argument over defective form or intention, even though the encyclical gives due attention to both; it is the condemnation of the overriding character and spirit of the English Reformation, the total significance of Cranmer's new rite of ordination, and its unmistakable protest against the Catholic priesthood.[45]

However, there remain difficulties with *Apostolicae Curae*, both on the Catholic and Anglican sides. For one thing, the case was heard and decided without any presentations made by Anglicans. All that Rome allowed was for the Anglican case to be put forward by such Catholics (in almost every case by non-English Catholics) as were favourable to the Anglican position. Even the English Catholic priest, Fr. T. B. Scannell, who was added to the commission in order to provide the pro-Anglican case, admitted to an Anglican priest in Rome that he did not believe in the validity of Anglican orders.

John Jay Hughes, a former Anglican priest who managed to get himself ordained *conditionally* by a German bishop, made the claim that historical flaws underpin the encyclical, but he made the mistake of quibbling about intention and sacramental validity (*ex opere operato*), which was precisely what the encyclical avoided in its more general assault on the Church of England.[46]

Anglicans, for their part, have driven a large wedge into the ordination debate by ordaining women, over the strong objections of the Roman and Eastern Churches, and consecrating an actively homosexual bishop in New Hampshire. Thus, the debate of the 1890s has become academic and only a matter of historical curiosity. Attempts to revive it now, and there are some who want to declare *Apostolicae Curae* simply a "work in progress" and not a definitive statement, seem doomed from the start.

The mood of the Catholic Church at the end of the nineteenth century was not one of reconciliation and the recognition of nuances. The Church of England was facing its own crisis, much like it is today, and the Catholic response was to make merry at its difficulties. Msgr. J. Moyes, a canon of Westminster Cathedral, wrote scores of articles for the Catholic newspaper *Tablet* between 1891 and 1900, and underlined the contradictory nature of Anglicanism. One essay, entitled "Double-dealing in Worship" (3 January 1891), questioned a recent pastoral of Archbishop Benson of Canterbury. Benson had enjoined High Church priests to allow those members of their congregations who were not of the High Church persuasion to worship in their own fashion at least one Sunday per month. Moyes pointed out that this was not about a difference of style – the use or non-use of candles, incense, vestments, Eucharistic prayers – but one of substance. He began by saying that the Archbishop was not being insincere, but that the insincerity was in the Anglican system, "which harbours yes and no under the same formularies". The Anglican priest now is "to worship what he believes to be the Real Presence with those who worship it, and outwardly deny it with those who deny it". He can, Moyes concluded, imitate "Catholic Antiquity" for three Sundays, "provided he will play Cranmer" on the fourth.[47]

The aggressive attitude of Canon Moyes was typical of the Catholic reaction to the Church of England, both historically in the person of Thomas Cranmer and his *Book of Common Prayer*, and contemporaneously to issues which concerned both Anglican and Roman Churches. And this attitude would continue into the twentieth century. But the arguments over liturgy and ordination would become muted in favor of the one argument towards which this was all leading: the argument from authority. Just as Lingard had cautioned Cardinal Wiseman to avoid the mire of minute points and to concentrate on the larger picture, so now Catholic historians began to argue less about individual popes and specific papal actions and to focus more on the whole idea of papal authority.

Chapter VII

THE CHURCH OF ENGLAND AND THE PAPACY

O nly when the issue of liturgical continuity had been settled, at least as far as Catholics were concerned, did the papacy emerge as the central issue of the English Reformation. The late nineteenth century was a time of particular discomfort for Anglicans in terms of their internal liturgical debate, and Catholic writers delighted in their plight, but in doing so pointed to the papacy as the final arbiter in disputed questions. The Anglican Bishop of Lincoln, for example, was a High Churchman who had caused a great stir by promoting several "Romish" practices, such as using sanctuary candles and the eastward position in prayer. The Archbishop of Canterbury declared that he could use some of these practices, but must discontinue others.[1] This quickly became a question of authority. High Church advocates qualified the decision and said that it applied only to the Bishop of Lincoln, and not to everyone in all places. The High Church organ, *The Church Times*, then did a curious thing: it appealed to the "Church at large" and to the "Supreme Ordinary" and said, "There are points of Catholic usage which no part of the Church can decide for itself, and which, therefore, no Anglican authority could forbid." This was all the Catholics needed. Canon Moyes wrote to remind Anglicans that *praemunire* laws existed which punished those who carried ecclesiastical appeals outside of England. "We have been told so often that the Church of England is a 'National Church' absolutely 'free and independent of foreign control'. Now it turns out that in all important matters of worship and ritual the Church of England is to be governed . . . by the 'Church at large'." Moyes then expressed relief at the "breaking down of the theory of insularity in which the Establishment has been ice-bound since the days of the Reformation".[2]

However much fun Moyes was having, he was also making a serious point, namely that authority was important in liturgical decisions. Years later, Francis Clark would write about the Anglican Orders controversy, "When the sufficiency or insufficiency of a rite is in question, the decisive norm is the acceptance or rejection of it by the Catholic Church."[3] In a similar vein, Edward Schillebeeckx wrote to Clark in 1958:

> It belong to the true Church to determine whether a rite performed in given circumstances is an "exteriorisation" of her own faith, that is, whether it is *her own act*; or whether it is, on the contrary, an act expressing the faith of another, separated church, qua separated. In the latter case the rite is not valid.[4]

The argument from authority had been building within the Reformation debate all during the nineteenth century. While more local discussions were taking place over specific issues such as apostolic succession, liturgical practice, and monasticism, the more general topic of the papacy was never far in the distance. Questions about continuity ultimately became questions about the papacy.

For some Catholics it was important to defend the reputations of individual popes or men who had given individual examples of loyalty to the popes. The Catholic *Dublin Review*, founded in 1836, was unrestrained in this regard. By mid-century it had become, in the words of Newman, "a dreary publication . . . which wakes up to growl or to lecture, and then goes to sleep again".[5] It was particularly dreary in the area of Reformation history. One looks through its pages in vain for a critical remark about the history of the Catholic Church. Examples are numerous. One writer, C. W. Russell, the most frequent contributor to the *Dublin Review* in the years 1836–56, sought to resurrect the good name of Pope Pius V, whom he enthusiastically called, "The Father of Christendom". Nowhere in one article about Pius V did he find a single fault with the pope, nor is the possibility of a fault mentioned.[6]

Canon Thomas Flanagan, another frequent contributor, brought out a *Handbook of Church History* and a two-volume *History of the Church in England*, which were no more than attempts to make Lingard's *History* more unpalatable to Protestant readers. The latter two volumes have more than their share of distortion. In describing the Benedictine abbots of Reading, Glastonbury, and Colchester, Flanagan insisted that they were all "uncompromising in their fidelity to the Holy See".[7] He failed to note that all of these men had signed the Oath of Supremacy when it was first tendered, and supported the king in his suppression of the Pilgrimage of Grace. This is not to say that these abbots were disloyal to the pope, or doubted his supremacy; only that their support for the Holy See was pragmatic at best, cowardly at worst, and certainly far from uncompromising. Flanagan did not complicate his text by introducing such facts; nor did he attempt to reconcile his unqualified admiration for these abbots with his approval of the Pilgrimage of Grace.[8]

Flanagan defended the Bull deposing Elizabeth with two casual remarks: "it was then usual" and "it had long been usual" for excommunicated princes to be deposed. This was true enough, but we are then given a triumphal pronouncement: "It was time for the warning voice of St. Peter to be heard; it was time to show what the See of Peter thought of the changes in the Church of England."[9] Any Catholic who differed with this enthusiasm for the popes was suspect. When Ignaz von Döllinger's *Die Reformation* appeared in 1846–48, claiming as it did that the corruption of several popes was partly to blame for the events of the Reformation, the *Dublin Review* attacked it as being "too candid".

Lord Acton was nearly excommunicated for holding similar sentiments. Yet his case, and that of his confrere Richard Simpson, was revealing in light of their distrust of papal authority and their simultaneous adherence to the Catholic Church. An examination of this seeming contradiction also reveals the extent of Roman Catholic disdain for the Church of England.

Richard Simpson and the Temporal Authority of the Pope

The Temporal Power of the pope – his control over the Papal States – was in its death throes in the 1860s, with Catholics divided about its various merits. Both Acton and Simpson saw this power as archaic and troublesome, and the sooner it was laid to rest the better. Simpson used his discussion of the Reformation to attack the temporal pretensions of the popes as intrinsically harmful to Catholicism.

Simpson (1820–76) was an Oxford graduate, a Shakespearean scholar, and an Anglican priest who converted to Catholicism in 1845, the same year as Newman, although he was never ordained as a Catholic priest. He contributed to the journal *Rambler*, which had been founded in 1838 by John Moore Capes, and served as editor from 1857 to 1859. After his removal (he was replaced by Newman), he worked behind the scenes and served as an unofficial editor under Lord Acton.

He was a throwback to the Cisalpine era, but with a difference. Cisalpines tended to whitewash the reign of Elizabeth, and saw only the pope as the villain. But, because of Lingard's monumental history, that position was no longer tenable. So Simpson, while he shared this aversion to the pope's meddling in temporal matters, also saw that Elizabeth shared some of the blame for the persecution of Catholics. He closely identified Elizabeth with her ministers and the Anglican clergy in a manner not seen before in books with an anti-papal bent. When Dr. Storey was put to death, after being kidnapped on the continent and brought back to England, many Protestant writers claimed that he acted in a manner unbecoming a martyr – boxing the executioner's ears and roaring "like a hell-hound". Simpson had a different opinion, namely that the term "hell-hound" was more applicable to those who would "come and gloat their vengeance over the sufferings of a dying man" and to "Elizabeth and her infamous ministers, and to the Protestant bishops and clergy who were continually urging them on to still further atrocities".[10]

Innocent people suffered under this regime as well, and Simpson placed much of the blame for this on Tudor "principles", which went back at least as far as Henry VIII. If Henry could not punish the real culprit, punishment would be inflicted on the nearest substitute; when he was scorned abroad, he would revenge himself on his subjects, "hanging a few of his favourites, or repudiating his wife, and beheading her if he dared". Elizabeth, he concluded, "refined on her father's example".[11] She did this either by putting to death the tools of her own crimes – occasionally hanging her own spies – or by punishing victims vicariously. "As she could not catch Sanders, or Allen, or the Pope, she was willing to hang Campion instead of them, though she did not believe that he was in the secret of their designs against her."[12]

But back to the pope. Simpson repeated the Cisalpine claim that Elizabeth was lenient and almost pro-Catholic, even after the excommunication of 1570, and even considered marrying the Catholic Duke of Anjou, when news of further intrigues began to arrive – the Desmond Rebellion and the arrival of the first Jesuits. "Toleration", Simpson noted, was scarcely possible".[13] Before Campion had written his famous "Brag" in 1580, Elizabeth had been content to issue proclamations; now, considering the urgency of events, "very different measures seemed necessary". Simpson added that the fear of a conspiracy, "when we consider the state of England and Ireland at the time . . . do not seem utterly unreasonable".[14]

Popes Paul III and Pius V, who had respectively drawn up the excommunications and depositions of Henry VIII and Elizabeth, were guilty of trying to maintain temporal prerogatives which had been claimed or exercised in the past. If they had "simply relinquished that temporal suzerainty . . . they would have given confidence to their friends, and disarmed their merely political foes". But, as affairs were managed, "they rendered simply impossible the coexistence of the government of Henry VIII and Elizabeth with the obedience of their subjects to the supreme authority of the Pope". Those princes had no choice but to abdicate, "or to hold their own in spite of the Popes".[15]

Edmund Campion, in other words, did not have a chance. He, and the rest of the English missionaries, were put in the impossible position of having "to profess to be true, and yet to *be* false, to Elizabeth; and at the same time not only to profess, but to be true to the Pope in his actions against her". This, he added "was a problem incapable of any moral or rational solution".[16] Campion could not even deny the validity of the Bull by which Elizabeth was deposed, "and could only show that he and the Catholics were for the present dispensed from attempting to enforce it".[17]

Campion was made a hero by Simpson, a fact which was a serious break from the Cisalpine canon. Simpson saw Campion was a prophet in refusing to profess any positive belief in the temporal pretensions of the pope: "In refusing their deepest assent to the medieval views of the temporal prerogatives of the Holy See, [Campion and his companions] were pioneers in the true path of the development of doctrine."[18]

But in his haste to ally himself with Campion, Simpson overlooked a significant question: Did Campion refuse to confess a belief in the temporal authority of the pope because he did not believe in it, or because he knew that such a refusal was his only escape? Simpson assumed the former. In fact, he assumed that Campion agreed with him about the temporal power of the pope. He did not offer any evidence, nor have I discovered any, to support this assumption. Campion may have been among the first to see difficulties with the maintenance of papal temporal power in a changed world, but that was much more likely due to his own predicament rather than to any theological doubts about the wisdom of temporal sovereignty. Simpson made the leap from one to the other far too easily.

It was necessary for him to do this if he was to make Campion into the genuine martyr he thought him to be. The Cisalpines did not regard those who had died – like Thomas Becket, "martyrs to the temporal power", or like Campion, "martyrs to the deposing power" – to be martyrs at all. Simpson, in attempting to create Campion in his own image, needed to correct this stance, and claimed Campion as a martyr to the Catholic faith – a victim of the inherent contradiction in the body of doctrine delivered to the English by the missionary priests, a contradiction not of his own making. He wrote, "the eternal truths of Catholicism were made the vehicle for a quantity of speculative and practical opinions about the temporal authority of the Holy See which could not be held by Englishmen loyal to the government".[19]

Simpson's biography of Campion, which incidentally served as the main source book for Evelyn Waugh's historical novel about Campion in

1935, aside from making too much of Campion's "repudiation" of the temporal power, also failed to see the spiritual implications of Elizabeth's Oath of Supremacy. Simpson may have made a few references to Elizabeth's exaggerated claims in the spiritual realm, but greater weight was given to the pope's offenses. Elizabeth's supremacy, after all, was no longer an issue in the middle of the nineteenth century, and the practice of Catholicism was no longer treason, but the pope was still making claims that bore some resemblance to those of the sixteenth century.

The most cogent criticism of Simpson's work on the Reformation was that he ignored theological problems, much like the Cisalpines had ignored them seventy years earlier. But he had less excuse than they had. He saw authority as a problem, but was so taken with the pope's current problems, that he never ventured into the deeper waters of spiritual authority. He could have pointed out that Elizabeth had deliberately held to a middle line in religion which was necessarily gray, and thus inge-niously susceptible to an interpretation which, she thought, could be either Catholic or Protestant. But he did not do so. Thereby, he showed he was quite capable of seeing the complexity of some issues, such as Campion's dilemma of double allegiance, but not others. We were to sympathize with the queen because of the circumstances she found herself in, the view she took of her role, the pressures brought upon her; but we were not to extend the same sympathy to the pope.

Campion was too sympathetic a figure to dismiss, as had the Cisalpines, who regarded him as a tragic product of his own wrong-headed Society of Jesus. So Simpson sought to fasten on the good name of the martyr Campion, while using it to attack the Ultramontanists (and the Jesuits), who were agitating for more authority in the pope. It was a delicate position to hold, and Simpson was not a delicate thinker. It was also a clever ploy by Simpson, to take up the cause of a Jesuit "saint" and use it against the very religious order Campion belonged to. It was a disreputable use of history, and too fraught with contradictions for Simpson to succeed, and a more formidable historian than he would be needed to make a more convincing case. His name was John Emerich Edward Dalberg, otherwise known as Lord Acton.

Lord Acton and the Authority of the Pope

Lord Acton (1834–1902) had studied under the great German historian Ignaz von Döllinger for six years, beginning in 1848. In 1859 he took over the editorship of the *Rambler* from John Henry Newman. In 1862, under heavy ecclesiastical pressure, he changed the name of the journal to the *Home and Foreign Review*, and promised to limit its pages to political matters. In 1864, after a controversial essay appeared named "The Munich Congress", the journal folded, again under ecclesiastical pressure. In 1895 he became the first Roman Catholic to become Regius Professor of Modern History at the University of Cambridge. While he did not publish a book, he edited the first *Cambridge Modern History* series, helped in the founding of the *English Historical Review*, and wrote several essays which later appeared as collections, such as *Lectures on Modern History* (1906) and *Essays on Church and State* (1952).

Lord Acton saw the pope's temporal power, as it was exercised over the centuries, as part of a larger picture of authoritarian papalism. Everywhere that he saw restrictions on liberty – censorship, harassment, tyrannical control – he rebelled. At first, in his younger days, his rebellion was directed against Protestants, whom he saw as the enemies of freedom. The Reformation was evil because it eliminated the sole check on state despotism, i.e. the Catholic Church. Personal freedom of conscience, which had been guaranteed to a far greater degree in a world ruled jointly by Church and state, all but disappeared in a world governed by the state alone. In sweeping away the Church (Acton's estimate of the Church of England was low indeed) the Reformation had swept away freedom of conscience. As a result, the future was dim with the prospect of dictators and the divine right of the state.

But as Acton matured, his disquiet at absolute authority was directed at the notion of papal infallibility. His well-known maxim, "Absolute power corrupts absolutely", applied to political and spiritual domains alike, and he was as nervous about the Church wielding this power as he was about the state. Infallibility was becoming the issue of the day, at the midpoint of the nineteenth century. And the battle lines within the Catholic Church were being drawn between those who wanted a strong definition, and those who wanted no definition at all. Acton was nervous that the advocates for a definition saw infallibility in every papal pronouncement or action. And he knew that popes had been wrong, or had acted wrongly, before. And thus he plunged into the debate with all of his energy.

Earlier in the century, Joseph de Maistre had written, "L'Infaillibité dans l'ordre spirituel, et la souveraineté dans l'ordre temporel, sont deux mots parfaitement synonymes".[20] Cardinal Manning thought that the temporal sovereignty would be solemnly defined as a doctrine of the Church.[21] William George Ward, the long-standing editor of the *Dublin Review* at the time, was the most outspoken adherent of unrestricted papal power. He originally opposed a definition because he thought it would be too restrictive of what he thought was a wide and beneficent power. He wrote, "To hold that the Church's infallibility is confined to her definitions of faith seems to us among the most fatal errors of the day". He added, "No one can limit [the Church's] infallibility to her definitions [of faith] without the most preposterous blunder; because that very infallibility is undefined. So long as she refrains from defining it, she testifies most unmistakably to her infallibility in things undefined."[22]

Ward's understanding of infallibility was so wide as to be laughable. He made a remark that he would like to have a papal Bull each morning with his eggs and *Times*, and Bishop Dupanloup circulated Ward's article at the Vatican Council as the best argument against the doctrine.

But the Vatican Council went ahead and committed this most "preposterous blunder", and said that papal statements, in order to be considered infallible, needed to concern themselves with faith and morals, and be issued by the pope *ex cathedra*, or in his role as the successor of Peter and universal head of the Church (and not merely as Bishop of Rome). This it must have come to men like Ward as a setback, though they tried to salvage their previous position as honourably as possible. Ward wrote of the definition, "It is accompanied by no single qualifying clause or explanation, which is not most heartily accepted by those who used to be called 'the extreme ultramontanists'."[23] Ward, however, could no longer define a vague notion himself, but now had to defend a written document, and one which was phrased so carefully and placed such limits on infallible statements that even Newman was satisfied with it, though he still begrudged the need for a definition at all.

Simpson reacted quickly by trying to shift the grounds of the argument from the nature of infallible statements to that of *ex cathedra* statements. He wrote to William Gladstone, the Prime Minister, that the Vatican Council had done nothing new: "[The definition] simply forbids us to contradict the proposition that the pope speaking *ex cathedra* is infallible. It leaves us perfectly free to form our own ideas as to what is *ex cathedra*."[24]

Lord Acton let his fear of an unqualified infallibility dictate his judgment about what was actually defined. He was disappointed that Newman had backed down in actively opposing a definition, and misunderstood Newman's point altogether. It was almost as if Acton *needed* to misunderstand the issue. He saw history as an uncomplicated dialectic between intransigents and conciliators, and theological subtleties only got in the way. For the most part, as in the Reformation, Acton saw the popes as the guilty parties, or as falling sway to the intransigents. Erasmus, and Cardinals Pole and Contarini were conciliators, but were eclipsed by Cajetan and the intransigents, reverting "to the old tradition of indefeasible authority wielding irresistible power".[25] The Catholic response to the Reformation was indeed a "counter-Reformation" for Acton, inasmuch as it was essentially negative, repressive, and reactionary. For Acton, there was no question that it ultimately related to the contemporary conflict between Ultramontanes and Liberal Catholics. The latter were Catholics dedicated to intellectual scholarship independent of the authority of the Church. Originally they emerged in France under Lamennais and Lacordaire, and sought some accommodation between the Church and the values of freedom found in the United States's Bill of Rights. In Germany they took a more intellectual turn and spawned such scholars as Johann Möhler and Döllinger. Joseph Altholz said that they were "neither liberal enough to please the Liberals, nor quite Catholic enough to please the Pope".[26] In any case, Lord Acton included himself among their number and regarded the group as in good historical company.

Opposed to these "conciliators" were the likes of Charles Borromeo, whom Acton claimed had complained that not enough Protestants were being murdered. With reckless facility, Acton connected Borromeo to Cardinal Manning, who joined a fraternity known as the Oblates of St. Charles, thus holding up to veneration "the authority that canonised this murderer".[27] Men such as Borromeo and Manning were in the tradition of the Inquisition, which Acton came to regard as *the* decisive ecclesiastical tragedy and the principal obstacle to conversion. Acton wrote that the Inquisition was the principal thing with which the papacy is identified, and by which it must be judged. He called the principle of the Inquisition "murderous" and "religious assassination" and then makes another leap: "If [one] accepts the Primacy with confidence, admiration, unconditional obedience, he must have made terms with murder."[28]

Lord Acton did not restrict these opinions to private letters. He wrote four letters to the *Times* in 1874, accusing Pius V of sanctioning the murder of heretics. Cardinal Manning took this personally and tried to obtain from Acton a formal submission to the definition of infallibility. Acton dodged this demand narrowly, by claiming that he lived in the Shrewsbury diocese, and was thus under the jurisdiction of Bishop Brown, and not Manning. Manning then pressured Brown to obtain the submission, but Brown settled for an explanation from Acton of his views. Acton said that his letters to the *Times* were strictly limited to historical matters, and did not delve into theological questions at all. This "satisfied" Brown, who was probably as anxious as Acton to be done with Manning. The cardinal persisted until 1875, when he threatened to ask Rome for an excommunication, but he desisted and the matter was dropped.

But Acton's obvious anti-papalism had another side. Once the Papal

States were finally gone in 1870, Acton was insistent that the pope remain politically free. What this meant, of course, was not clear, and Acton made no concrete proposals. However, he was definitely opposed to any schemes which would have placed the Roman curia in another country such as France or Spain. And therein he betrayed feelings about the papacy which were in sharp contradistinction to his anti-papal views. He spoke in Kidderminster (England) in 1871 and strongly defended the liberty of the pope. He said, "It is certain that the Catholic world will never rest content if the Pope is unable to discharge his spiritual powers without impediment, or without suspicion of undue influence."[29] In a lengthy article, he defended the papacy by contending that, whenever things went wrong in Italy, it was usually the fault of the French. The popes had wanted to make Italy a free and united country in the fifteenth and sixteenth centuries, but were thwarted in this by the French, who "over and over again marched their armies across the Alps when Italy had risen to a flourishing and prosperous condition, only to leave it an impoverished and desolate ruin".[30]

Furthermore, despite Acton's apparent distrust of popes and his repeated problems with ecclesiastical authority, he was never tempted in the least to join the Church of England or defend it. His contempt was for a national establishment which had deliberately secluded itself from the rest of the ecclesiastical world and had the presumption to call itself "catholic".[31] Acton believed along with Leibniz, whom he quoted in his famous inaugural lecture at Cambridge, that "History is the true demonstration of religion". In light of other things he wrote, it is difficult to believe other than that he felt history was a true demonstration of Catholicism. Certainly, his confidence in both history and his religion were unbounded. "I rest unshaken in the belief", he wrote to the *Times*, "that nothing which the inmost depths of history shall disclose in time can ever bring to Catholics just cause of shame or fear."[32]

One might well wonder what happened to the Inquisition and the murdering Charles Borromeo and Pius V and even Manning. But Acton was not speaking about individuals. He was quite ready to concede that there were several bad characters in the mix. He was talking about the truth of the Catholic religion. And he was talking about the falsehood of Protestantism: "Whilst we [Catholics] are content to rely on the laws of historical evidence applied with utmost rigour, the Protestant must make them bend to the exigencies of his case. His facts must be as false as his theory; he is obliged to be consistent in his perversion of the truth."[33]

Acton overestimated the value of history, calling it the "final arbiter of truth" on the one hand, and by thinking that "purposeless history" was possible on the other.[34] He wrote, "In a few years, all these publications will be completed, and *all will be known that ever can be known*. In that golden age our historians will be sincere, and our history certain."[35] This was far more preposterous than anything Belloc would contrive to claim, and Belloc was a debater and often said things for effect. But Acton really believed this stuff.

What he did not see was the plank of presupposition and prejudice in his own eye, and that he could be as intolerant as the "intransigent" he so facilely condemned. When he wrote of the role of historians – "Our business is to know what contemporaries could not tell us because they did not see it" – he was unwittingly passing a stern judgment on himself.[36] Had he written one substantial history, he could have shown by example how the thing was to be done, rather than by petulant theorizing. Belloc's theorizing is just as solid, and shows that between theory and practice there is a wide gulf.

Focus on the Papacy: Aidan Gasquet

After Lord Acton, Catholic historians called more and more attention to the spiritual authority of the pope. Discussion of individual papal actions, such as Pius V's excommunication of Elizabeth, shifted to a discussion about the papacy in the abstract. For most, the temporal authority of the pope was a dead issue. Aidan Gasquet was a good example of this shift. He said that the Reformation changed the papacy insofar as the papacy had, until then, been "fully and freely recognised by all" in England.[37] The reformers deliberately exaggerated the abuses in temporalities so as to be able to effect a greater change.[38] One good example was in the bidding prayer, or the prayer of petition, which had, before the Reformation, included mention of the pope. But when the pope's authority was rejected by the king, it was necessary to justify the removal of the pope's name from the bidding prayer (and canon) "by turning men's thought to the temporal aspect of the Papacy, and making them think that it was for the national profit and honour that this foreign yoke should be cast off".[39]

Gasquet was quite prepared to abandon any claims to a temporal authority in the pope, and attack its misuse in England, but not without suggesting that it was not as evil a power as people believed. He cited Gairdner and Maitland in their praise of the Roman Curia as a court of international and ultimate appeal. The Church was indeed an *imperium in imperio* throughout the world. Yet this very power and worldliness weakened the Church's spiritual hold. The dazzling display of Renaissance art and architecture "made it difficult to recognize the divinely-ordered spiritual prerogatives which are the enduring heritage of the successor of St. Peter".[40]

Gasquet did not entirely excuse the pope and, at least on one occasion, drew conclusions which made him suspect of Liberalism. He suggested, in one case, that had the pope surrendered some of his temporal prerogatives in England in the early 1500s, as he had in France in the Gallican Concordat in 1516, trouble might have been avoided. Had the pope removed the source of genuine English grievances over his temporal power, the pretext for the religious change and assault on his spiritual power might also have been removed.

Such sentiments cast Gasquet as a Liberal Catholic and probably cost him the election to the archbishopric of Westminster in 1903.[41] He certainly had friends among Liberal Catholics, and one chronicler of the period called Gasquet a "closet Modernist", but this would be to ignore the whole of his historical work, his conclusions about Anglican Orders, and his being made a cardinal by no less than Pope Pius X.[42] One encounter with a real Modernist, George Tyrrell, proved to be considerably awkward. Gasquet presided over the Eucharistic Congress of 1908 as the Papal Legate and was carrying the Eucharist under his cloak through the streets of London (public exposition was forbidden by law), when the procession finally arrived at a hall. There waited George Tyrrell, the Jesuit who had been excommunicated *ad vitandum* for his Modernist views on a few theological points. The *ad vitandum* excommunication was very serious, and meant "to the point of shunning". Catholics were not allowed, in other words, to be in the same room with him. Gasquet, when informed of Tyrrell's presence, stopped the procession and decided that either Tyrrell would have to leave the place, or the Eucharistic Congress would go somewhere else. Frantic negotiations convinced Tyrrell to leave, and the Congress went on.

John Hungerford Pollen

But the days of questioning the pope's temporal authority were over (for Catholics), and Gasquet stood out alone as one who continued to do so. Instead, most Catholic historians focused on the pope's spiritual authority in the widest sense, staying away from the specific issue of infallibility. In doing this, they reversed the Cisalpine position and praised the popes for their moderation during the turbulent Reformation period, and blamed Elizabeth for her excesses. John Hungerford Pollen, a very capable Jesuit historian, held that Pope Paul IV, by initially refusing to excommunicate

Elizabeth and her ministers, which "they so richly deserved", was moderate to a fault – "always treating Elizabeth's Government with the greatest deference".[43] Elizabeth had made a deliberate choice against Roman Catholicism, and held to it. Pius V was left with no alternative, such was the pressure the queen and the English government had put him under, but to excommunicate her. Pollen left no doubt about his opinion of the pope: "Michele Ghislieri, Pope St. Pius V, was beyond question the greatest Pope of the Counter-Reformation period."[44]

Evelyn Waugh, in his biography of Campion, echoed this adulation. He wrote that the See of Peter was occupied by a saint, and that the saint in his prayer and meditation realized that "there was to be no easy way of reconciliation, but that it was only through blood and hatred and derision that the faith was one day to return to England".[45]

It was a feeble defense of the excommunication and deposition to say that the pope who issued them was a saint. Pollen's approach made more sense because it relegated the deposition to insignificance and treated only of the excommunication. Seen in this light, the Bull of Excommunication cleared the air. Finally, a pope had pointed out to the Tudors, "with their miserable proclivity to give up religious liberty at the sovereign's whim", that attendance at Protestant services was iniquitous.[46] Although it may have been politically disastrous, the excommunication was successful from a religious point of view because it spawned "a fresh enthusiasm for the ancient cause" and began "to produce permanent good fruit, especially among the Catholic exiles".[47]

Pollen saw Campion and Persons as attempting to mitigate the excommunication, requesting from Rome a qualification, "The Catholics desire it to be understood in this way: it obliges them in no way, while affairs stand as they do."[48] The resulting Mitigation permitted Catholics to call Elizabeth their queen, a fact which Pollen felt should have been sufficient. But Cecil, her prime minister, commented that the qualifying phrase "while affairs stand as they do" was suspicious and meant "that you are loyal while you cannot resist, and that you will rebel at the first opportunity".[49] Pollen condemned Cecil for misconstruing the facts, but said nothing about the pope blundering into a trap wherein Catholic loyalty became first impossible, then temporary and conditional.

Robert Hugh Benson

Another product of this time, Robert Hugh Benson (1871–1914), the convert son of the Archbishop of Canterbury – he was ordained in the

Church of England in 1895 and became of Roman Catholic priest in 1903 – wrote a series of historical novels about the English Reformation. In one of them, *By What Authority*, he summarized Pollen's point quite well. Benson wrote that Elizabeth's excommunication, while unfortunate, "may have been a necessity". It was difficult to see what else the pope could do. He had tried a gentle appeal, but she had "repudiated and scorned him". Benson added, "Nothing was left but to recognize and treat her as an enemy of the Faith, an usurper of spiritual prerogatives, and an apostate." Benson admitted that this would bring trouble on those who were still within her power, "but to pretend that the Pope alone was responsible for their persecution, was to be blind to the fact that Elizabeth had already openly defied and repudiated his authority".[50]

Benson and Pollen drew attention to an aspect of Elizabeth's claims which Cisalpines had traditionally ignored: the spiritual nature of the Oath of Supremacy. The choice for Catholics in England, because of this Oath, was between loyalty to their sovereign or loyalty to God. Henry VIII had created this ultimatum, and Elizabeth had acquiesced in it. The pope's deposition, according to this argument, was no more than a formal recognition on his part of what Henry and Elizabeth had done on theirs. This Oath was best understood when reduced to its logical extreme, which Benson puts in the mouth of one of his characters (Mr. Buxton) in the same novel. While he admits that a national Church may be powerful and number thousands of holy men and women among her ministers and adherents, still her foundation is insecure:

> Christ's Kingdom is not of this world. Can you imagine, for example, St. Peter preaching religious obedience to Nero to be a Christian's duty? I do not say (God forbid) that her Grace is a Nero, but there is no particular reason why some successor of hers should not be.[51]

Hilaire Belloc (1870–1953)

This tendency to emphasize the pope's spiritual authority increased in the work of Hilaire Belloc. Born in the same year as the definition of infallibility, he never ceased to interpret history in terms of the centrality of papal authority. His message was as simple as it was all-encompassing: Europe is the Faith and the Faith is Europe. This was the famous final line of a book written soon after World War I, and it was that event, probably more than any other, which influenced Belloc's view of history.

The Great War had shocked a complacent Europe into the realization that its very extinction was a possibility. Several writers, Belloc among them, began to look at the foundations of Europe and wonder what was at stake. Acton had written before the war that religion was the determining force of society, and Belloc used this to explain what was happening to Europe. He narrowed Acton's statement to mean that the Catholic religion was the determining force of European society. As the one was threatened, so was the other. In fact, European society was threatened precisely because Catholicism was being forgotten. The crisis had become one of fundamentals: the existence of God and the authenticity of the Bible were being questioned. It was now a matter of belief or unbelief, and the bickering over various nuances of belief seemed an irrelevance. What was urgently needed was an interpretation of history which might explain how the crisis of civilization had come about, and how it might yet be averted.[52]

For Belloc, the explanation was elementary: everything pointed to Rome. Neither Europe nor Christianity could be understood apart from Rome. The Christian relation to Rome was almost genetic: where Rome had ruled, Christianity had thrived. And Christianity had preserved whatever of Rome was worthwhile. The Catholic Church had gathered up the social traditions of the Greco-Roman world and had given them new life. "It was the Catholic Church which made us, gave us our unity and our whole philosophy of life."[53]

Belloc did not invent this thesis; E. A. Freeman before him, and Belloc's contemporaries Christopher Dawson and Herbert Butterfield held similar views. But Belloc gave it a particularly Catholic twist, and thus saw more to the Reformation than did the others. When the Reformation came about, only those countries which had grown up within the boundaries of the Roman Empire remained faithful to the Catholic Church. England was the only exception, and thus held the key to the success of the Reformation. Without England's defection, the Reformation would simply not have happened; the other countries could not have sustained it. And that is why he claimed that the English Reformation was the most important thing to have happened in history in the last one thousand years.[54]

The exact nature of the Reformation, for Belloc, was disobedience to papal authority. Granted, all of the temporal and political entanglements of the popes, as well as their worldly and sometimes scandalous behaviour, provided an impetus to the Reformation, but "it needed the experience of disunion to prove the necessity of union, and to prove in especial that the test of unity was obedience to the See of Peter".[55]

This resonates with Chesterton's thesis that great men, from Chaucer to Thomas More and Erasmus, had complained about how the Church was run – and ridiculed its running ruthlessly. But they did not want to get rid of the popes or the monks; they only wanted better popes and monks. Chaucer satirized the monk "for not being sufficiently monastic" and priests for not being sufficiently priestly.[56] When the Reformation sought to eliminate them, it had crossed a dangerous, and, Belloc thought, a fatal line. The Reformation, in extinguishing the pope's spiritual authority, had caused both Europe and the Faith to lose their unity. "When England became Protestant", he wrote, "she became a new thing and the old Catholic England of the thousand years before the Reformation is, to the Englishman after the Reformation, a foreign country."[57] This same theme would be taken up later by Eamon Duffy, who concluded his *Stripping of the Altars* in similar language: "By the end of the 1570s, whatever the instincts of their seniors, a generation was growing up which had known nothing else, which believed the Pope to be Antichrist, the Mass a mummery, which did not look back to the Catholic past as their own, but another country, another world."[58]

Belloc's was Ultramontanist history with a vengeance. Item after item of the cisalpine corpus was reversed by Belloc. Judgments on specific characters of the Reformation, as well as interpretations of a more general nature, were offered by Belloc as counterpoints to Cisalpine doctrine. Individual popes were judged much more sympathetically than they had been previously; they were lauded for their strength, their correctness, their sanctity, their defense of the Catholic "thing". Only one pope was criticized and he, Clement VII, for exactly the same reasons the Cisalpines had praised him: he played for time which, while it had been termed caution and moderation by the Cisalpines, became a defect of character under Belloc. This pope was weak, lacked straightforwardness, was irresolute, created delay for its own sake, and was cowed by the prospect of losing England. If anything, he was too indulgent towards Henry.[59]

The world of the early twentieth century was only reaping the fruits of the Reformation, and the only solution was a return to the Faith, i.e. a reversal of the Reformation process. Better historians than Belloc had engaged in this sort of moralizing. Christopher Dawson's thesis was surprisingly similar and became even more explicit after his conversion to Catholicism in 1914. Both Acton and Froude saw the historian as a moral judge, though Froude saw the Reformation in opposite terms from Belloc – as the revival of the creative civilizing element in Europe.[60]

Froude resembled Belloc in one particular, namely in the notion that history was accidental. One historiographer of the period noticed that Froude's history "was essentially spasmodic, unpredictable in a fashion which went beyond a commonplace rejection of determinism".[61] Froude had written, "The temper of each generation is a continual surprise."[62] Belloc, for his part, wrote that "The breakdown of our civilization in the sixteenth century, with its difficult saving of what could be saved, and the loss of the rest, was an accident."[63] The ever-vigilant Coulton ridiculed this in Belloc, writing, "Real Catholic history at last is being written, upon an impregnable basis; there is no god but accident, and Mr. Belloc is its prophet."[64] Coulton had not noticed that Mr. Froude had established Protestant history on a similar basis, long before the bigoted Belloc. A more recent historian, Christopher Haigh, has also proposed the accidental nature of the Reformation – that Protestants were in Henry's good graces when he died in 1547, that Mary Tudor died so young in 1558, etc.

Belloc's thesis contained both his attraction as a theorist and stylist, but also the seeds of his destruction as a historian. He was always the teacher attempting to simplify the material ("Now there are three points about Cromwell which you must remember",) and the aphorist tossing out memorable phrases such as "No Calvin, No Cromwell", but these qualities often got the better of his history. The sweeping judgments so necessary to the grand and readable style often failed to take in disturbing precisions.

Furthermore, Belloc knew how things *had* to happen. Accident became inevitability. Elizabeth must have had a weak character because she was the daughter of a weak king. Her ministers must have acted as they did because they were Calvinists, or were rich. They must have been avaricious because Calvinism, by its very nature, is avaricious.

Belloc had not always written such bad history. In fact, he came to the discipline with impressive credentials. He was highly regarded as a debater and was elected president of the Oxford Union in 1894, and in June of the following year took a First in History at Balliol College. His official biographer said of his historical ability, "A glance at Belloc's history notes for the Oxford History Schools reveals the width of his reading, his power of analysis, his quickness of assimilation, the extreme precision of his method."[65]

His first two biographies, *Danton* (1899) and *Robespierre* (1901), were highly praised and represent the results of his recent Oxford training. But they also betrayed a fault which would haunt Belloc for the remainder of his writing career: they include no authorities and no documentation. This is not to say that Belloc did not appreciate the need for detail. He could be as eloquent as Acton on the subject: "The external actions of man", Belloc wrote in one essay, "the sequence in dates and hours of such actions, and their material conditions and environment must be strictly and accurately acquired."[66] But the accumulation of detail was only a starting point, to which other qualities – proportion and imagination – had to be applied.[67]

The difficulty was not that Belloc failed to supply details; it was that he refused to say where he got them from. This made his details suspect. H. G. Wells could not resist having fun in noticing that Belloc did not quote his source: "It does not exist for him to quote; but he believes that it exists. He waves his hand impressively in the direction in which it is supposed to exist."[68] Wells continued, "There is a placard in one corner of my study which could be rather amusingly covered with the backs of dummy books. I propose to devote that to a collection of Mr. Belloc's authorities."[69]

Coulton, with far less humour, carefully catalogued twenty errors to be found in one of Belloc's histories, *How the Reformation Happened*:

> [Belloc's] builds his argument upon a ludicrously mythical assertion as to the effect of the Black Death on Oxford's University. His account of the Indulgence system is grossly misleading. His version of Zwingli's attitude to Church art is, in one most important point, the very opposite of the truth. Again, it is quite false to represent the early Reformation movement as simply destructive; Mr. Belloc evidently knows scarcely anything of Luther and Zwingli at first hand. His attempt to separate Henry VIII's antipapalism from heresy is pure nonsense . . .[70]

The quarrel with Belloc's negligence was by no means limited to non-Catholics. E. E. Reynolds, the Catholic biographer of Thomas More, found a glaring example of Belloc's recklessness in *The Servile State*, where Belloc stated that in the England of Henry VIII, "the great mass of men owned the land they tilled and the houses in which they dwelt". Reynolds commented, "Such a statement (unsupported by evidence) makes the student of Tudor England gasp. It simply isn't true."[71]

Herbert Thurston, another Jesuit historian of the period, was especially exasperated by Belloc's sloppiness, since he thought Belloc's admirable attempt to correct Protestant history was undermined by his failure to face facts. In his review of Belloc's *History of England*, Thurston stated, "Mr. Belloc is chary of references, but many, I think, would like to know the evidence on which these statements are based." He added that Belloc tried to convince the reader less by evidence than by "emphatic assertion and persistent reiteration", concluding, "It seems a pity that Mr. Belloc . . . should have no indication that anything worthy of attention has been written on the subject in the past forty years."[72]

According to Robert Speaight, Belloc refused to let a friend see the proofs of his *History of England* because he "was afraid that niggling criticism would spoil the sweep of his work".[73] Belloc, at least, knew that he was not writing very good history. When Philip Hughes asked him why he refused to give references, Belloc replied, "I am not an historian, I am a publicist."[74] He wrote to a friend to tell of his *Richelieu*: "It is a bad book. I would not be seen dead in a field with it."[75] A. N. Wilson related

one story he had heard from several sources, where a man sitting opposite Belloc in a railway carriage was reading a volume of his *History of
England*: "Belloc leaned forward and asked the man how much he had
paid for the volume, and, being informed, fished the sum out of his pocket.
He then gave the money to his companion, snatched the book from his
hand, and tossed it out of the carriage window."[76]

One thing that must be remembered is that even academic historians
were reacting to over-documentation in a way similar to Belloc's. Perhaps
Belloc's popularity had them reconsidering their approach. When J. E.
Neale came out with his *Queen Elizabeth* in 1934, he shocked the scholarly world by including neither footnotes nor bibliography. The difference
was, of course, that Neale consciously left out the references; Belloc often
did not have them to begin with. As time went on, he did less and less
research, and his biographies began to look more and more like reactions
or re-interpretations of other people's work. His biographies of Wolsey
and Elizabeth, for example, appeared suspiciously soon after those of
Pollard and Neale. He once said, "Pay me twice as much and I'll do twice
as much research."[77]

Belloc's excuses were many. Having neither a university job nor the
money that went with it, he complained that he did not have the leisure
to produce a first-rate history. He told Mrs. Raymond Asquith in 1929,
"Shall I before I die have strength or leisure to write real history all aflame
with life? I could do it, but I haven't yet and probably never shall."[78] A.
N. Wilson suggested that "with sufficient leisure and incentive, he could
have written some supremely great biographies".[79]

But, as we know, he did not. The fact is that Belloc did not have the
leisure because he did not have the incentive. He was temperamentally
incapable of sustained scholarship; he did not have the disposition to stay
in one place and write books. Did the Oxford Fellows and Tutors suspect
this when they turned him down for a fellowship in 1895? E. E. Reynolds
thought so and wrote, "The Fellows and Tutors must have detected that
he did not have the qualifications for real scholarship."[80] However, it
seems more probable that they were reacting more to his irritating manner than to any incipient wanderlust.

Belloc maintained that his poverty forced him to travel, lecture, and
write newspaper articles or hack biographies, simply to support his family. But the reality is probably that Belloc traveled so much in order to
satisfy his own restlessness rather than to provide a living for his family.
One extraordinary point made by Wilson in his biography of Belloc is that,
for all of Belloc's protestations of love for his wife and county of Sussex,
he was hardly at home to enjoy either one. In 1912, Wilson calculated that
Belloc cannot have spent more than five weeks at home, a figure which is

rather typical of a man he described as "one of the most restless beings who ever crashed about the surface of the earth".[81]

Neither did his facility in debate serve him well in historical writing. Arguing a point in debate was much easier than arguing a point of historical research. In fact, his historical works read more like debaters' manuals than they do definitive studies of a particular subject. He knew the advantages of attack as well as the weaknesses of too much defense. Defects in his own argument or evidence did not concern him because they could be disguised by bluster. Thus his books were often accusatory, bullying, threatening. Basil Blackwell, his English publisher, addressed Belloc once as "Dear Mr. Hilaire Bullock", a statement fairly descriptive of his pose.[82] When Belloc replied to an opponent's argument with a particularly astonishing fact, Douglas Woodruff asked him if it were true. "Oh, not at all", said Belloc, "but won't it annoy Coulton".[83]

Given all of this negative criticism of his historical work, Belloc's contribution to Catholic historiography would appear to be negligible, perhaps even counter-productive. One cannot write a biography of James II in eight days in a hut at the edge of the Sahara Desert and expect to be taken seriously. But such was the force of Belloc's writing that he was taken seriously, at least by Catholics. Granted, he was known for much more than his history, but his history and historical biographies were a significant part of his total impact. Edward Dutton, in an essay on Catholic literature, explained that Belloc's history was "among the least insular of our time" and that he influenced a generation of writers. It was Belloc's pen, Dutton continued, which had "widest and surest influence in our day on the side of Catholicism".[84]

Christopher Hollis suggested that Catholic historians who came after Belloc owe him a considerable debt of gratitude because Belloc broke down walls of prejudice: "If today history is taught in the English universities fairly and without bias, in a vastly different fashion from that in which it was taught in the last century, we must remember that a large part of the credit is due to Belloc."[85]

Certainly Belloc shaped Catholic consciousness about the English Reformation. And what he shaped was quite different than Catholic historical writing one hundred years before him. Belloc was an important part of the process which had begun with Nicholas Sanders and continued through Bishop Milner: the process of an increasing emphasis on the papacy as the determining factor in the English Reformation. It was a process which would not end with Belloc, but continue with the next generation of Catholic historians and culminate in the work of Fr. Philip Hughes. In fact, Belloc could not have received a greater tribute than Hughes's monumental *Reformation in England* (1950–54).

Philip Hughes (1895–1967)

Philip Hughes was ordained in 1920 and spent seven years in a parish before being appointed archivist for the Archdiocese of Westminster, a post which he held from 1931 to 1943. In 1955 he was appointed Professor of Church History at the University of Notre Dame, and died in South Bend in 1967. Hughes made respectable what Belloc had been preaching irresponsibly or, at least, unprofessionally. The Bellocian theme that the spiritual power of the papacy was the key to the English Reformation, Hughes had made his own, but had also supplied the footnotes.

Hughes has been criticized for avoiding some important topics, such as Cranmer's cruel end and the question of Anglican Orders. He spoke little about the politics, economics, and sociology of the Reformation, and tended toward polemics on the subject of religion and could descend to special pleading. In regard to the king's supremacy, Hughes commented too frankly, "Did anyone believe this blasphemous rubbish?"[86] And after describing a piece of propaganda put out by the government in 1533, Hughes commented, "There follows an amazing piece of humbug . . . "[87] He could also be sarcastic. He refered to Henry as "the Supreme Head" and then, on Henry's death, wrote, "The new Supreme Head of Christ's Church is a little boy of nine."[88]

But there is much to say in favour of Hughes's three volumes. It was the first Catholic attempt to write about the Reformation in a complete way since Lingard more than one hundred years before. Every other Catholic had written about various moments in the Reformation or about various characters within the Reformation, but no one since Lingard had attempted a broad-based evaluation of the English Reformation from start to finish, and even Lingard avoided the monasteries.

Secondly, even though he differed from Lingard in that he did not introduce very much original material to the debate, he brought a certain perspective which made his contribution unique.[89] J. J. Scarisbrick's review of the history noted, "Fr. Hughes succeeds in providing an astonishingly new version of the old. Even if all controversy is not stayed, at last the picture is in focus; at last the story has been told in the right way; everything has been re-aligned – and, one feels instinctively, correctly." What was perhaps more important was that Hughes was "a theologian fully competent to unravel the doctrinal intricacies that are at the heart of his story".[90]

Hughes was especially insightful and fair in his treatment of the Marian persecution, placing it as he did in the greater perspective of sixteenth-century criminal justice. He pointed out that human life was cheaper then,[91] that heresy was considered to be among the greatest of crimes,[92] that Protestants also burned heretics,[93] that many of the Marian victims were Anabaptists and were just as likely to suffer from Anglicans as Catholics,[94] that the Catholic bishops had far less of a role in the Marian heresy trials than they did under Henry.[95] But Hughes also blamed Mary for assuming that her realm was a thoroughly Catholic country – desiring to be set free of the Protestant yoke. Instead, Hughes wrote, "the religious situation was . . . confusion itself", and the common people, whom he categorized as conscientious heretics, the puzzled, and the indifferent, were the unfortunate victims of a body of men who had had nothing better to do than simulate conformity in order to save their own skins.[96]

Thirdly, what stands out in Hughes's history is the fact that it brings together the work of Aidan Gasquet in his defense of the monasteries and the claims of Hilaire Belloc about the papacy. He echoed many of Gasquet's themes – that the monastic visitators were "moral monsters";[97] that their reports could make no logical claim on reform since on their "own showing, the 'lesser' houses were, as a class, morally healthier than the greater";[98] that the principal motive of the dissolution had been "plunder";[99] that scholarly life virtually came to an end as a result of the dissolution;[100] that the poor and those who depended on monasteries for their livelihood were neglected after the dissolution;[101] that the business of Reformation was unpopular and had to be forced on the populace.[102]

Hughes pushed this beyond the bounds even Gasquet had set for himself. For Hughes, the connection between the king's actions in the matter of the divorce and the dissolution of the monasteries and the royal repudiation of the ancient religion was no coincidence. It was "the great business in the English Reformation". All else was secondary. It was "the repudiation of the doctrine, and the fact, that the pope is primate over the Church of Christ wherever this be found, that is the really substantial change, but the side of which all other changes are mere detail".[103]

What bothered Hughes so much was that a king had taken away from the English people their ancient religion. His Act of Supremacy was

the act by which the mass of Englishmen cease to be what all Englishmen have been for a thousand years nearly; here is what matters most, in the whole mass of changes, namely that the English are now, by their own act, outside a particular religious society, to wit, the pope-governed Church, which society, so they have all believed until now, was founded by God as the shrine and guardian and interpreter of the doctrines revealed to mankind through Christ Our Lord.[104]

What mattered to Hughes, then, was that "the religion had changed entirely" and had done so during the reign of Henry VIII – an early Reformation indeed. This had occurred as a result of the various acts of Parliament, the *Bishops' Book* of 1537, and the *King's Book* of 1543. Parliament, under the badgering of Cromwell, had given Henry the authority which for so long had resided in the Church. Step by step, beginning with the Submission of the Clergy (1532) and the Act in Restraint of Appeals (1533), the body of legislation was built up, handing over to Henry the ecclesiastical authority it was simultaneously taking away from the Church. This culminated in the Act of Supremacy and the Act of Succession, both passed in 1534. The *Bishops' Book* of 1537 addressed a number of doctrinal and devotional issues, and declared that the "non-scriptural" sacraments of Confirmation, Matrimony, Holy Orders, and Extreme Unction were subordinate to those of Baptism, Eucharist, and Penance. Significantly, the book interpreted the "Universal Church" to mean a Church consisting of free and equal national churches. The *King's Book* of 1543 was a shorter version of the *Bishops' Book*, with a few important differences.

A. G. Dickens commented on the *Bishops' Book* that, "Taken as a whole it looked a Catholic rather than a Lutheran document",[105] and saw the *King's Book* as even more Catholic, remarking, "Had Stephen Gardiner [an outspoken Catholic-leaning bishop] written the whole work himself it could scarcely have been more to his taste."[106] But Hughes saw in these two books something sinister and essential to the Reformation. Try as the conservatives might, they could not make the *Bishops' Book* palatable to Catholics. While there is a repudiation of the Lutheran teaching on Justification, some of the old problems remained – among them the notion that "Christ never gave unto St. Peter, or to any of the apostles or their successors, any such universal authority over all the others" so that "the bishop of Rome hath no such primacy, nor any such can challenge by any words in scripture".[107]

Finally, in its teachings about the efficacy of Extreme Unction, the Eucharist as a sacrifice, and Penance as a sacrament (and not merely a virtue), the *King's Book* was not acceptable to Catholic theologians. Hughes wrote, "Henry, whatever he is, is not a Catholic."[108]

Hughes's critique of the theological aspects of the English Reformation was probably the most thorough ever written. Yet it suffers from a certain post-Tridentine clarity which may not have been present during Henry's reign. For a long time, the missing piece of the Reformation puzzle had been what Catholics actually believed before the Reformation. Current research has focused more on the sociological (because it is more easily obtained) than on the theological, though Eamon Duffy's masterpiece, *The Stripping of the Altars*, has gone a long way in establishing the beliefs of Catholics prior to the Reformation, and (by the way) in supporting Hughes's conclusions.

Perhaps more important than the argument about to what extent these ideas, voted on by Henrician bishops, were Catholic or Lutheran is the overriding fact that matters of universal concern were being discussed and decided by a national hierarchy or, if the Act of Supremacy has any theological weight, by the prince. Hughes touched on this, but did not give it the attention it deserved. He complimented the *King's Book* for having described the Church of England as a Catholic Church, but noticed its admonition that all Christians are bound to honour and obey the "Christian kings and princes, which be the head governors under him in the particular churches". He commented mischievously:

> It is, then, a man's duty in 1543, a thing commanded him by Christ our Lord, to be what is nowadays called a Roman Catholic, if he be a Spaniard or a Frenchman or a Scot – to be a Lutheran if the Elector of Saxony is his prince – or, if he is English or Irish, to be whatever at this moment Henry VIII is.[109]

Not surprisingly, Catholic reviewers greeted Hughes's effort enthusiastically, and one commented that Hughes "has killed, once and for all, the idea that the Church of England remained Catholic in doctrine until the death of Henry VIII".[110] But even non-Catholics critics saw in Hughes's *Reformation* a valuable contribution. E. Harris Harbison of Princeton University wrote, "The most useful thing Father Hughes has done is to measure precisely the deviations from orthodox Roman doctrine in the successive dogmatic and liturgical changes. He effectively exposes the practical absurdity of Henry VIII's 'Catholicism without the Pope'."[111]

Hughes had bigger game in mind, as he devoted one entire chapter to the close relationship between the continental reformers and their English counterparts, but he singled out Henry VIII because he not only began the Reformation process in England; to a great extent he completed it. Henry was to blame not only because he changed the religion, but even more because he regarded himself as the one who *could* change the religion if need be. Elizabeth only followed Henry's lead in re-imposing the Act of Supremacy in 1559, which Hughes thought was clear: it was "the plain fact that the Royal Supremacy meant, in law, under Elizabeth and under her successors for three hundred years nearly, all that it had meant under King Henry VIII".[112]

Catholic historians had finally come to realize not only that this had happened, but that this was the very core of the English Reformation.

CONCLUSION

The achievement of Philip Hughes in regard to the English Reformation marks the end of an era. His is really the last Catholic (or pro-Catholic) historical work which would be so outspoken in regard to the centrality of theology in the English Reformation.[1] The works of David Knowles, E. E. Reynolds, and J. J. Scarisbrick have dealt with similar but narrower topics in more cautious ways. Even the latest defense of Catholic continuity, seen in the work of Eamon Duffy, has been restrained by comparison. Hughes's *Reformation in England* is a testimony to the pre-Vatican II English Catholic Church not only because of what the work accomplished, which was a professionally-written monumental statement about the causes of the English Reformation, but because of what it says about how far that Church (and historical writing) had come since the days of the first histories written in the late 1500s, and even since the days of Joseph Berington in the late 1700s.

I would like to draw several conclusions. First, Philip Hughes's conclusion – that papal authority was the central issue in the English Reformation – did not appear out of a vacuum. While Hughes's work could not have been written a century before, and certainly not two centuries before, the Catholic community had been moving gradually in Hughes's direction. What occurred was a development, an unfolding of Catholic opinion, affected by political events and a simultaneous reflection on doctrinal matters. Emancipation, once obtained in 1829, allowed Catholics to look elsewhere than politics for the causes of the Reformation – since one of its principal effects had been removed. The issue of the Temporal Power of the pope, once solved forcibly by Italian revolutionaries in 1870, placed in much clearer light the spiritual authority of the papacy unencumbered by temporal concerns. The vindication of the monasteries by Aidan Gasquet exposed other issues which were closer to the heart of the Reformation. The Anglican liturgy, shown by Edmund Bishop and Gasquet to be a liturgy *essentially and intentionally* different from the ancient liturgy, allowed Hilaire Belloc to strike home with his assertion that the English Reformation, when you came down to it, was about the pope. Philip Hughes did more than second this opinion. He produced a synthesis of the preceding opinions and demonstrated that, as the various layers were peeled away, they exposed the core of the matter – the spiritual authority of the papacy. He did not write about economic, political, or sociological issues during the Reformation because he felt that they all followed from the religious issue and were subordinate to it.

Catholics had not always agreed about these topics, and herein lies my second conclusion. The common and even current prejudice that Catholic historical writing is of one piece is refuted by an examination of those Catholic histories produced between the years 1585 to 1954. These works show that it is largely a mistake to speak about "the Catholic version" of the English Reformation, though this is still done today. Right from the very first accounts of the Reformation, two very different opinions surfaced about the political causes and effects of the Reformation. In the one camp were the Exile priests and Jesuits who saw English events in the larger light of the continental Reformation, and thus as an assault on the papacy and traditional Christianity. The pope was thus misunderstood, wronged, and responded nobly. The other camp, the Appellant priests, saw themselves as victims of an irresponsible Society of Jesus, who had misled the pope with their intrigues. For them, Elizabeth was a beneficent queen who had no choice but to react forcefully to the unnecessary pressure brought against her. These two camps remained stubbornly in place for more than two hundred years, and came out fighting anew in the late 1700s as the discussion about Catholic Emancipation heated up. All of the histories written by Catholics between 1780 and 1820 were pre-occupied with Emancipation – but even here disagreement was strong. While the Cisalpines Berington, Joseph Butler, John Lingard, and the various Catholic Committees searched desperately for a political solution to the disabilities imposed on Catholics because of the Oath of Allegiance, and proposed ingenious accommodations in their negotiations with the government, the Ultramontanists Charles Plowden and Bishop John Milner argued that religious considerations could not honestly be excluded.

Once the political question of Emancipation was laid to rest, the Cisalpine focus on politics also disappeared and other concerns, long neglected because of the political feuding, now came to the surface. Only when the Temporal Power of the pope became a pressing issue in the 1850s did this disagreement about the political aspects of the Reformation reappear, this time under the pen of Richard Simpson and Lord Acton. Here, too, the emphasis on politics faded quickly when the issue simply disappeared in the summer of 1870. So what we see is both a contemporaneous debate within Catholicism about the political ramifications of the Reformation, as well as a long-term shift in Catholic sympathies. Thus, while Plowden and Milner fought it out with Berington and Butler, and Simpson and Acton debated fiercely with Manning and the *Dublin Review* over the limits of the authority of the pope, the entire debate changed by the time we come to Belloc and Hughes. As a consequence, the Cisalpine sentiment of the late eighteenth century – "I am no papist" – became almost unthinkable by the middle of the twentieth century. Berington and Butler thought the Reformation had happened in England because individual popes had intruded where they should not have; Belloc and Hughes thought the Reformation happened in England because heads of the English government had intruded where *they* should not have.

Another area in which Catholic historians were divided was in their estimate of individual characters of the Reformation. For the most part, this divergence of opinion followed political lines. Those writers, for example, who opposed the Society of Jesus – the Appellants, Dodd, Berington, Tierney – tended to find fault with the Society and individual Jesuits of the sixteenth century, especially Robert Persons. Those writers who favoured either the abolition of religious orders or severe restrictions on religious orders, such as Berington, trod heavily on the monastic activity and individual religious of the sixteenth century. On the other hand, members of religious orders, such as Gasquet and Pollen, took care to defend their own and, at times, even attack the complacency of the secular clergy. But even here we find the notable exception of Richard Simpson, who was opposed to papal power and would have been expected to oppose the Jesuit intrusion after 1580, but who consistently maintained a very high estimate of both Campion and Persons, the latter of whom was a great exponent of papal politics.

Related to this, the opinions about various Reformation characters changed with time. Elizabeth had been regarded by the Appellants and Cisalpines (who had more perspective) as one of the most important monarchs ever to have ruled England, and certainly as the centerpiece of the English Reformation. Berington wrote that her reign was "the real era of the Reformation".[2] But as the emphasis on the Reformation ran more to the theological, Elizabeth's importance to Catholic historians faded correspondingly, so that by the time we come to Belloc, we find Elizabeth dismissed as "the puppet or figurehead of the group of new millionaires established upon the loot of religion begun in her father's time".[3]

Thirdly, as the political issues of the English Reformation faded in the distance, first after 1829 and finally after 1870, there was a growing unanimity within Catholic ranks precisely because the issues over the Reformation were increasingly theological ones. Several events (Emancipation, Irish Immigration, the Gothic Revival, the Oxford Movement) came to bear on the Catholic Church and turned Catholic attention to the religious aspects of the Reformation, and it is here that we find Catholics closely united. Not only was there a confidence that their Church, which Henry VIII and Cranmer had attacked, was the true Church, but there was a corresponding assurance that the Church of England had no claim to be a continuation of the ancient Faith. No matter how Catholic writers might disagree about the political policies of their Church, they never wavered from this assertion.

This attitude, which became more and more explicit as the twentieth century approached, first took the form of a detailed refutation of Anglican claims: the monasteries had not been as corrupt as had been thought; the Anglican liturgy was not a reform, but something entirely new; Anglicans were not validly ordained. After the First World War this assault on the Church of England became more general – with Belloc it became a question of absolutes: the papacy versus barbarism. Anglicanism, by this way of thinking, became, like Elizabeth, almost unimportant and a distraction from the real battle. Hughes joined in this sweeping condemnation: "The fact that a worldly generation got rid of monasticism was not merely an evidence of what was wrong with that generation: it was to be the one principal cause of why its worldliness grew and grew until it became the actual religion of the mass of the country."[4]

There was a confidence in the Catholic position which can still be found today. One well-respected Catholic historian at Cambridge University, a convert, told me that my research might show that the Protestants were right. Then, as he reflected on what he had just said, he leaned over the table and said, almost confidentially, "But it won't". That sentiment fairly well sums up Catholic historical writing in the period under consideration. While it would be inaccurate to say there was a Catholic "version" of the English Reformation, since there was such a range of disagreement, it would certainly be accurate to characterize what was written as "Catholic".

This is not necessarily a bad thing. Even though the Catholic historical writing of the period 1585–1954 is not, collectively, one of the great moments in Catholic thought, and at times even falls to the level of the embarrassing, still there were important discoveries made and cogent arguments raised by Catholic historians which furthered the historiography of the English Reformation. These writers, in their various ways, forced the scholarly world of England to realize that there was a second

— 150 —

opinion that could not honestly be ignored. If the history of the English Reformation is written more accurately today, it is due partly to these Catholic historians. That is reason enough not to ignore them.

NOTES

Introduction

1 Christopher Dawson, *Progress and Religion* (New York, 1938), p. 184.
2 Christopher Dawson, "Edward Gibbon and the Fall of Rome", in John Mulloy, ed., *Dynamics of World History* (New York, 1956), p. 333.
3 Hilaire Belloc, *Characters of the Reformation* (London, 1936), p. 1.
4 Geoffrey Elton, *The Practice of History* (London, 1969), p. 192. He continued, "All those booklets and pamphlets which treat historical problems by collecting extracts from historians writing about them give off a clear light only when a match is put to them."
5 G. P. Gooch, *History and Historians of the Nineteenth Century* (London, 1913), p. 569.
6 Jasper Ridley: *Elizabeth I: The Shrewdness of Virtue* (New York, 1988).
7 For a discussion of these oaths, see Ann Forster, "The Oath Tendered", *Recusant History* 14 (October 1977), pp. 86–96.
8 Forster, "The Oath Tendered", p. 93.
9 Forster, "The Oath Tendered", p. 92. The italics are mine.
10 Bernard Ward, *The Dawn of the Catholic Revival* (London, 1909), vol. 1, pp. 165–66.
11 Ward, *Dawn*, vol. 1, p. 282.
12 John Lingard to Bishop Poynter, 18 March 1821, WAA – Poynter Papers, IV, p. 5.
13 Sanders did not finish the book, but left notes for its completion in 1579, when he set out on an ill-fated mission to Ireland, which would become known as the Desmond Rebellion. Edward Rishton, a priest in exile on the continent, edited the manuscript and added new material, publishing it in Cologne in 1585. It was translated by David Lewis in 1877 and published as *The Rise and Growth of the Anglican Schism*.
14 See Henry Hallam, *The Constitutional History of England from the Accession of Henry VII to the Death of George II* (London, 1827); Edward Babington Macaulay, "Hallam's Constitutional History", *Edinburgh Review* 48 (September 1828), pp. 96–169, and Robert Southey, "Hallam's Constitutional History", *Quarterly Review* 37 (January 1826), pp. 194–260.

15 Gilbert Burnet, *Letter . . . to the Lord Bishop of Coventry and Lichfield* (1693), pp. 15–16. Cf. Edwin Jones, *English Historical Writing on the English Reformation, 1680–1730* (Ph.D. Dissertation, Cambridge, 1959), pp. 20, 113.

16 G. P. Gooch, *History and Historians*, p. 11.

17 Joseph Berington, *State and Behaviour of English Catholics* (London, 1780), Introduction.

18 Nicholas Wiseman, "The Apostolic Succession", *Dublin Review* 4 (April 1838), p. 327.

19 Dawson, "Edward Gibbon", p. 352.

I Exiles and Appellants

1 The college at Douai was founded in 1568, the English College in Rome was founded in 1579, and a third college was later established at Valladolid in 1589. Douai was moved temporarily (1578) to Rheims.

2 See John O'Malley, *Trent and All That: Renaming Catholicism in the Early Modern Era* (Cambridge MA, 2000).

3 There were always exceptions to this. The Dominicans continued to have their own rite until 1968, when they voted to accept the Roman Rite.

4 David Lewis, Introduction to Nicolas Sanders's *The Rise and Growth of the Anglican Schism* (London, 1877), p. xv. There also existed a York Rite in England. Pius V was not canonized until 1712.

5 In Sanders, p. 10.

6 Most modern writers favour "Persons", a practice followed here, except in quotations.

7 For Edmund Campion, see Peter Lake with Michael Questier, *The Antichrist's Lewd Hat* (New Haven, 2002).

8 John Allen, *Admonition to the Nobility and People of England*, 1588, in John Lingard, *History of England* (London, 1819–1830), vol. 5, pp. 660–63.

9 Sanders, pp. 25–26.

10 Sanders, p. 25. He adds, curiously, that she was "handsome to look at" and admits that she had a pretty mouth (presumably if one overlooked the projecting tooth), "was amusing in her ways, playing well on the lute, and was a good dancer". E. W. Ives claimed she "radiated sex" (*Anne Boleyn* [New York, 1986]). See also Maria Dowling, "Anne Boleyn and Reform", *Journal of Ecclesiastical History* 35 (January 1984). Robert Persons was also adept at the personal smear, as when he described Anne Askew (burnt in 1546) as "a heifer untied to any yoke," suggesting that she was sexually unbridled. There was no evidence for this allegation.

11 Allen, *Admonition*, p. 661.

12 In Introduction to Sanders (1877), pp. xxii–xxiii.

13 See John Foxe's *Acts and Monuments* (a.k.a. *The Book of Martyrs*), (London, 1583). It is interesting to note that the *Oxford Dictionary of the Christian Church* (Oxford, 1974) remarked about Sanders's history, "Though sharply criticized at the time, it is now admitted to be accurate in many of its controverted statements", p. 1234.

14 Sanders, pp. 307–8.
15 Sanders, p. 136.
16 A. G. Dickens, *The English Reformation* (London, 1964), p. 124.
17 J. J. Scarisbrick, *The Reformation and the English People* (Oxford, 1984), p. 83.
18 William Watson, *Important Considerations*, in D. M. Rogers, ed., *English Recusant Literature* (Menston, 1970), vol. 31, p. 6.
19 Watson, *Important Considerations*, p. 9.
20 Watson, *Important Considerations*, p. 10.
21 Watson, *Important Condiderations*, p. 14.
22 Watson, *Important Considerations*, p. 10.
23 Watson, *Important Considerations*, p. 17.
24 William Watson, *A Sparing Discovery* (1601), p. 6.
25 One Jesuit was accused of taking £500, another of taking £57.17s one year and £27 the next, in addition to the Jesuit "general pillage" of England and Scotland. See Watson, *A Sparing Discovery*, p. 20.
26 Watson, *A Sparing Discovery*, pp. 10–31.
27 Watson, *A Sparing Discovery*, p. 42. Watson also called Persons "their chief Polypragmon" [an officious meddler] and a "prowde Nemrod" [a tyrant].
28 Watson, *A Sparing Discovery*, Introductory Epistle.
29 Watson, *Important Considerations*, p. 9.
30 Robert Persons, *A Temperate Ward-Word*, in Rogers, ed., *English Recusant Literature*, vol. 31, p. 36.
31 See J. B. Code, *Queen Elizabeth and the English Catholic Historians* (Louvain, 1935), p. 85.
32 Watson, *Important Considerations*, p. 5.
33 Cf. John Bishop, *Courteous Conference* (1598).

II The Quest for Catholic Emancipation

1 See Antonia Fraser's *Faith and Treason* (New York, 1996) for a very readable and balanced account.
2 See Alexandra Walsham's *Church Papists* (New York, 1993).
3 Charles Dodd, *The History of Douay College* (London, 1713), p. 14.
4 Dodd, *Douay College*, p. 17.
5 Charles Dodd, *Church History of England, 5 vols. (Brussels, 1737–42)*
6 Owen Chadwick, *The Popes and European Revolution* (Oxford, 1984), p. 368.
7 Eamon Duffy, *Saints and Sinners* (New Haven, 1997), p. 195.
8 The Gordon Riots of 1780, which occurred when the government refused to abrogate the Relief Bill of 1778, saw 285 people killed and fifty-eight Catholic residences destroyed, including those of Bishops Hay in Glasgow and Walmesley in Bath.
9 Wilfrid Ward, *The Life and Times of Cardinal Wiseman* (London, 1899), vol. 1, p. 202.

10 127 signed by proxy.
11 Philip Hughes, *The Catholic Question* (London, 1929), p. 148.
12 Forster, "The Oath Tendered", p. 94
13 In other words, in canon law, there was no such thing as a proper English hierarchy, or bishops who presided over dioceses. Rather, four "bishops" were assigned to the Northern, Western, Midlands, and London District, until such time as the hierarchy could be restored. In 1840 the number of these districts was increased to eight, in anticipation of a full restoration of the hierarchy. In 1850, the hierarchy was restored.
14 Walmesley to Butler, 28 September 1789, Clifton Archives.
15 Berington to Carroll, in Peter Guilday, *The Life and Times of John Carroll* (New York, 1922), p. 132.
16 Alexander Geddes, *A Modest Apology for the Roman Catholics of Great Britain* (London, 1800), p. 80.
17 Berington, *State and Behaviour*, p. vi.
18 Joseph Berington (q.v. "Candidus"), "The Principles of Roman Catholics Stated", *Gentleman's Magazine* 57 (February 1787), p. 108.
19 Bernard Ward, *Dawn*, vol. I, p. 176.
20 See Eamon Duffy, "Ecclesiastical Democracy Detected (Part 2)", *Recusant History* 10 (1970), p. 324.
21 Joseph Berington, *The Memoirs of Gregorio Panzani* (Birmingham, 1793), p. vii.
22 Berington, *State and Behaviour*, p. 14.
23 Berington, *Panzani*, p. 18.
24 Berington, Panzani, p. 29.
25 Berington, *Panzani*, p. 14.
26 Berington, *Panzani*, p. 3. Cf. Peter Heylyn, *Ecclesia Restaurata* (London, 1661), p. 103.
27 Berington, *Panzani*, p. 4.
28 Berington, *Panzani*, p. xix.
29 Berington, *Panzani*, p. 7.
30 Berington to John Kirk, 26 December 1794, BAA, c. 1310. The italics are Berington's. Cf. Eamon Duffy, *Joseph Berington and the English Catholic Cisalpine Movement, 1782–1803* (Ph.D. Dissertation, Cambridge, 1972), p. 239. Berington's "fact" is wrong – popes did exercise this jurisdiction frequently in the first three hundred years. But if he believed it to be true, one can understand the force of his argument.
31 Joseph Berington, *Gentleman's Magazine* 69 (August 1799), pp. 653–54.
32 Berington, *Panzani*, p. 11n. The italics are Berington's.
33 Berington, *Panzani*, pp. 32–33.
34 Berington, *Panzani*, p. 34. The italics are Berington's.
35 Berington, *Panzani*, pp. 68–69.
36 Berington, *Panzani*, pp. 27–28.
37 Berington, *Panzani*, p. 51.
38 Berington, *Panzani*, p. 25.
39 Berington, *Panzani*, p. 25.

40 Berington, *Panzani*, p. 24.

41 Bernard Ward, *Dawn*, vol. 2, pp. 44–45.

42 Plowden also denounced Berington to Propaganda, which promptly confused Joseph with Bishop Charles Berington, "and the case of both of them became intricately involved in consequence" (Bernard Ward, *Dawn*, vol. 2, p. 45).

43 Charles Plowden, *Remarks on a Book Entitled "Memoirs of Gregorio Panzani"* (Liege, 1794), pp. 176, 209.

44 Plowden, *Remarks*, p. 31.

45 Plowden, *Remarks*, p. 19.

46 Plowden, *Remarks*, p. 136.

47 Plowden, *Remarks*, p. 136.

48 Berington, *Panzani*, p. xiv.

49 Bernard Ward, *Dawn*, vol. 2, p. 45n.

50 Philip Hughes, *The Reformation in England* (London, 1950–54), vol. 3, pp. 270–71. See also Marvin O'Connell, "Protestant Reformation in the British Isles", *New Catholic Encyclopedia* (New York, 1967), vol. 12, p. 180.

51 Berington, *Panzani*, p. 66.

52 For an interesting discussion of this issue, see Walsham, *Church Papists*.

53 Berington, *Panzani*, p. xxii.

54 Berington, *Gentleman's Magazine* 69 (August 1799), pp. 653–54.

55 Duffy, *Berington*, p. 289.

56 Berington, *Gentleman's Magazine* 69 (December 1799), p. 1023.

57 Berington, *Gentleman's Magazine* 69 (August 1799), p. 654.

58 Duffy, *Berington*, pp. 244–46. The manuscript detailing this schism is entitled "Reasons for altering our Church Government, or for withdrawing from it". It is unsigned, but is written in Berington's hand.

59 Berington to John Kirk, 22 April 1797, BAA, *c.* 1389. Cf. Duffy, *Berington*, p. 272.

60 Lord Acton would find this a distinct advantage many years later.

61 Charles Butler, *Historical Memoirs respecting the English, Irish, and Scottish Catholics* (London, 1819), vol. 1, p. 39.

62 Butler, *Historical Memoirs*, vol. 1, p. 40.

63 Butler, *Historical Memoirs*, vol. 1, pp. 45–46.

64 Butler, *Historical Memoirs*, vol. 1, p. 154.

65 Robert Persons, *Responsio Edictum* (1593), pp. 149, 151–53.

66 Code, *English Historians*, p. 125.

67 Butler, *Historical Memoirs*, vol. 1, p. 158.

68 Butler, *Historical Memoirs*, vol. 1, p. 158.

69 Code, *English Historians*, p. 124.

70 John Milner to Peter Gandolphy, 26 December 1817, ECA, 59.1. Gandolphy was a Jesuit who made a name for himself preaching at the Spanish Chapel in London, where he made many converts. Somehow, this letter ended up with Propaganda Fide.

71 Martin Haile and Edwin Bonney, *Life and Letters of John Lingard* (London, 1913), p. 101.

72 John Milner, *Supplementary Memoirs of the English Catholics* (London, 1820), p. v.
73 Milner, *Supplementary Memoirs*, pp. 2–3.
74 Milner, *Supplementary Memoirs*, p. 18.
75 Milner, *Supplementary Memoirs*, p. 4.
76 Hughes, *The Catholic Question*, pp. 167–68.
77 Milner, *Supplementary Memoirs*, p. 13.
78 Milner, *Supplementary Memoirs*, p. 20. Milner reinforces this in another passage by calling Pius "a canonized Pope" (p. 17).
79 Butler, *Historical Memoirs*, vol. 1, pp. 199–209.
80 In William Barry, "Milner and His Age", *Dublin Review* 150 (April 1912), p. 237.
81 William Amherst, *The History of Catholic Emancipation* (London, 1886), vol. 1, pp. 6–7.
82 Edward Norman called Milner "one of the great ecclesiastics of modern English Catholic history", *English Catholic Church in the Nineteenth Century* (Oxford, 1984), p. 36.
83 Bernard Ward, *Dawn*, vol. 1, p. 48.
84 Barry, "Milner", p. 237.
85 Milner to Gandolphy, 26 December 1817, ECA, 59.1.
86 Hughes, *The Catholic Question*, p. 168. Hughes also reported the comment of a "typical admiring contemporary" of Milner's, who described a Milnerian sermon: "Dr. Milner in a few sentences then disposed of all the calumnies of our opponents and proved conclusively the chief truths of our Holy Faith" (p. 168).
87 Butler to Robert Gradwell, 4 April 1823, ECA, 67:6.
88 Joseph Gillow, *A Literary and Biographical History, or Biographical Dictionary of the English Catholics* (London, 1885–1902), vol. 2, p. 411.
89 Milner, *Supplementary Memoirs*, p. 53.
90 Milner, *Supplementary Memoirs*, p. 53n.
91 The government wanted two assurances if it passed an emancipation act: the veto would give the crown power to approve nominations to the English Catholic episcopate; *exequator* gave the government power to examine official correspondence between the bishops and Rome. The Catholic Board recommended the acceptance of these assurances, while the bishops opposed them. When emancipation became law in 1829, these assurances were not included.
92 Hughes, *The Catholic Question*, pp. 270–71. There are different versions of these words. Hughes borrows from Bernard Ward's account (*The Eve of Catholic Emancipation* [London, 1911–12], vol. 2, p. 55). Haile and Bonney relate his closing words as "Gentlemen, you consider me unfit for your company on earth, may God make me fit for your company in heaven" (*Life of Lingard*, p. 124). Milner frequently phrased his arguments and questions in terms of God. He once wrote to Bishop Douglass, "Did you think it would be more for the honour and glory of God, that I should not be your Co-

adjutor?" Douglass replied, "I did think so, and I do think so" (Bernard Ward, *Eve*, vol. 1, p. 33).

93 Butler to Gradwell, 27 March 1819, ECA, 67:2.

94 Poynter to Gradwell, 4 May 1819, ECA, 59:4. "Msgr. Milner has provoked the Duke of Norfolk, and offended almost all of the Members of Parliament with a cheap and vulgar article just before the debate on Catholic Emancipation, which had already been published in the Orthodox Journal. This pope has noticed (?) the nasty effect." Why this letter is in Italian (and not very good Italian) is anyone's guess.

95 Philip Hughes, "The Centenary of Lingard's History", *Dublin Review* 167 (October–December 1920), p. 271.

96 J. C. H. Aveiling, *The Handle and the Axe* (London, 1976), p. 342.

97 William Roberts, *Memoirs of the Life of Hannah More* (London, 1834), vol. 3, p. 273. Cf. Duffy, Barrington, p. 314.

III *John Lingard and the Cause of Catholicism*

1 See Joseph Chinnici, *The English Catholic Enlightenment* (Shepherdstown, 1980), pp. 108–17, and Edwin Jones, *John Lingard and the Pursuit of Historical Truth* (Brighton & Portland, 2001), pp. xvi–xix.

2 John Lingard, Journal, UCA, sec. 18, F.2.11.a.

3 Lingard, *The Antiquities of the Anglo-Saxon Church* (London, 1810), p. iv. He also mentions the name of Edmond Martène (1654–1739).

4 It must be said in Lingard's favor that a re-interpretation which was, and still is, badly needed. Recently Michael Lynch has posited an identical "revision" for the Scottish Church, claiming that a Protestant descent from a Celtic (i.e. non-Roman) Church is a fiction. Cf. Michael Lynch, *Scotland: A New History* (London, 1991), pp. 26–38.

5 *Quarterly Review* 7 (1812), p. 93.

6 Lingard to Gradwell, 3 June 1819, in Haile and Bonney, p. 2.

7 Lord Acton, "The Catholic Press," *The Rambler* 11 [N.S.] (February 1859), pp. 75–76.

8 Lingard, *History*, vol. 1, pp. xvii–xviii. All quotations from Lingard's *History* are from this First Edition, unless otherwise noted.

9 John Allen, *Edinburgh Review* 42 (1825), p. 27.

10 Lingard to J. Mawman, 23 November 1820, UCA, Lingard Correspondence.

11 Lingard to Gradwell, 3 June 1819, in Haile and Bonney, *Lingard*, p. 2.

12 Haile and Bonney, *Lingard* (London, 1913), p. 109. See John Lingard, *Documents to Ascertain the Sentiments of British Catholics in Former Ages respecting the Power of the Popes* (London, 1812) and *A Review of Certain Anti-Catholic Publications* (London, 1813).

13 Lingard to John Kirk, 18 December 1819, in Haile and Bonney, *Lingard*, p. 166.

14 Lingard, *Antiquities*, p. iv.

15 Lingard was in Rome in 1817 and 1825. The rest of the time he relied on Fr. Robert Gradwell, the Rector of the English College to serve as his agent in

NOTES TO PP. 56–60

obtaining documents from both the Vatican Archives and those of Propaganda.

16 See Owen Chadwick's fascinating account in *Catholicism and History: The Opening of the Vatican Archives* (Cambridge, 1978).

17 Gradwell to Lingard, 31 July 1819, FSA – Lingard Correspondence.

18 Haile and Bonney, *Lingard*, pp. 152–153. Cardinal Consalvi prevailed, however, and Lingard was eventually admitted.

19 Lingard to Mawman, ibid., p. 195. G. P. Gooch said Froude was the first Englishman to use Simancas (*History and Historians*, p. 335) and, similarly, Macaulay claimed to have been the first to see the Barillon papers in France, and was praised by the *Times* for this. Lingard had seen them years before. See Edwin Jones, "John Lingard and the Simancas Archives", *The Historical Journal* 10 (1967), pp. 57–76.

20 Cf. Edwin Jones, *A Study of John Lingard's Historical Work* (M.A. Dissertation, University of Wales [Swansea], 1956), pp. 26–31. Lingard thought Wolsey was the originator of the conscience motif.

21 Lingard, *History*, vol. 4, pp. 121, 126.

22 Lingard, *History*, vol. 4, p. 127.

23 Lingard, *History*, vol. 4, p. 149–50.

24 Lingard, *History*, vol. 4, p. 142. Ethelred Taunton, in a later biography of Wolsey, said that Campeggio suffered from "diplomatic gout" (*Thomas Wolsey: Legate and Reformer* [London, 1902], p. 192).

25 Lingard, *History* (Sixth Edition), vol. 4, p. 249.

26 Lingard, *History*, vol. 4, p. 222.

27 Lingard, *History*, vol. 5, p. 382.

28 Lingard, *History*, vol. 5, p. 298.

29 Lingard, *History*, vol. 5, p. 300.

30 Lingard, *History*, vol. 5, p. 206.

31 Lingard, *Sentiments of British Catholics*, p. 10.

32 Lingard, *History*, vol. 5, p. 146. Later on, Lingard found evidence that this exchange never occurred (See his Fourth Edition, vol. 8, p. 251), but it is still possible that the supposed slight had entered the popular "demonology" about the pope.

33 For Mary Stuart's claim to the English throne, see M. H. Merriman, "Mary, Queen of France", *Innes Review* 38 (1987), pp. 30–52 and Jenny Wormald, *Mary Queen of Scots: A Study in Failure* (London, 1988).

34 Lingard, *History*, vol. 5, p. 147.

35 Lingard, *History*, vol. 5, pp. 384–85.

36 Lingard to E. Price, 10 January 1847, in Haile and Bonney, *Lingard*, p. 26. This refers specifically to the conduct of Campion and Persons.

37 Lingard to Gradwell, 17 October 1822, ECA, 66:9.

38 "Incestuous" because Anne Boleyn, the mother of Elizabeth, was thought by some (e.g. Nicholas Sanders) to have been the daughter of Henry VIII as well as his wife.

39 The complete text is in Lingard, *History* (Sixth Edition), vol. 6, pp. 357–59.

40 Lingard to Gradwell, 17 October 1822, ECA, 66:9.

41 Lingard to Gradwell, 17 October 1822, ECA 66:9. Cf. Lingard, *History* (Sixth Edition), vol. 6, p. 359.

42 Lingard, *History* (Sixth Edition), vol. 6, p. 359. See also Lingard to Gradwell, 30 December 1822, ECA, 66:9.

43 Lingard, *History* (Sixth Edition), vol. 6, p. 359.

44 John Allen, *Edinburgh Review* 42 (1825), p. 6. His word was not to be taken lightly, since, in the same article, he recommends Lingard's work as the best general history of England to date.

45 *Eclectic Review* 27 (March 1827), p. 251.

46 Thomas Babington Macaulay, *Edinburgh Review* 47 (May 1828) p. 361.

47 Patrick McMahon, "Lingard's History of England", *Dublin Review* 12 (May, 1842), pp. 361–62. Admittedly, McMahon is reviewing a later edition of the *History*, but he is consistent with general Catholic praise of Lingard from the beginning.

48 Mark Tierney, "Memoir of the Rev. Dr. Lingard," included in Lingard, *History* [Sixth Edition]), vol. 1, pp. 33–34.

49 In Philip Hughes, "Centenary of John Lingard's History," *Dublin Review* 167 (December 1920), p. 274.

50 Shane Leslie, *Cardinal Gasquet: A Memoir* (London, 1953), p. 7; Donald Shea, *The English Ranke: John Lingard* (New York, 1969).

51 Edwin Jones, *John Lingard and the Pursuit of Historical Truth* (Brighton & Portland, 2001), p. 207.

52 Norman Davies, Foreword to Jones, *Lingard and Historical Truth*, p. x.

53 John Kenyon, *The History Men* (London, 1983), p. 86.

54 See John Vidmar, "John Lingard's History of the English Reformation: History or Apologetics?" *Catholic Historical Review* 85, No. 3 (July 1999), pp. 383–419.

55 *Quarterly Review* 56, p. 13.

56 Sharon Turner, *The History of the Reign of Henry VIII comprising the Political History of the Commencement of the English Reformation*, 2 vols (London, 1828).

57 Rosemary O'Day, *The Debate on the English Reformation* (London, 1986), pp. 76, 79.

58 O'Day, *The Debate on the English Reformation*, p. 79.

59 Lingard, *History*, vol. 4, p. 245.

60 Lingard, *History*, vol. 4, p. 245.

61 Lingard, *History*, vol. 4, pp. 245–46.

62 See Ives, *Anne Boleyn*, pp. 383–408. Ives contends that Thomas Cromwell masterminded the adultery charge in order to save his own career. Froude, the apologist for Henry, thought that Anne was guilty only because the alternative was too unthinkable in terms of his hero-king.

63 *Eclectic Review*, 27 (March, 1827), p. 250.

64 Professor Scarisbrick claims that Henry did not mourn for Catherine. In fact, his actual response to the news of her death seems to have been quite the opposite. Scarisbrick writes, "When news of her death at Kimbolton reached London, Henry – dressed from head to toe in exultant yellow – celebrated the

event with Mass, a banquet, dancing and jousting" (*Henry VIII*, London, 1968, p. 335).

65 Lingard, *History*, vol. 4, p. 293. The italics are mine.
66 Lingard, *History* (Sixth Edition), vol. 5, p. 259.
67 Lingard, *History*, vol. 5, p. 102.
68 Lingard to Mawman, April 1823, in Haile and Bonney, *Lingard*, p. 195.
69 Lingard to Mawman, 21 December 1820, in Haile and Bonney, *Lingard*, p. 186.
70 Lingard, *History* (Sixth Edition), vol. 1, p. 3.
71 These include the papers of De la Mothe Fenelon, the French Ambassador from 1568–74.
72 Agnes Strickland, *Lives of the Queens of England* (London, 1840–48).
73 Lingard, *History* (Sixth Edition), vol. 1, p. 10. See Mark Tierney, *Dodd's Church History of England* (London, 1839–43).
74 Lingard, *History* (Sixth Edition), vol. 4, p. 232: (First Edition), vol. 4, p. 119.
75 Lingard, *History* (First Edition), vol. 4, p. 229.
76 Lingard, *History* (Sixth Edition), vol. 5, pp. 26–27.
77 Haile and Bonney, *Lingard*, pp. 183–84.
78 Aidan Gasquet, "Autobiography", in Leslie, *Gasquet*, p. 35.
79 G. R. Elton, *Reform and Renewal* (Cambridge, 1973), p. 159. Elton elaborated on this with the statement: "Of late, the inwardness of the dissolution has always been studied from the point of view of the monks; surprising things might emerge if that of the reformers were substituted and the matter considered in the light of social renewal" (p. 159).
80 Lingard, *History* (First Edition), vol. 5, p. 152: (Fourth Edition), vol. 7, p. 259.
81 Lingard, *History* (Sixth Edition), vol. 5, p. 137.
82 Lingard, *History* (First Edition), vol. 5, p. 155: (Fourth Edition), vol. 7, p. 261: (Sixth Edition), vol. 6, Note DD, pp. 326–30.
83 Lingard, *History* (First Edition), vol. 4, p. 26: (Sixth Edition), vol. 4, pp. 14, 21.
84 Jones, *A Study of John Lingard's Historical Work*, p. 11.
85 Newman saw the same problem thirty years later when he gave a series of lectures on the position of Catholics in England. He said, "I am neither assuming, nor intending to prove, that the Catholic Church comes from above . . . ; but here I am only investigating how it is she comes to be so despised and hated among us; since a religion need not incur scorn and animosity simply because it is not recognised as true . . . She is considered too absurd to be inquired into, and too corrupt to be defended, and too dangerous to be treated with equity and fair dealing. She is the victim of a prejudice which perpetuates itself, and gives birth to what it feeds upon" (John Henry Newman, *The Present Position of Catholics in England*, London, 1908, pp. 11–12).
86 Lingard, *History*, vol. 5, pp. 98–99.
87 Lingard, *History*, vol. 5, p. 99.
88 Lingard, *History*, vol. 5, p. 86.

89 Lingard, *History*, vol. 2, p. 231.

90 Appointments *riservati in petto* are those which are not made public until circumstances permit. Often these circumstances are political, wherein the public recognition of a priest's work (e.g. in Mainland China today) could jeopardize whatever work he is doing. At other times the appointment is given as an honor pending the completion of a work. The important thing about *in petto* appointments is that they take effect retroactively on their publication. Thus Lingard, assuming he was made a cardinal *in petto* in 1826, would, when his appointment was made public, have had seniority over cardinals created later. One theory is that Lingard was not made a cardinal at the time because there were no other cardinals in England, and he would have been the ranking ecclesiastic, creating awkwardness all around. The *in petto* aspect of this appointment would have had less to do with the completion of his work than with the restoration of the hierarchy, still twenty-four years away. In any case, when the pope died in 1829, the secret, and the appointment, died with him.

91 Bishop Poynter, who accompanied Lingard, felt snubbed because he had only received a silver medal.

92 Bernard Ward, *Eve*, v. 3, p. 199, and its Appendix N (pp. 350–54) for a full account.

93 Lingard to Walker, 14 September 1840, in Haile and Bonney, *Lingard*, p. 229.

94 Jones, *John Lingard and the Pursuit of Historical Truth*, pp. 202, 205.

95 Lingard, *History*, vol. 4, p. 391–2, fn. 3. Lingard relies mostly on the testimony of Thomas More. Cf. Peter Gwyn, *The King's Cardinal* (London, 1992), pp. 31–32.

96 Lingard, *History*, vol. 4, 407; Gwyn, pp. 165, 168, 172.

97 Lingard, *History*, vol. 4, p. 416; Gwyn, p. 156; Scarisbrick, *Henry VIII*, p. 107–9.

98 *Eclectic Review* 16 (July 1821), p. 11.

99 *Eclectic Review* 16 (July, 1821), p. 11.

100 *Eclectic Review* 27 (March 1827), p. 239.

101 Norman Davies, *The Isles* (London, 1999), p. 519.

IV   The Jesuits and Mark Tierney

1 Edward Norman, *The English Catholic Church in the Nineteenth Century* (Oxford, 1984), p. 64.

2 Even though the Jesuits were still suppressed in England, they continued to function, especially in areas of education. Stonyhurst, for example, had begun in 1794 when Thomas Weld had provided a house for the Jesuits exiled consecutively from St. Omers and Liege.

3 Robert Peel to John Ambrose Woods, 4 April 1829, English Dominican Archives, Woods Papers; Duke of Wellington to Woods, 20 March 1829, English Dominican Archives, Woods Papers.

4 Berington, *Panzani*, p. 459.

5 Berington, *Panzani*, pp. xvi, xvii.
6 Lingard to Walker, 13 October 1843, UCA – Lingard Papers, 1358, 1360.
7 Lingard to E. Price, 6 July 1848, FSA – Lingard Correspondence.
8 Lingard to Walker, 5 November 1849, UCA – Walker Papers.
9 Lingard to Walker, 25 December 1843, UCA – Lingard Papers, 1365.
10 Stonyhurst Archives, *Glover's Excerpts*, vol. 3, p. 189. Cf. Norman, *The English Catholic Church*, pp. 82ff.
11 Gradwell to Lingard, 31 July 1819, FSA – Lingard Correspondence.
12 Gradwell to Lingard, 31 July 1819, FSA – Lingard Correspondence.
13 See W. J. Amherst, *The History of Catholic Emancipation: 1771–1820* (London, 1886), vol. 1, p. 107.
14 William Wilds to Bramston, 25 November 1814, in Joan Connell, *The Roman Catholic Church in England, 1553–1850* (Philadelphia, 1984), p. 133.
15 Gradwell to Consalvi, 2 September 1818, ECA 59:3.
16 Tierney to Poynter, 22 April 1838, WAA – Poynter Papers. When it became apparent that the bishops would not be elected, Tierney was disconsolate and wrote, "The cause of religion, I am convinced, is thrown back at least a century by these proceedings" (Richard Schiefen, *Nicholas Wiseman and the Transformation of English Catholicism* [Shepherdstown WV, 1984], p. xii).
17 John Lingard, "Dodd's Church History of England", *Dublin Review* 6 (May 1839), p. 397.
18 Kirk to Berington, Catholic Miscellany, VI (1826), p. 262. Kirk (1760–1851) was a friend of Lingard, but even Lingard thought Kirk was "growing an old woman" (Lingard to Gradwell, 17 October 1831, WAA – Poynter Papers, IV).
19 *Dodd's Church History*, vol. 1, pp. viii–ix.
20 Tierney to Kirk, *Catholic Miscellany* 6 (October 1826), p. 332. Kirk had been discreet enough not to mention the Society of Jesus by name.
21 Tierney to Kirk, *Catholic Miscellany* 6 (October 1826), p. 332.
22 Tierney to Kirk, *Catholic Miscellany* 6 (October 1826), p. 331.
23 Lingard to Tierney, 27 March 1841, FSA – Lingard Correspondence.
24 SAA – Tierney Papers, 169, 3 September 1840.
25 Lythgoe to Tierney, 18 January 1842, FSA, SB/1
26 Lythgoe to Tierney, 23 March 1840, FSA, Package 2/1/2. Lythgoe wrote: "You may rest assured my dear Dr. Mr. Tierney that Fr. Bird, as well as every member of the Society, is most anxious that you should have every means of information that can be put within your reach, respecting the facts, touched upon in Dodd's History, and we all of us sincerely hope that the result of your labours maybe, to secure for you, the Character, of a high minded and honest Historian".
27 FSA, Package 2/1/2.
28 The fifth and final volume has an appendix of documents three times longer than the text.
29 A case could be made here that Tierney was cautioning Kirk not to insert his own views, rather than telling him the documentation precluded such inser-

tion, but the evidence remains that Tierney did not imagine that documents could be accumulated in a partisan way.

30 *Dodd's Church History*, vol. 1, p. 221.
31 *Dodd's Church History*, vol. 1, p. 221.
32 *Dodd's Church History*, vol. 3, p. 14, n. 1.
33 *Dodd's Church History*, vol. 3, p. 12, n. 1.
34 *Dodd's Church History*, vol. 3, p. 28.
35 *Dodd's Church History*, vol. 3, p. 29n.
36 *Dodd's Church History*, vol. 3, p. 13, n. 2. The only three who answered "satisfactorily" – the priest Rishton, the Jesuit Bosgrave, and the layman Orton – were "immediately pardoned", thus providing further evidence of the queen's lenience.
37 *Dodd's Church History*, vol. 3, p. 31, n. 1 (continued from p. 29).
38 *Dodd's Church History*, vol. 3, pp. 4–5.
39 *Dodd's Church History*, vol. 3, p. 45n.
40 *Gentleman's Magazine* 12 (April 1862), p. 509.
41 Lingard to Tierney, 21 April 1846, FSA – Lingard Correspondence.
42 Tierney to Lythgoe, 20 January 1842, FSA, SB/1.
43 Tierney to Oliver, c. 1842, FSA, SB/1. The italics are Tierney's. Ironically, Tierney had written to Lythgoe two years before to complain that Oliver was planning to attack the re-edition of Dodd (Tierney to Lythgoe, 27 March 1840, FSA, 2/1/2).
44 Tierney to Bodenham (son), 14 April 1840, SAA – Tierney Papers, 169.
45 Bodenham to Tierney, 9 May 1840, SAA – Tierney Papers, 169.
46 Jones to Tierney, 1 April 1835, SAA – Tierney/Rock Collection, 153.
47 SAA – Tierney Papers, Wiseman Manuscript, p. 1.
48 SAA – Tierney Papers, Wiseman Manuscript, p. 2.
49 It also proves, parenthetically, that Tierney did not stop writing his history because of paralysis in the hand. The exchange with Wiseman took place in 1857, and there are two drafts of the article, both running to twenty-four pages, written in a faintly trembling hand.
50 Wilfrid Ward, *Cardinal Wiseman*, vol. 1, p. 300.
51 Ward, *Eve*, vol. 3, p. 354.
52 Ward, *Eve*, vol. 3, p. 354.

V *The Restoration of the Middle Ages and Monasticism*

1 William Amherst, *Catholic Emancipation*, vol. 1, p. 71.
2 John Henry Newman to Edward Pusey, *Letters and Diaries*, vol. 23, p. 288.
3 William George Ward, *The Ideal of a Christian Church* (London, 1844), pp. 44, 45n. The title of this book earned for the author the nickname "Ideal" Ward.
4 John Henry Newman, *Apologia pro Vita Sua* (London, 1913), p. 217.
5 Newman to Robert Wilberforce, 26 January 1842, in Ian Ker, *John Henry Newman* (New York, 1988), p. 243.
6 William Palmer, *Treatise on the Church of Christ* (London, 1838), vol. 1, p. 455.

7 Walter Farquhar Hook, *Hear the Church* (London, 1838). This is essentially the same point as was made by the other reformers of the sixteenth century.
8 See above, p. 8.
9 See Peter Lake's *Anglicans and Puritans* (Boston, 1988).
10 Richard Simpson, *Edmund Campion* (London, 1896), p. 392. The italics are mine.
11 Some would claim that Eamon Duffy's last chapters of his *Stripping the Altars* (New Haven, 1992) continue the assault to the present.
12 Kenneth Clark, *The Gothic Revival* (London, 1928), pp. 86, 127–28. Cf. *Essays on Gothic Architecture* (London, 1802). Clark added that the chapel was built in the "most completely unattractive architectural style ever employed" (p. 86).
13 Aveling, *The Handle and the Axe*, p. 340.
14 Edward Norman, *The English Catholic Church*, p. 236.
15 Bernard Ward, *Sequel of Catholic Emancipation* (London, 1915), vol. 1, p. 87.
16 Augustus Welby Pugin, *Apology for the Contrasts*, in Ward, *Sequel*, vol. 1, p. 87.
17 Augustus Welby Pugin, *Contrasts* (London, 1841), p. 7.
18 Pugin, *Contrasts*, p. 7.
19 Pugin, *Apology for the Contrasts*, in Ward, *Sequel*, vol. 1, p. 87. He retracted this statement in the 1841 edition of *Contrasts*, admitting that he overstated his opinion that Protestantism was the primary cause of this degraded condition, while he should have said that Protestantism was the effect of some more powerful agency, i.e. Catholic degeneracy (p. 111).
20 In John Glen Harries, *Pugin: An Illustrated Life of Augustus Welby Northmore Pugin, 1812–1852* (Princes Risborough, 1994), p. 10.
21 Clark, *The Gothic Revival*, p. 188.
22 Pugin, *Contrasts*, p. 29.
23 Pugin, *Contrasts*, p. 30.
24 David Knowles, "Cardinal Gasquet as an Historian", in *The Historian and Character* (Cambridge, 1963), p. 244. This essay was originally given as the Creighton Lecture in History at the University of London in 1956.
25 Aidan Gasquet, "Autobiography", in Leslie, *Gasquet*, p. 35.
26 Gooch called Froude's *History* "the most brilliant historical work produced in England in the middle of the [nineteenth] century, with the single exception of Macaulay" (*History and Historians*, p. 334).
27 James Anthony Froude, *History of England* (London, 1856–70), vol. 2, p. 413.
28 For a discussion of the finality of the Henrician Reformation, see Christopher Haigh, *English Reformations* (Oxford, 1993) and Susan Brigden, *New Worlds, Lost Worlds: The Rule of the Tudors 1485–1603* (New York, 2001). Haigh's thesis is that *none* of the Reformations (Henrician, Edwardian, or Elizabethan) was conclusive. For a critique of Haigh's work, see John Vidmar's review in the *Thomist* 62 (July 1995) and Susan Wabuda's review in the *Journal of British Studies* 35 (April 1996).

29 See John Hatcher, "England in the Aftermath of the Black Death", *Past & Present* 144 (August 1994), for a good overview of the debate.

30 Aidan Gasquet, *Henry VIII and the English Monasteries* (London, 1888–89), vol. 1, p. 9. A study about the French capitulation in World War II makes a similar claim – that the generation which had experienced Verdun did not want to fight anymore (Alistair Horne, *The Price of Glory* [London, 1977]).

31 Aidan Gasquet, *The Eve of the Reformation* (London, 1900), pp. 184–85.

32 The friars were unquestionably the most popular preachers in England, but could often live in houses large enough to be confused with "monasteries". See Susan Wabuda, *Preaching during the English Reformation* (Cambridge, 2002), especially Chapter 3, "Flocking companies of Friars", pp. 107–46.

33 Scarisbrick, *Henry VIII*, p. 248.

34 Gasquet, *Henry VIII*, vol. 1, p. 248.

35 Knowles, "Gasquet", p. 245.

36 Gasquet, *Henry VIII*, vol. 1, p. 437.

37 Gasquet, *Henry VIII*, vol. 1, pp. 439–40.

38 Gasquet, *Henry VIII*, vol. 1, pp. 391–92.

39 Gasquet, *Henry VIII*, vol. 1, p. 423. Cf. Samuel Maitland, *Essays on the Reformation* (London, 1899), p. 182. Maitland (1792–1866) was the librarian of Lambeth Palace and a professional historian who espoused High Church views of the English Reformation.

40 Gasquet, *Henry VIII*, vol. 1, p. 387n.

41 Gasquet, *Henry VIII*, vol. 1, pp. 387–88.

42 Gasquet, *Henry VIII*, vol. 1, p. 384. Even more bizarre was the case of Robert Burgoyne, cited in Scarisbrick's *Reformation and the English People* (Oxford, 1984), pp. 8–9. Burgoyne was an auditor for the Court of Augmentations, the agency in charge of the dissolution. Yet he, just a few weeks before the first act for the dissolution of the chantries, provided for a chantry to be set up in his native parish, "with a priest who could sing 'playne songe and deskante well', and teach grammar". See also Alan Kreider, *English Chantries: the Road to Dissolution* (Harvard, 1979).

43 Gasquet, *Henry VIII*, vol. 1, p. 430.

44 Belloc, *Characters of the Reformation*, pp. 96, 123.

45 Scarisbrick, *Henry VIII*, p. 380.

46 Gasquet, *Henry VIII*, vol. 1, pp. 469–70.

47 Gasquet, *Henry VIII*, vol. 1, p. 469.

48 Gasquet, *Henry VIII*, vol. 1, p. 378.

49 Gasquet, *Henry VIII*, vol. 2, p. 446.

50 Gasquet, *Henry VIII*, vol. 2, p. 491.

51 Gasquet, *Henry VIII*, vol. 1, p. 420. The italics are Gasquet's.

52 Gasquet, *Henry VIII*, vol. 1, ch. 9.

53 Gasquet, *Henry VIII*, vol. 1, p. 355.

54 Knowles, "Gasquet", p. 262, and Leslie, *Gasquet*, p. 38.

55 Henry Manning, "Henry VIII and the English Monasteries", *Dublin Review* 102 (April 1888), p. 244.

56 Maisie Ward, *The Wilfrid Wards and the Transition* (London, 1934), pp. 211, 213.
57 Gasquet, *Henry VIII*, vol. 1, p. xi.
58 In Gasquet, *Henry VIII*, vol 2, p. 497.
59 Lord Acton, *Lectures on Modern History* (London, 1906), p. 318.
60 Acton to Gasquet, 12 June 1890, in Leslie, *Gasquet*, p. 113.
61 Knowles, "Gasquet", p. 260.
62 Aidan Gasquet and Edmund Bishop, *Edward VI and the Book of Common Prayer* (London, 1890), p. 118.
63 Knowles, "Gasquet", p. 257.
64 Gairdner to Gasquet, 23 October 1908, DA – Gasquet Papers, no. 964.
65 Haile and Bonney, *Lingard*, pp. 183–84.
66 David Knowles, *The Religious Orders in England* (Cambridge, 1959), vol. 3, p. 302.
67 Knowles, *Religious Orders*, vol. 3, pp. 302–3.
68 Gasquet, *Eve*, p. 8. See Edwin Jones, *The English Nation: the Great Myth* (Phoenix Mill, Gloucestershire, 2000) for an interesting discussion of England's isolation from the continent after the Reformation.
69 Knowles, *Religious Orders*, vol. 3, p. 90.
70 Gasquet, *Eve*, p. 337.
71 Knowles, *Religious Orders*, vol. 3, pp. 260–63.
72 Much more effective was Lingard's suspicion of government duplicity in its treatment of the monks at Canterbury: "[They] have suffered the most in reputation: they are charged with habitually indulging the most immoral and shameful propensities. Yet, when archbishop Cranmer named the clergy for the service of his cathedral, he selected from these very men no fewer than eight prebendaries, ten minor canons, nine scholars, and two choristers" (Lingard, *History*, vol. 4, p. 261). See Barrie Dobson, "The Monks of Canterbury in the Later Middle Ages" and Patrick Collinson, "The Protestant Cathedral, 1541–1660" in Patrick Collinson; Nigel Ramsey; and Margaret Sparks, eds., *A History of Canterbury Cathedral* (Oxford, 1995), pp. 154–203. Dobson observed that Canterbury "has the unusual distinction of being the only ex-monastic cathedral of Tudor England whose first dean was not its last prior" (p. 152).
73 Gasquet became Abbot-President of the Benedictines in 1900, in which capacity he served until 1914. Other duties included membership on the Commission on Anglican Orders, membership on the Commission on the Vulgate (1907), Prefect of the Vatican Archives (1917), and Vatican Librarian (1919).
74 Knowles, "Gasquet", p. 254.
75 G. R. Elton, *Reform and Renewal* (Cambridge, 1973), p. 159.
76 Elton, *Reform and Renewal*, p. 159.
77 Elton, *Reform and Renewal*, pp. 158–66.
78 A. G. Dickens has given a convincing case that even Cromwell was, in some sense, motivated by religious concerns (*The English Reformation*, pp. 135–38).

79 Knowles, *Religious Orders*, vol. 3, p. ix.
80 Knowles, *Religious Orders*, vol. 3, p. 318.
81 Knowles, *Religious Orders*, vol. 3, pp. 294, 414.
82 Knowles, *Religious Orders*, vol. 3, p. 291.
83 Knowles, *Religious Orders*, vol. 3, pp. 321–22.
84 Gasquet, *Henry VIII*, vol. 2, p. 324.
85 Knowles, *Religious Orders*, vol. 3, p. 387.
86 See Elton, *Reform and Renewal*; Dickens, *English Reformation*, pp. 167–81, and *Thomas Cromwell and the English Reformation* (London, 1959).
87 Elton, *England under the Tudors* (London, 1974), p. 484. O'Day, *The Debate on the English Reformation*.

VI *Archbishop Cranmer and the Anglican Liturgy*

1   A. F. Pollard, *Henry VIII* (New York, 1966), p. 187. The work was originally published in 1902.
2   Lingard, *History*, vol. 4, pp. 242–43.
3   Lingard, *History*, vol. 4, p. 263.
4   Hilaire Belloc, *Characters of the Reformation* (London, 1936), pp. 139, 143.
5   Belloc, *Characters*, pp. 131–32.
6   Hilaire Belloc, *Cranmer* (London, 1931).
7   Belloc, *Cranmer*, p. 157.
8   Belloc, *Cranmer*, p. 159.
9   Belloc, *Cranmer*, pp. 109–14.
10 Hughes, *Reformation in England*, vol. 1, p. 243.
11 Hughes, *Reformation in England*, vol. 1, pp. 243–44.
12 Dowling, "Anne Boleyn and Reform", p. 45.
13 Dowling, "Anne Boleyn and Reform", p. 45.
14 Diarmaid MacCulloch, *Thomas Cranmer: a Life* (New Haven, 1996), p. 157.
15 Martin Haile, *The Life of Reginald Pole* (London, 1910), p. 485.
16 Mary Jean Stone, *The Church in English History* (Edinburgh, 1907), p. 199.
17 Stone, *The Church in English History*, p. 199.
18 Belloc, *Characters*, p. 137.
19 In Nigel Abercrombie, *The Life and Work of Edmund Bishop* (London, 1959), p. 156. For further details on Bishop's life, see Cuthbert Butler's article in the *Dictionary of National Biography, 1912–1921* (London, 1927), p. 47.
20 Leslie, *Gasquet*, p. 43.
21 Edmund Bishop and Aidan Gasquet, *Edward VI and the Book of Common Prayer* (London, 1890), p. 182.
22 Bishop and Gasquet, *Edward VI*, pp. 2–3.
23 Bishop and Gasquet, *Edward VI*, p. 36. Subsequent revisions of the *Prayer Book* corrected this, adding "a breadth or even a certain dignity" (p. 36).
24 Bishop and Gasquet, *Edward VI*, p. 217.
25 Bishop and Gasquet, *Edward VI*, p. 217.
26 Bishop and Gasquet, *Edward VI*, p. 228.
27 Bishop and Gasquet, *Edward VI*, p. 196. The authors add mischievously, "Only the collection remained".

28 Bishop and Gasquet, *Edward VI*, p. 234.
29 Bishop and Gasquet, *Edward VI*, p. 235.
30 Bishop and Gasquet, *Edward VI*, pp. 130–31.
31 Bishop and Gasquet, *Edward VI*, p. 129.
32 Bishop and Gasquet, *Edward VI*, pp. 42–43.
33 Bishop and Gasquet, *Edward VI*, p. 12.
34 Bishop and Gasquet, *Edward VI*, p. 252.
35 Bishop and Gasquet, *Edward VI*, p. 106.
36 Bishop and Gasquet, *Edward VI*, p. 155.
37 Gasquet, Memorandum, 14 August 1896, DA – Gasquet Papers, no. 942.
38 In Wilfrid Ward, *Cardinal Wiseman*, vol. 1, p. 300.
39 Lingard to Wiseman, 25 February 1840, UCA – Lingard Papers, 350.
40 SAA – Tierney Papers, no date.
41 SAA – Tierney Papers, no date (*c.* 1857).
42 Bishop's biographer stated that, while *Edward VI* hardly mentioned the question of Anglican Orders, "the whole book demonstrates incidentally the historical fact that Cranmer and his associates were moved by the single impulse to eradicate from the formularies of the church of England, as foreign to the very basis of her doctrinal structures and essence, the idea of the Mass" (Abercrombie, *Edmund Bishop*, p. 154).
43 In Abercrombie, *Edmund Bishop*, pp. 228–29.
44 In Francis Clark, *Anglican Orders* (London, 1960), p. 5.
45 The encyclical never said *whose* intention was defective, nor what was specifically defective about it.
46 See John Jay Hughes, *Absolutely Null and Utterly Void* (Washington, 1968). The only other Anglican to have himself ordained was the Bishop of London in the 1990s.
47 Canon J. Moyes, "Double-Dealing in Worship", in the *Tablet*, 3 January 1891. These essays were gathered together in one volume, entitled *Aspects of Anglicanism* (London, 1906).

VII *The Church of England and the Papacy*

1 What he permitted were altar candles, the Agnus Dei, the eastward position in prayer, and the ablutions. Prohibited were the public mixing of the chalice, the concealment of the manual acts at the Consecration, and the Final Blessing.
2 Moyes, *Aspects of Anglicanism*, pp. 36–37.
3 Clark, *Anglican Orders* (London, 1956), p. 10.
4 In Clark, *Anglican Orders*, p. 10.
5 Newman to Capes, 19 January 1857, in Aidan Gasquet, *Lord Acton and His Circle* (London, 1906), p. xxiv.
6 C. W. Russell, "St. Pius V, "the Father of Christendom", *Dublin Review* 59 (October 1866), pp. 273–304.
7 Thomas Flanagan, *History of the Church in England* (London, 1857), vol. 2, p. 80.

8 Flanagan, *Church in England*, vol. 2, pp. 77–78.

9 Flanagan, *Church in England*, vol. 2, pp. 181, 180.

10 Richard Simpson, *Under the Penal Laws* (London, 1930), p. 27.

11 Simpson, *Campion*, p. 331.

12 Simpson, *Campion*, p. 331–32.

13 Simpson, *Campion*, p. 281.

14 Simpson, *Campion*, pp. 233–34.

15 Simpson, *Campion*, pp. 88–89.

16 Simpson, *Campion*, p. 482.

17 Simpson, *Campion*, p. 228.

18 Simpson, *Campion*, p. 489.

19 Simpson, Campion, p. 486.

20 Joseph de Maistre, *Du Pape* (Paris, 1872 [New Edition]), p. 13. The first edition was published in 1819.

21 Henry Manning, *The Temporal Power* (London, 1862), pp. xxiv ff., and *The Temporal Sovereignty of the Popes* (London, 1860).

22 William George Ward, "Minor Doctrinal Judgements", *Dublin Review* 61 (October 1867), pp. 364–65.

23 William George Ward, "The Definition of Papal Infallibility", *Dublin Review* 68 (January 1871), p. 205.

24 Simpson to Gladstone, 28 December 1874, in Joseph Altholz, *The Liberal Catholic Movement in England, 1848–1864* (Montreal, 1962), p. 246.

25 Lord Acton, "The Counter-Reformation", in *Lectures on Modern History*, pp. 109–10.

26 Altholz, *Liberal Catholics*, p. 1.

27 Acton to Mary Gladstone, 30 March 1884, in *The Letters of Lord Acton to Mary Gladstone*, ed. Herbert Paul (London, 1904), pp. 186–87.

28 Acton to Mary Gladstone, 30 March 1884, in *Letters of Lord Acton*, pp. 185–86.

29 Lord Acton, Kidderminster *Shuttle*, 31 January 1871, in Damien McElrath, *Lord Acton: the Decisive Decade* (Louvain, 1970), p. 33.

30 Lord Acton, "Political System of the Popes", in *Essays on Church and State*, ed. Douglas Woodruff (London, 1952), pp. 136–37.

31 Lord Acton, "Political System of the Popes", in *Essays on Church and State*, p. 159.

32 Lord Acton, Letter to the *Times*, 24 November 1874.

33 Lord Acton, "The Catholic Press", *Rambler*, New Series 11 (February 1859), p. 74.

34 Lord Acton, *English Historical Review* 3 (October 1888), p. 788.

35 Lord Acton, *Lectures on the French Revolution* (London, 1910), p. 373. The italics are mine.

36 Lord Acton, in Herbert Butterfield, "Acton: His Training, Methods and Intellectual System", *Studies in Diplomatic History and Historiography*, ed. A. O. Sarkissian (London, 1961), p. 196.

37 Gasquet, *Eve*, p. 81.

38 Gasquet, *Eve*, p. 93.

39 Gasquet, *Eve*, p. 98.
40 Gasquet, *Henry VIII*, vol. 2, p. 333. For Gairdner and Maitland on the Roman Curia, see Gasquet, *Eve*, p. 72.
41 See Leslie, *Gasquet*, pp. 80–90. Gasquet was also considered for the see of Southwark in 1904.
42 William Schoenl, *The Intellectual Crisis in English Catholicism* (New York, 1982).
43 John Hungerford Pollen, *English Catholics in the Reign of Elizabeth* (London, 1920), p. 38.
44 Pollen, *English Catholics*, p. 142.
45 Evelyn Waugh, *Edmund Campion* (London, 1935), pp. 42, 44.
46 Pollen, *English Catholics*, p. 156.
47 Pollen, *English Catholics*, p. vii.
48 Pollen, *English Catholics*, p. 293.
49 Pollen, *English Catholics*, p. 297.
50 Robert Hugh Benson, *By What Authority* (London, 1904), p. 47.
51 Benson, *By What Authority*, p. 234.
52 This position is essentially the same as Rome's today, in its protest to the European Economic Community's "mission statement", which leaves out all mention of Christianity in its description of Europe's formation and development.
53 Hilaire Belloc, *The Crisis of Civilisation* (New York, 1937), pp. 1–2.
54 Belloc, *Europe and the Faith* (London, 1920), p. 289.
55 Belloc, *Characters of the Reformation*, pp. 144–45.
56 G. K. Chesterton, *Chaucer: A Study* (New York, 1932), p. 238.
57 Belloc, *Characters of the Reformation*, p. 193.
58 Duffy, *The Stripping of the Altars*, p. 593.
59 Belloc, *Characters of the Reformation*, pp. 115–21.
60 J. R. Burrow, *A Liberal Descent: Victorian Historians and the English Past* (Cambridge, 1981), pp. 254–55.
61 Burrow, *A Liberal Descent*, p. 251.
62 J. R. Froude, *Short Studies on Great Themes* (London, 1882), vol. 1, p. 27.
63 Belloc, *Europe and the Faith*, p. 4. The italics are Belloc's.
64 G. G. Coulton, "Mr. Belloc as Historian", *Medieval Studies*, 19 (London, 1930), p. 3. Froude saw the accumulation of accidents as adding up to "Providence".
65 Robert Speaight, *The Life of Hilaire Belloc* (New York, 1957), p. 94.
66 Hilaire Belloc, "On the Method of History", in *Selected Essays*, ed. J. B. Morton (New York, 1957), p. 135.
67 Hilaire Belloc, "The Character of the Historical Novel", in *One Thing and Another*, ed. Patrick Cahill (London, 1955), p. 25.
68 H. G. Wells, *Mr. Belloc Objects to "The Outline of History"* (London, 1926), p. 8.
69 Wells, *Mr. Belloc Objects*, p. 10.
70 Coulton, "Mr. Belloc as Historian", p. 6
71 E. E. Reynolds, "The Chesterbelloc", *The Tablet* (21 October 1978), p. 1016.

72 Herbert Thurston, S. J., "Celt, Roman or Teuton", *The Month* 146 (July 1925), pp. 23, 24, 25.

73 Robert Speaight, *The Life of Hilaire Belloc* (New York, 1957), p. 410. Chesterton, whose opinions about history depended almost entirely on those of Belloc, was no better. He prided himself that his *Short History of England* did not include a single date.

74 In Speaight, *Life of Belloc*, p. 392.

75 Belloc to Duff Cooper, 17 January 1930, BC – Belloc Collection.

76 A. N. Wilson, *Hilaire Belloc* (London, 1984), p. 318.

77 Wilfrid Sheed, *Frank and Maisie* (New York, 1985), p. 68.

78 In Speaight, *Belloc*, p. 429.

79 Wilson, *Belloc*, p. 321.

80 Reynolds to the author, 7 February 1979.

81 Wilson, *Belloc*, p. 203.

82 Blackwell to Belloc, *c.* 1895, BC – Belloc Collection.

83 Wilson, *Belloc*, p. 350.

84 Edward Hutton, "Catholic Literature, 1850–1950", in *The English Catholics*, ed. George Andrew Beck (London, 1950), p. 541.

85 Christopher Hollis, *The Mind of Chesterton* (Coral Gables, FL, 1970), p. 20.

86 Hughes, *Reformation*, vol. 1, p. 342.

87 Hughes, *Reformation*, vol. 1, p. 254.

88 Hughes, *Reformation*, vol. 1, p. 290; vol. 2, p. 342.

89 This was not through any neglect on the part of Hughes. Several learned societies had been publishing manuscripts of state papers and letters, so that most of what Hughes needed was in public libraries. Unfortunately for Hughes, the great explosion of local records (chantry accounts, burial records, tax returns, church census reports, etc.) was a few years away.

90 J. J. Scarisbrick, "Religio Depopulata", *Dublin Review* 228 (Third Quarter, 1954), p. 361.

91 Hughes, *Reformation*, vol. 2, p. 275.

92 Hughes, *Reformation*, vol. 2, p. 278.

93 Hughes, *Reformation*, vol. 2, pp. 279–86.

94 Hughes, *Reformation*, vol. 2, pp. 260–62.

95 Hughes, *Reformation*, vol. 2, pp. 265–73.

96 Hughes, *Reformation*, vol. 2, pp. 301–2.

97 Hughes, *Reformation*, vol. 1, p. 286. Hughes also wrote, "So far, indeed, we have not met, among those who favour 'the king's proceedings', his counselors, his agents, one single leading character who is really a good man – they are wicked from ambition, or from greed, or from cowardice, or wicked from the deliberate consent to evil in the hope that 'good' may ultimately be achieved" (p. 75).

98 Hughes, *Reformation*, vol. 1, p. 288.

99 Hughes, *Reformation*, vol. 1, pp. 322, 328.

100 Hughes, *Reformation*, vol. 2, p. 156. "It is not surprising that when the government's only interest in colleges was the profit to be made by confis-

cating their properties, university life seemed about to disappear altogether" (p. 156).

101 Hughes, *Reformation*, vol. 1, pp. 45–46; vol. 2, pp. 161–62.
102 Hughes, *Reformation*, vol. 1, pp. 296–320.
103 Hughes, *Reformation*, vol. 1, p. 196.
104 Hughes, *Reformation*, vol. 1, p. 196.
105 Dickens, *English Reformation*, p. 176.
106 Dickens, *English Reformation*, p. 184.
107 Hughes, *Reformation*, vol. 2, p. 48.
108 Hughes, *Reformation*, vol. 2, p. 56.
109 Hughes, *Reformation*, vol. 2, p. 47.
110 K. M. Booth, "The English Reformation", *Month* 197 (May 1954), p. 309.
111 E. Harris Harbison, *Church History* 23 (December 1954), p. 374.
112 Hughes, *ReformationReformation*, vol. 3, p. 73.

Conclusion

1 Derek Holmes, whose *Short History of the Catholic Church* (New York, 1984) can be seen as an updated version of Fr. Hughes's own *Popular History of the Catholic Church* (New York, 1949), commented to me in private conversation, "It was amazing what Hughes got away with".
2 Berington, *State and Behaviour*, p. 14.
3 Belloc, *Characters of the Reformation*, p. 166.
4 Hughes, *Reformation*, vol. 1, p. 323.

BIBLIOGRAPHY

1. Manuscript Sources

Archives of the Archdiocese of Southwark   Tierney Collection
Archives of the Archdiocese of Westminster   Poynter Papers
     Wiseman Papers
Archives of Downside Abbey   Gasquet Papers
Archives of the Duke of Norfolk   Tierney Papers
Boston College Library   Belloc Collection
Cambridge University Library
English Dominican Archives   Woods Papers
English College Archives
Jesuit Archives at Farm Street   Tierney Papers

The Jesuit Archives also contain many of Lingard's letters on subjects unrelated to the Society of Jesus. The archivist of the collection thought that these letters came to Farm Street in the confusion following Tierney's death. Tierney had not returned several collections and it was uncertain to whom they belonged. Westminster, in order to compensate those religious orders who were missing material lent to Tierney, may have given them whatever material was at hand.

National Library of Scotland
Ushaw College Archives   Lingard Papers

2. Early Printed Books

Allen, William. *Admonition to the Nobility and People of England.* Antwerp, 1588. Reprinted in Lingard's *History*, vol. 5. Pp. 660–63.

Bishop, John. *Courteous Conference.* 1598.

Cecil, William. *A Declaration of the Favourable Dealing of her Majesties Commissioners Appointed for the Examination of Certain Traitors.* London, 1583.

Persons, Robert. *A Temperate Ward-Word.* In Rogers, D. M., ed. *English Recusant Literature.* Vol. 31. Menston, 1970.

Watson, William. *Important Considerations*. 1601. In Rogers, D. M., ed. *English Recusant Literature*. Vol. 31. Menston, 1970.

——. *A Sparing Discoverie of our English Jesuits*. 1601.

3. Other Primary Printed Sources

Acton, Lord John. "The Catholic Press". *Rambler*, N.S. 11, February 1859, pp. 73–90.

——. *Essays on Church and State*. Ed. Douglas Woodruff. London, 1952.

——. *Lectures on Modern History*. Eds. J. N. Figgis and R. V. Lawrence. London, 1906.

——. *The Letters of Lord Acton to Mary Gladstone*. Ed. Herbert Paul. London, 1904.

Allen, John. *Reply to Dr. Lingard's Vindication*. London 1827. Lingard replied to this in the second edition of his *Vindication*.

Belloc, Hilaire. *The Case of Dr. Coulton*. London, 1938.

——. *Characters of the Reformation*. London, 1936.

——. *Cranmer*. London, 1936.

——. *Europe and the Faith*. London, 1920.

——. *Elizabethan Commentary*. London, 1942.

——. *The Great Heresies*. London, 1938.

——. *A History of England*. Vol. 5. London, 1931.

——. *How the Reformation Happened*. London, 1928.

——. *One Thing and Another*. Ed. J. B. Morton. New York, 1957.

——. *Wolsey*. London, 1930.

Benson, Robert Hugh. *By What Authority*. London, 1904.

——. *Come Rack! Come Rope!* London, 1912.

——. *The King's Achievement*. London, 1905.

——. *The Queen's Tragedy*. London, 1906.

Berington, Joseph. *The Memoirs of Gregorio Panzani*. Birmingham, 1793.

——. "The Principles of Roman Catholics Stated (Part 1)". *Gentleman's Magazine*, 57, January 1787, pp. 25–26.

——. "The Principles of Roman Catholics Stated (Part 2)". *Gentleman's Magazine*, 57, February 1787, pp. 107–8.

——. *State and Behaviour of English Catholics*. London, 1780.

Bridgett, Thomas. "The Defender of the Faith". *Dublin Review*, 96, April 1885.

——. *Life and Writings of Sir Thomas More*. London, 1891.

——. *Life of Blessed John Fisher*. London, 1890.

——. and T. F. Knox. *Queen Elizabeth and the Catholic Hierarchy*. London, 1889.

Butler, Charles. *Historical Memoirs Respecting the English, Irish, and Scottish Catholics, From the Reformation to the Present Time*. London, 1819.

——. *The Execution of Justice*. London, 1583.

Cobbett, William. *A History of the Protestant Reformation*. London, 1824.

Coulton, G. G. *Five Centuries of Religion*. Cambridge, 1923–1950.

——. *A Premium upon Falsehood*. Taunton, 1939.

——. *Roman Catholic History*. London, 1925.

——. *Roman Catholic Propaganda*. Taunton, 1936.

——. *The Scandal of Cardinal Gasquet*. Taunton, 1937.

Dawson, Christopher. *The Dividing of Christendom*. New York, 1965.

——. "Edward Gibbon and the Fall of Rome". In Mulloy, John, ed. *Dynamics of World History*. New York, 1956.

Dodd, Charles. *The Church History of England*. 3 Vols. Brussels, 1737–42.

——. *The History of the English College at Doway*. London, 1713.

——. *The Secret Policy of the English Society of Jesus*. London, 1715.

Finlason, W. F. "The Age of Morton, Wolsey, and More". *Dublin Review*, 40, March 1856, pp. 1–66.

——. "An Anglican Apology for Tyranny". *Dublin Review*, 41, December 1856, pp. 307–44.

——. "Catholic Fiction". *Dublin Review*, 31, October 1878, pp. 439–62. It states that all fiction is bad in principle (because it is necessarily fictitious and therefore false), but that Catholic fiction is acceptable because it is Catholic.

——. "History in Fiction". *Dublin Review*, 45, December 1858, pp. 328–64.

——. "Froude's History of England". *Dublin Review*, 44, June 1858, pp. 445–85.

——. "The Reformation, the Result of Tyranny". *Dublin Review*, 41, September 1856, pp. 1–27.

Flanagan, Thomas. "The Anglo-Saxon and Ancient British Churches". *Dublin Review*, 18, March 1845, pp. 128–74.

——. *A History of the Church in England*. 2 Vols. London, 1857.

——. "Mary Queen of Scots". *Dublin Review*, 19, September 1845, pp. 195–229.

——. "Suppression of Monasteries". *Dublin Review*, 16, March 1844, pp. 237–60.

Gasquet, Aidan. "Archbishop Morton and St. Albans". *Tablet*, 17, October 1908, pp. 603–4.

——. *Cardinal Pole and His Early Friends*. London, 1927.

——. and Edmund Bishop. *Edward VI and the Book of Common Prayer*. London, 1890.

——. *England's Breach with Rome*. London, 1920.

——. *The Eve of the Reformation*. London, 1900.

——. *Henry VIII and the English Monasteries*. 2 Vols. London, 1888–89.

——. *The Last Abbot of Glastonbury*. London, 1895.

——. *Lord Acton and His Circle*. London, 1906.

Geddes, Alexander. *A Modest Apology for the Roman Catholics of Great Britain*. London, 1800.

Haile, Martin. *The Life of Reginald Pole*. London, 1910.

——. and Bonney, Edwin. *Life and Letters of John Lingard*. London, 1913.

Hughes, Philip. *The Catholic Question: 1688–1829*. London, 1929.

——. "The Centenary of John Lingard's History". *Dublin Review*, 167, December 1920, pp. 259–74.

——. *The Reformation in England*. 3 Vols. London, 1950–54.

Keough, E. S. and Doyle, Thomas. "Replies to Lord Acton". *Dublin Review*, 24, January 1875, pp. 127–53.

Knowles, David. "Cardinal Gasquet as an Historian". In *The Historian and Character and Other Essays*. Cambridge, 1963. Pp. 240–63.

——. *The Religious Orders in England*. Vol. 3. Cambridge, 1959.

Lingard, John. "The Ancient Church of England, and the Liturgy of the Anglican Church". *Dublin Review*, 9, August 1841, pp. 167–96.

——. *Antiquities of the Anglo-Saxon Church*. 2 Vols. Newcastle, 1806.

——. "Did the Anglican Church Reform Itself?" *Dublin Review*, 8, May 1840, pp. 334–73.

——. *Documents to Ascertain the Sentiments of British Catholics in former ages respecting the Power of the Popes*. London, 1812.

——. "Dodd's Church History of England". *Dublin Review*, 6, May 1839, pp. 395–415.

——. *History of England*. 8 Vols. London, 1819–30.

——. *A Review of Certain Anti-Catholic Publications*. London, 1813.

——. *A Vindication of Certain Passages in the Fourth and Fifth Volumes of the History of England*. London, 1826.

McCabe, W. B. "Recent Writers on the Temporal Sovereignty of the Pope". *Dublin Review*, 41, December 1856, pp. 344–82.

Manning, Henry. "Henry VIII and the English Monasteries". *Dublin Review*, 102, April 1888, pp. 243–56.

——. "Henry VIII and the Suppression of the Greater Monasteries". *Dublin Review*, 104, April 1889, pp. 243–59.

——. *The Temporal Power*. London, 1862.

——. *The Temporal Sovereignty of the Popes*. London, 1860.

Milner, John. *Essays on Gothic Architecture*. London, 1802.

——. *The History, Civil and Ecclesiastical, and Survey of the Antiquities of Winchester*. Winchester, 1801.

——. *Supplementary Memoirs of English Catholics*. London, 1820.

Morris, John. "Jesuits and Seculars in the Reign of Elizabeth". *Dublin Review*, 106, April 1890, pp. 243–55.

___ *Troubles of Our Catholic Forefathers*. London, 1872.

Moyes, J. *Aspects of Anglicanism*. London, 1906.

Newman, John Henry. *The Present Position of Catholics in England*. London, 1908.

O'Leary, Arthur. *Miscellaneous Tracts on Several Interesting Subjects*. London, 1791.

Plowden, Charles. *Considerations on the Modern Opinion of the Fallibility of the Holy See*. London, 1790.

——. *Remarks on a Book Entitled Memoirs of Gregorio Panzani*. Liege, 1794.

Pollen, John Hungerford. "The Alleged Papal Sanction of the Anglican Liturgy". *Month*, 100, September 1902, pp. 274–80.

——. *The English Catholics in the Reign of Queen Elizabeth*. London, 1920.

——. *The Journey of Edmund Campion*. London, 1897.

——. *The Memoirs of Fr. Robert Parsons*. London, 1906.

——. *Memoirs of Missionary Priests*. London, 1924.

——. "Religious Terrorism under Queen Elizabeth". *Month*, 105, June 1905, pp. 271–87.

Pugin, Augustine Welby. *Contrasts*. London, 1841.

Russell, C. W. "St. Pius V, the Father of Christendom". *Dublin Review*, 7 N.S., October 1866, pp. 273–304.

Sanders, Nicholas. *Rise and Growth of the Anglican Schism*. Trans. David Lewis. London, 1877. This was originally published in 1585 with a continuation by Edward Rishton.

Simpson, Richard. *Edmund Campion*. London, 1896.

——. *Under the Penal Laws*. London, 1930.

Stevenson, Joseph. "The Ecclesiastical Policy of Queen Elizabeth". *Month*, 79, September 1893, pp. 24–41.

Stone, Jean Mary. *The Church in English History*. Edinburgh, 1907.

——. *Mary, the First Queen of England*. London, 1901.

——. "Philip and Mary". *Dublin Review*, 107, July 1890, pp. 110–30.

——. "Progress and Persecution under Elizabeth". *Dublin Review*, 109, October 1891, pp. 311–32.

——. "Queen Elizabeth and the Revolution (Part 1)". *Dublin Review*, 113, June 1893, pp. 599–625.

——. "Queen Elizabeth and the Revolution (Part 2)". *Dublin Review*, 115, October 1894, pp. 358–81.

——. *Reformation and Renaissance*. London, 1904.

Talbot, John. "The Reformation and its Consequences". *Dublin Review*, 14, May 1843, pp. 379–411.

Taunton, Ethelred. *The History of the Jesuits in England*. London, 1901.

——. *Thomas Wolsey, Legate and Reformer*. London, 1902.

Throckmorton, John. *A Letter Addressed to the Catholic Clergy of England on the Appointment of Bishops, by a Layman*. London, 1790.

——. *A Second Letter Addressed to the Catholic Clergy of England on the Appointment of Bishops*. London, 1791.

Thurston, Herbert. "Celt, Roman or Teuton? Some Comments on our Latest Catholic History of England". *Month*, 146, July 1925, pp. 20–35.

Tierney, Mark. "Did Dr. Lingard Actually become a Cardinal?" *Rambler*, 9 (June 1858), pp. 425–32.

——. Ed. *Dodd's Church History of England*. 5 Vols. London, 1839–43.

Ward, Wilfrid. "English Catholic Literature". *Dublin Review*, 151, December 1912, pp. 269–76.

——. "Leo XIII and Anglican Orders". *Dublin Review*, 151. July 1912, pp. 94–117.

Ward, William George. "The Definition of Papal Infallibility". *Dublin Review*, 68, January 1871, pp. 171–205.

——. "The Encyclical and Syllabus". *Dublin Review*, 56, April 1865, pp. 441–99.

——. *The Ideal of a Christian Church*. London, 1844.

——. "Minor Doctrinal Judgements". *Dublin Review*, 61, October 1867, pp. 333–81.

Waugh, Evelyn. *Edmund Campion*. London, 1935.

Wells, H. G. *Mr. Belloc Objects to the "Outline of History"*. London, 1926.

Wiseman, Nicholas. "Anglican Claims of Apostolic Succession (Part 1)". *Dublin Review*, 4, April 1838, pp. 307–55.

——. "Anglican Claims of Apostolic Succession (Part 2)". *Dublin Review*, 5, October 1838, pp. 285–309.

4. Secondary Sources: Books

Abercrombie, Nigel. *The Life of Edmund Bishop*. London, 1959.

Altholz, Joseph. *The Liberal Catholic Movement in England, 1848–1864*. London, 1962.

Amherst, W. J. *The History of Catholic Emancipation: 1771–1820*. London, 1886.

Aveling, J. C. H. *The Handle and the Axe: the Catholic Recusants in England from Reformation to Emancipation*. London, 1976.

Avis, Paul. *Anglicanism and the Christian Church*. Edinburgh, 1989.

Barry, William. "Milner and His Age". *Dublin Review*, 150, April 1912, pp. 230–55.

Basset, Bernard. *The English Jesuits*. London, 1967.

Billington, Ray Allen. *The Protestant Crusade*. New York, 1938.

Bossy, John. *The English Catholic Community, 1570–1850*. London, 1975.

Brigden, Susan. *New Worlds, Lost Worlds: The Rule of the Tudors, 1485–1603*. New York, 2001.

Burrow, John. *A Liberal Descent*. Cambride, 1981.

Butterfield, Herbert. "Acton: His Training, Methods and Intellectual System". In Sarkissian, A. O. ed. *Studies in Diplomatic History and Historiography*. London, 1961. Pp. 169–98.

——. *The Historical Novel*. Cambridge, 1924.

——. *Lord Acton*. London, 1948.

——. *Man on His Past*. Cambridge, 1955.

——. *The Whig Interpretation of History*. London, 1931.

Chadwick, Owen. *Catholicism and History: the Opening of the Vatican Archives*. Cambridge, 1978.

——. *From Bossuet to Newman*. Cambridge, 1957.

——. *The Popes and European Revolution*. Oxford, 1981.

——. *The Reformation*. London, 1965.

——. *The Victorian Church*. 2 Vols. London, 1966–70.

Chinnici, Joseph. *The English Catholic Enlightenment: John Lingard and the Cisalpine Movement, 1780–1850*. Shepherdstown, WV, 1980.

Clark, Francis. *Anglican Orders*. London, 1956.

Clark, Kenneth. *The Gothic Revival*. London, 1928.

Cochrane, Eric. "What is Catholic Historiography?" In McIntire, C. T., ed. *God, History, and Historians*. New York, 1977. Pp. 444–65.

Code, Joseph Bernard. *Queen Elizabeth and the English Catholic Historians*. Louvain, 1935.

Collinson, Patrick; Ramsey, Nigel; and Sparks, Margaret, eds. *A History of Canterbury Cathedral*. Oxford, 1995.

Connell, Joan. *The Roman Catholic Church in England, 1553–1850*. Philadelphia, 1984.

Cowling, Maurice. *Religion and Public Doctrine in Modern England*. Cambridge, 1980.

Creighton, Mandel. Review of Gasquet's Henry VIII. *English Historical Review*, 3, April 1888, pp. 373–79.

Cross, F. L. and Livingstone, E. A., eds. *Oxford Dictionary of the Christian Church*. Oxford, 1974.

Culkin, Gerard. "The Making of Lingard's History". *Month*, 192, July 1951, pp. 7–18.

Davies, C. S. L. "The Pilgrimage of Grace Reconsidered". *Past and Present*, 41, December 1968, pp. 54–76.

DeCastro, Paul. *The Gordon Riots*. Oxford, 1926.

Delaney, John and Tobin, J. E., eds. *Dictionary of Catholic Biography*. London, 1962.

Dickens, A. G. *The English Reformation*. London, 1964. A second revised edition was published in 1989.

——. and Tonkin, John. *The Reformation and Historical Thought*. Oxford, 1985.

——. "Religious and Secular Motivation in the Pilgrimage of Grace". In Cumming, G. J., ed. *Studies in Church History*, 10, Leiden, 1968. Pp. 39–54.

Dowling, Maria. "Anne Boleyn: Reformer". *Journal of Ecclesiastical History*, 35, January 1984, pp. 30–46.

Drabble, John. *The Historians of the English Reformation: 1780–1850*. New York University, 1975.

Duffy, Eamon. "Ecclesiastical Democracy Detected (Part 1)". *Recusant History*, 10, 1969–70, pp. 193–209.

——. "Ecclesiastical Democracy Detected (Part 2)". *Recusant History*, 10, 1969–70, pp. 309–31.

—— *Joseph Berington and the English Catholic Cisalpine Movement, 1772–1803*. Cambridge University, 1972.

——. *The Stripping of the Altars*. New Haven, 1992.

Edwards, Francis. *The Jesuits in England: From 1580 to the Present Day*. Tunbridge Wells, 1985.

Ellis, John Tracy. *Cardinal Consalvi on Anglo-Papal Relations*. Washington, 1942.

Elton, G. R. *England Under the Tudors*. London, 1974.

——. *Modern Historians on British History*. London, 1970.

——. *The Practice of History*. London, 1969.

——. *Reform and Renewal*. Cambridge, 1973.

Forster, Ann. "The Oath Tendered". *Recusant History*, 14, October 1977, pp. 86–96.

Gillow, Joseph. *A Literary and Biographical History, or Bibliographical Dictionary of the English Catholics, from the Breach with Rome, 1534, to the Present Time*. 5 Vols. London, 1885–1902.

Gooch, G. P. *History and Historians in the Nineteenth Century*. London, 1913.

Gray, Robert. *Cardinal Manning*. London, 1985.

Gwynn, Denis. *The Second Spring, 1818–52*. London, 1942.

Haigh, Christopher. "The Continuity of Catholicism in the English Reformation". *Past and Present*, 93, November 1981, pp. 37–69.

———. *The English Reformation Revisited*. Cambridge, 1987.

———. *English Reformations*.

———. *Queen Elizabeth I*. Cambridge, 1984.

———. "The Recent Historiography of the English Reformation". *Historical Journal*, 25, December 1982, pp. 995–1007.

———. "Revisionism, the Reformation and the History of English Catholicsm". *Journal of Ecclesiastical History*, 36, July 1985, pp. 394–406.

Hollis, Christopher. *The Mind of Chesterton*. Coral Gables, FL, 1970.

Hughes, John Jay. *Absolutely Null and Utterly Void*. Washington, 1968.

Husenbeth, F. C. *The Life of John Milner*. Dublin, 1862.

Ives, E. W. *Anne Boleyn*. Oxford, 1986.

Jones, Edwin. *English Historican Writing on the English Reformation, 1680–1730*. Cambridge University, 1959.

———. *The English Nation: The Great Myth*. Phoenix Mill, 1998.

———. *John Lingard and the Pursuit of Historical Truth*. Brighton & Portland, 2001.

———. "John Lingard and the Simancas Archives". *The Historical Journal*, 1, 1967, pp. 57–76.

———. *A Study of John Lingard's Historical Work*. University of Wales (Swansea), 1956.

Kenyon, John. *The History Men*. London, 1983.

Ker, Ian. *John Henry Newman*. Oxford, 1990.

Kirk, John. *Biographies of English Catholics in the Eighteenth Century*. Eds. John Hungerford Pollen and Edwin Burton. London, 1909.

Leslie, Shane. *Cardinal Gasquet: a Memoir*. London, 1953.

Linker, R. W. "English Catholics in the Eighteenth Century". *Church History*, 25, 1966, pp. 288–310.

MacCulloch, Diarmaid. *The Boy King: Edward VI and the Protestant Reformation*. New York, 1999.

———. *Thomas Cranmer*. New Haven, 1996.

MacDougall, Hugh. "The Later Acton: The Historian as Moralist". In Hasting, Adrian, ed. *Bishops and Writers*. Wheathampstead, 1977. Pp. 35–49.

McElrath, Damien, ed. *Lord Acton: The Decisive Decade*. Louvain, 1970.

McGrath, Patrick. "The Bloody Questions Reconsidered". *Recusant History*, 20, May 1991, pp. 305–19.

Mascall, E. L. *Theology and History*. Westminster, 1962.

Mathew, David. *Catholicism in England*. London, 1936.

Norman, Edward. *Anti-Catholicism in Victorian England*. London, 1968.

———. *The English Catholic Church in the Nineteenth Century*. Oxford, 1984.

———. *Roman Catholicism in England from the Elizabethan Settlement to the Second Vatican Council*. Oxford, 1985.

O'Day, Rosemary. *The Debate on the English Reformation*. London, 1986.

Peardon, T. P. *The Transition in English Historical Writing, 1760–1830.* Columbia University, 1933.

Reynolds, E. E. *The Life and Death of St. Thomas More*. London, 1968.

Rowell, Geoffrey. *The Vision Glorious*. Oxford, 1983.

Scarisbrick, J. J. "Catherine of Aragon". *Tablet*, 25 January 1986, pp. 85–86.

——. "England's Catholic Revolt". *Tablet*, 4 October 1986, pp. 1038–40.

——. *Henry VIII*. London, 1968.

——. *The Reformation and the English People*. Oxford, 1984.

Schiefen, Richard. *Nicholas Wiseman and the Transformation of English Catholicism*. Shepherdstown, WV, 1984.

Schoenl, William. *The Intellectual Crisis in English Catholicism*. New York, 1982.

Shea, Donald. *The English Ranke: John Lingard*. New York, 1969.

Sheed, Wilfrid. *Frank and Maisie*. New York, 1985.

Speaight, Robert. *The Life of Hilaire Belloc*. New York, 1957.

Ward, Bernard. *The Dawn of the Catholic Revival*. London, 1909.

——. *The Eve of Catholic Emancipation*. 3 Vols. London, 1911–12.

——. *The Sequel of Catholic Emancipation*. 2 Vols. London, 1915.

Ward, Maisie. *Insurrection versus Resurrection*. New York, 1937.

——. "W. G. Ward and Wilfrid Ward". *Dublin Review*, 198, April–June 1936, pp. 235–52.

——. *The Wilfrid Wards and the Transition*. London, 1934.

Ward, Wilfrid. *The Life and Times of Cardinal Wiseman*. 2 Vols. London, 1899.

——. *William George Ward and the Catholic Revival*. London, 1893.

——. *William George Ward and the Oxford Movement*. London, 1889.

Watkin, E. I. "Gasquet and the Acton-Simpson Correspondence". *Cambridge Historical Journal*, 10, 1950.

——. *Roman Catholicism in England from the Reformation to 1950*. London, 1957.

Wilson, A. N. *Hilaire Belloc*. London, 1984.

Wormald, Brian. "The Historiography of the English Reformation". In Williams, T. Desmond, ed. *Historical Studies*, vol. 1. London, 1958. Pp. 50–58.

INDEX

INDEX

Gibbon, Edward, 1, 52, 72
Gradwell, Robert, 56, 60, 77–8
Gregory XIII, 12–13, 41
Gunpowder Plot, 23

Haile, Martin, 115
Hallam, Henry, 7, 72
Hay, Bishop, 25–6
Henry VIII, 3–4, 8, 12–14, 16, 19, 42, 45–6,
    48, 57–8, 63–5, 67–8, 70, 72–3, 81,
    94–8, 102, 112–16, 119, 126, 136, 138,
    140, 143–6, 150
Hughes, Philip, 2–3, 8, 46, 50, 115, 140,
    142–50
Hume, David, 7, 52, 54–5, 63, 72–3

Infallibility of the Pope, 5, 129–30
Inquisition, 131–2

James I, 17
Jane Seymour, 65
Joan of Arc, 69–70
Josephism, 25

King's Book, 145–6
Kirk, John, 32, 36, 39, 78–81
Knowles, David, 2–3, 68, 100, 105–10, 147

Liberal Catholicism, 131, 134
Lingard, John, 3, 5, 7–8, 15, 17, 31, 50–74,
    76–8, 83–6, 114, 118–25, 143, 148
Luther, Martin, 11, 117–18, 145

Mcaulay, Thomas Babington, 7, 61, 72
Manning, Henry Edward, 51, 96, 103–4,
    129, 131–2, 149
Mary, Queen of Scots, 5, 47, 59–60, 82
Mary Tudor, 4, 15, 22, 42, 65–6, 70, 90,
    114–15, 121, 144
Middle Ages, 7, 42, 91–95
Milner, John, 38–40, 45–9, 52, 76–7, 91,
    148–9
Missionary Priests, 5, 33, 37, 40–2, 60, 82–3,
    127
Mitigation of Gregory XIII, 12, 135
Modernism, 134
More, Thomas, 4, 32, 42, 58, 65, 99, 137,
    140
Moyes, Canon James, 122–4

Neale, J. E., 141
Newman, J. H., 48, 89–90, 124–5, 128, 130

Oaths of Allegiance (Supremacy), 4–5, 17,
    30–2, 37, 41–4, 59, 65, 70, 124, 128,
    136, 148
Oxford Movement, 8, 89–90, 150

Panzani, Gregorio, 29–30, 35, 80–1
Paul III, 11, 31, 48, 58–9, 126
Paul IV, 31, 40, 59, 69–70, 134–5
Persons, Robert, 12–13, 16, 19–20, 22–3, 33,
    42, 56, 83, 135, 149

Pilgrimage of Grace, 4, 15–16, 105, 110, 125
Pius V, 11, 19, 29, 41, 47–8, 59, 124, 126,
    131–3, 135–6
Plowden, Charles, 34–6, 148–9
Pole, Reginald, 12, 56, 65, 99–101, 130
Pollen, John Hungerford, 3, 134–6, 149
Pugin, Augustus Welby, 92–5, 110–1

Relief Act of 1778, 6, 25–6
Relief Act of 1829 (Catholic Emancipation)
    5–6, 43, 55, 62–3, 67, 70, 75, 77, 88,
    148, 150
Religious Orders, 22, 42, 45, 64, 67–8, 73,
    75–6, 78, 91, 93–111, 144, 149–50.
Reynolds, E. E., 140–1, 147
Rising of the North, 18, 30–1, 37, 82
Russell, C. W., 124
Sanders, Nicholas, 2, 6, 12–16, 18, 126, 142
Savonarola, Girolamo, 11
Scarisbrick, J. J., 2–3, 16, 72–3, 99, 102,
    143–4, 147
Sheldon, William, 25
Simpson, Richard, 90, 125–8, 130, 148–9
Society of Jesus (Jesuits), 5–6, 10–12, 17–24,
    30, 32–5, 37, 45–6, 60, 69, 75–80, 82–5,
    91, 104, 126, 128, 148–9
Southey, Robert, 7, 61
Spanish Armada, 6, 13, 41, 82
Speaight, Robert, 140
Stone, Mary Jean, 115
Strickland, Agnes, 67
Stuart Kings of England, 17, 23–4, 47, 142

Temporal Authority of the Popes, 4–5, 20–1,
    29, 30–2, 37, 40–2, 44, 46–7, 70–1,
    112–13, 125–9, 131–4, 137, 147–8
Throckmorton, John, 26, 29
Thurston, Herbert, 140
Tierney, Mark, 17, 24, 36, 62, 67, 75–87,
    120, 149
Trent, Council of, 11, 13
Turner, Sharon, 7, 63

Ultramontanists, 22, 50, 131, 138, 148

Vatican Council I, 130
Vicars–Apostolic, 26–7, 34, 38–9, 45, 49–50,
    75–8, 83
Visitors of Monasteries, 68, 100–2, 144
Voltaire, François, 7, 91

War of the Roses, 98, 110
Ward, Maisie, 104
Ward, Wilfrid, 25
Ward, William George, 89, 129–30
Watson, William, 17–19
Waugh, Evelyn, 127, 135
Wells, H. G, 140
Wiseman, Nicholas, 8, 51, 62, 71, 77, 83,
    85–6, 90, 120, 122
Wolsey, Thomas, 72–3, 90, 97–9, 101, 141

Printed and bound by CPI Group (UK) Ltd, Croydon, CR0 4YY

09/06/2025

14685956-0001